**Towards
the Community
University**

Towards
the Community
University

Case Studies of Innovation
and Community Service

Edited by
David C B Teather

Associate Professor and Director,
Higher Education Development Centre,
University of Otago

Kogan Page, London/
Nichols Publishing Company, New York

First published in Great Britain in 1982 by
Kogan Page Ltd, 120 Pentonville Road, London N1 9JN

British Library Cataloguing in Publication Data
Towards the community university.
   1. Continuing education
   I. Teather, David C.B.
   370.19'4   LB2820
   ISBN 0-85038-496-6

First published in the USA by Nichols Publishing Company,
PO Box 96, New York, NY10024

Library of Congress Cataloguing in Publication Data
Towards the community university.
   Includes indexes.
   1. Community and college — United States — Addresses,
essays, lectures. 2. Continuing education —
United States — Addresses, essays, lectures.
   I. Teather, David C.B.
   LC238.T68   378'.103   81-22542
   ISBN 0-89397-130-8   AACR2

Printed in Great Britain by the Anchor Press Ltd
and bound by Wm Brendon & Son,
both of Tiptree, Essex.

Contents

Contributors

Professor Donald Bewley is Director of Extramural Studies at Massey University. Before becoming Director in 1967 he taught Education internally and extramurally at Massey and at the University of New England. He was a founder executive member of the Australian and South Pacific External Studies Association. His interest in education in developing countries resulting from three years at the Malayan Teachers College, Liverpool, led to visits to South-east Asian educational institutions, a semester as Visiting Professor of Education at Simon Fraser University, and his secondment for a year as Head of the School of Education to the University of the South Pacific. Professor Bewley has written several pamphlets and articles on distance education in New Zealand, and has published articles on aspects of South-east Asian education in books and journals.

Address: Centre for University Extramural Studies, Massey University, Palmerston North, New Zealand

Phil Bradbury has taught in the School for Independent Study of North East London Polytechnic for four years. Previously he was engaged in course and teaching evaluation at NELP, about which he has published various papers. He has had teaching experience of a wide variety of students whose interests range from the theoretical to the vocational. His academic interests are human social behaviour, social psychology and educational evaluation. His personal interest is in politics and political action. He lives in the East End of London, where for the last three years he has been Chairman of his local Labour party in Newham.

Address: School for Independent Study, North East London Polytechnic, Holbrook Road, London E15 3EA, England

Professor Derek Broadbent is Coordinator of Postgraduate Extension Studies of the University of New South Wales and has been Head of its Division of Postgraduate Extension Studies since its inception in 1961. The Division operates Radio University VL2UV and Television University VITU and a cassette correspondence service to provide continuing education for graduates and professional people. Professor Broadbent's research has been in the area of information theory in human communication and the application of media in distance learning. Prior to taking up his present position and installing the University's radio transmitter in 1961, he was Associate Professor of Electrical Engineering.

Address: Division of Postgraduate Extension Studies, University of New South Wales, PO Box 1, Kensington, New South Wales, Australia 2033

Richard Higham is Director of the Otago University Business Development Centre, and of its Resource Development Unit. He served as a consultant and as Deputy Director before becoming Director. Research interests include the problems of and training techniques for small businessmen (following a year's research under the

Sloan Fellowship Programme at the London Graduate School of Business Studies) and the impact of major developments in rural areas, as a result of which he has been asked to serve on the New Zealand Energy Advisory Committee.

Address: Otago University Business Development Centre, PO Box 56, Dunedin, New Zealand

Eunice Hinds is at the School for Independent Study of North East London Polytechnic. She has taught with the UK Open University and worked in industry. Her particular research interests are continuing education in relation to changing patterns of employment and the social policy of the European Economic Community.

Address: School for Independent Study, North East London Polytechnic, Holbrook Road, London E15 3EA, England

Maggie Humm is a senior lecturer in the School for Independent Study at North East London Polytechnic. She has taught at an art college and at a Bengali community language centre, as well as at the Polytechnic. Her main interests are in feminist criticism and libertarianism. During 1974 she conducted a research project on continuing education in the arts and helped to design a higher education access course for unqualified students. She has published articles on Paul Goodman, Thomas Hardy and issues in continuing education.

Address: School for Independent Study, North East London Polytechnic, Holbrook Road, London E15 3EA, England

Susan Knights worked in university adult education in England and community education in Scotland before moving to Australia in 1976. She worked at Murdoch University during 1977 and is now a consultant in adult education in Sydney.

Address: c/o Educational Services and Teaching Resources Unit, Murdoch University, Perth, Western Australia 6150

Jindra Kulich is Director of the Centre for Continuing Education at the University of British Columbia. Prior to becoming Director he held a number of continuing education positions in public school adult education, residential adult education and in the UBC Centre for Continuing Education (which he joined in 1966). His academic interest is the comparative study of adult education, with emphasis on Central, Eastern and Northern Europe; he has published widely in this area.

Address: Centre for Continuing Education, the University of British Columbia, 5997 Iona Drive, Vancouver, Canada V6T 2A4

Rod McDonald is foundation director of the Educational Services and Teaching Resources Unit at Murdoch University, which collaborates with academic staff and students throughout the University in promoting and improving teaching and learning. He has taught at the Australian National University, Canberra College of Advanced Education, the UK Open University, and the Ontario Institute for Studies in Education. Dr McDonald is the author of 40 papers; his main research interests are adult learners in higher education and the contribution of educational research to the improvement of teaching and learning.

Address: Educational Services and Teaching Resources Unit, Murdoch University, Perth, Western Australia 6150

Professor Daniel W McKerracher is Director of the Clinical and Special Services Unit in the Education Department at the University of Otago. Before this, he was Chairman of that Department, which he joined in 1973 from the Department of Educational Psychology at Calgary University, Alberta. Previous positions include that of senior research psychologist at Rampton State Hospital, England, and teacher-librarian in the Glasgow public school system. He has published more than 40 articles in scientific journals dealing with social deviance and special education. His major current interests are in biofeedback and computer simulations.

Address: Clinical and Special Services Unit, Department of Education, University of Otago, PO Box 56, Dunedin, New Zealand

Jane Oakshott, BA MA, is a practical theatre historian with a particular interest in medieval drama. In 1975 her production of the York Cycle on pageant wagons made theatre history, as did her Towneley Cycle production in the main shopping centre of Wakefield (1980). In 1977 she was appointed William Evans Lecturer in Drama at the University of Otago, New Zealand. Among her wide-ranging productions was the world première of the complete *Booke of Sir Thomas More* by Shakespeare and others; while at Otago she also initiated New Zealand's first course in radio drama. Miss Oakshott relinquished her teaching post in 1979 to join her husband in Leeds, England, where she is working on research projects in drama with the Centre for Medieval Studies.

Address: 5 Albert Grove, Leeds LS6 4DA, England

Lorne A Parker is Director of Instructional Communications Systems at the University of Wisconsin-Extension. In this capacity he heads three major statewide communications systems designed to provide continuing education for students throughout the state of Wisconsin. A member of the University of Wisconsin faculty for the past 16 years, Dr Parker played a significant role in the development and operation of these communications systems. His doctoral research was in mass communications and adult education, with specific focus on compressed speech. Among his books are *The Telephone in Education, Book II* and *A Design for Interactive Audio*; he has also written numerous articles for professional journals and provided consultation for major educational and electronic manufacturers.

Address: Instructional Communications Systems, University of Wisconsin-Extension, Radio Hall, Madison, Wisconsin 53706, USA

Richard Rastall, MA MusB PhD, teaches music at Leeds University, England, where he is also a member of the Centre for Medieval Studies. His doctoral thesis (1968) on minstrelsy in the late Middle Ages led to extensive work on the music in the English cycle-plays. He was responsible for the music in both the major cycle productions (1975 and 1980) by Jane Oakshott, to whom he is married.

Address: Department of Music, 14 Cromer Terrace, Leeds LS2 9JR, England

Derek Robbins taught English literature in the Faculty of Arts, North East London Polytechnic before joining the DipHE Development Unit in the same institution in 1973. His doctoral work on Samuel Taylor Coleridge stimulated his subsequent interest in the philosophy of knowledge and in the philosophy of education. He was involved in the development of the DipHE at NELP in 1973, was one of the first tutors on that course in 1974, and was responsible for the submission, in 1976, of proposals for the Degree by Independent Study. He is now Head of Research in the School for Independent Study.

Address: School for Independent Study, North East London Polytechnic, Holbrook Road, London E15 3EA, England

David Spikins has been Managing Director of Loughborough Consultants Limited since its formation in 1969. He was formerly a Senior Lecturer in the Department of Chemical Engineering at Loughborough University of Technology and obtained a PhD in Chemical Engineering at Birmingham University in 1959. He was Chairman of the informal group of University Directors of Industrial Liaison in the United

Kingdom from 1977 to 1979, has contributed articles on industrial liaison to a number of journals and addressed two OECD conferences on the subject.

Address: Loughborough Consultants Ltd, University of Technology, Loughborough, Leicestershire LE11 3TU, England

David C B Teather obtained a PhD at University College London. He taught at the Polytechnics of Wolverhampton and North East London, at Goldsmiths' College London and at the University of Liverpool before taking up his present position as Director of the Higher Education Development Centre, University of Otago, New Zealand. He has written some 40 papers on various aspects of higher education, and edited *Staff Development in Higher Education: an international review and bibliography* published by Kogan Page and Nichols. He has served on the councils of several learned societies and is currently President of the New Zealand College of Education.

Address: Higher Education Development Centre, University of Otago, PO Box 913, Dunedin, New Zealand

Dr J E Thomas is Reader in Adult Education, and Deputy Director of the Department of Adult Education at Nottingham University. He is a regular visitor to Australasia, not only in connection with education, but with prison administration, since he is an international authority on prisons. His particular interest in adult education is in the comparative field, and he is at present engaged upon an historical international biography of adult education.

Address: Department of Adult Education, University of Nottingham, 14-22 Shakespeare Street, Nottingham NG1 4FJ, England

Acknowledgements

I should like to thank the many people who have had a hand in creating this book. Not all who helped are known to me personally, but I am particularly aware of my indebtedness to Professor Michael Stephens, for his comments on the planning of the book as a whole; to Mrs Katrina Trevella for typing, and often retyping, large sections of the text; and to Mrs Jocelyn Diedrichs for preparing the author index.

David C B Teather
September 1981

Part 1:
Introduction

1. Contemporary universities: characteristics and challenges

David C B Teather

> There is a new dynamic trend which is changing the place of institutions of higher education within the economic, cultural and social system and more particularly changing the role of those institutions in the development of their region or their immediate environment. (OECD/CERI, 1978)

How best to employ their resources for the public good is a key question for universities today, and one which is commanding increasing attention. As one would expect from organizations which contain within them so great a diversity, such a question is answered in several ways. Some academics argue that a university will best serve the community by husbanding its resources in what they regard as its traditional areas, *viz* in research and scholarship in the fundamental disciplines[1] and in the teaching of undergraduate and graduate students of high calibre. Others, while not denying the importance of such activities, call for initiatives to open up more direct avenues of contact between universities and their local and regional communities; they press for a new balance to be struck between the amount of university resources committed to traditional activities and that committed to other more direct forms of community service.[2]

The ways in which universities can use their resources more directly in the service of their local and regional communities, however these communities may be defined,[3] vary with time and place. They vary with the particular strengths of the university itself,[4] with the needs and demands of its communities, and with the abilities of other institutions to respond to these community needs. For example, in considering the regional role of the University of Otago, in the South Island of New Zealand, the foundation Professor of Management at that University stated:

> The case for careful examination by the University of its role in the community is related to our size. We dwarf all other organizations and institutions. Our position is in marked contrast with that of universities in larger industrial societies where government departments, industries, and corporations contain a great deal of talent and may themselves be centres of excellence.
>
> In the South Island of New Zealand, government departments and statutory boards are small, key staff are often over-worked, and therefore are often unable adequately to serve the region.

> Frequently, it is the University and only the University to which
> organizations can turn for professional assistance, for research, and upon which
> the region relies for services and progress. In some cases, organizations are
> themselves so unaware of possibilities that the University may have to take
> the initiative. (Rossell, 1974)

The ways in which such initiatives can be taken are the focus of this
book. Of course, many members of university staff contribute to the local
and regional communities of which they are a part; but here we are
concerned not with the contribution of academics as individuals, but with
the commitment of universities as institutions to widening their
community roles. Examples of such institutional commitments have been
sought which relate to teaching, to research and to other forms of
professional service; they have come from a very wide range of universities
serving communities which differ in important characteristics. The
innovations described in the chapters which follow range from permanent
structures with many employees and seven-figure budgets to more
temporary ventures which rely largely on voluntary co-operation. They
have in common the effect of making selected resources of the university
more widely available to the community which the university serves and,
in a reciprocal way, drawing from the community in the furtherance of
the university's teaching, research and service functions.

The authors of these chapters are pioneers. In the majority of cases
they have been the driving force behind the innovation which they
describe, since its inception. Each case study describes the context in
which the innovation occurred, its aims, and the methods by which it
became established. In the case of all but the most recent initiatives,
accounts are given of the development of the innovation following its
formal establishment and attention is also paid to its evaluation.

The aim of drawing together these accounts, all of which have been
specially commissioned for this volume, is to increase knowledge and
awareness of the range of ways in which universities have, in recent years,
sought to respond directly to community needs over and above those
which are met by their accepted roles of pure research and the teaching
of students recently out of secondary schools. While many universities
now possess a department of continuing education and a structure for
liaison with industry concerned with applied research, few if any possess
the wide range of structures described in the following chapters. Some
readers may consider emulating, in their own institution, one or other of
the developments described here, or may see some other community need
which could be met by an initiative appropriate to their own university.
It was with such possibilities in mind that the authors of these case studies
were asked to describe in some detail the conditions obtaining in their
universities at the time at which their initiative was established. But before
moving to the individual case studies it is appropriate to consider, in a
general way, two aspects of the context shared by contemporary
universities which have a direct bearing on the establishment and success
of any such innovation. These are, first, the nature of university

governance and, secondly, the attitudes and orientations of university staff.

The nature of university governance

Two aspects of the contemporary university are essential to an understanding of its governance and decision-making processes: one is its size, the other is that it is staffed largely by professionals. The sheer size and complexity of the university now render the collegiate, democratic model of governance of little relevance. While the ideal of a self-governing community of scholars may have been appropriate to Oxford and Cambridge colleges a century ago, the governance of the contemporary university bears little relationship to the collegiate model. Nor can university governance be easily explained by likening universities to large business organizations. Although the imagery of bureaucracy adequately describes some of the more peripheral aspects of universities — their business administration, plant management, ancillary services — at the heart of the academic enterprise, in policy-making and professional teaching and research tasks, universities bear little resemblance to bureaucracies. Certainly the ultimate formal authority rests, in universities in the British tradition, with the council, beneath which there is an appearance of hierarchy; but effective power is widely dispersed throughout the institution.[5]

One of the most convincing recent accounts of university governance is that of Baldridge *et al* (1978). In this the authors suggest that universities can best be studied as miniature political systems, with interest group dynamics similar to those in cities, states or other political systems. Such a model becomes the more appropriate the larger and more complex the university, for with increase in size the dual allegiance of the faculty member, to the university as a whole or to his department and discipline, tips further in favour of the latter. Large academic organizations are splintered into groups with basically different lifestyles and political interests. These differences often lead to conflict, for what is in the best interests of one group may damage another.

The account given by Baldridge *et al* (1978) is worth quoting at length:

> The political model has several stages, all of which center around the university's policy-forming processes. Policy formation was selected as the central focal point because major policies commit the organization to definite goals, set the strategies for reaching those goals, and in general determine the long-range destiny of the organization. Policy-decisions are critical decisions, those that have a major impact on the organization's future.
>
> Since policies are so important, people throughout the organization try to influence their formulation in order to see that their own special interests are protected and furthered. Policy making becomes a vital focus of special interest group activity that permeates the university . . . with policy formation as its key issue, the political model then makes a series of assumptions about the political process:

Inactivity prevails. To say that policy making is a political process is not to say that everybody is involved. Quite the contrary. For most people most of the time, the policy making process is an uninteresting, unrewarding activity, so they allow administrators to run the show.

Fluid participation. Even when people are active they move in and out of the decision-making process. Individuals usually do not spend very much time on any given issue; decisions, therefore, are usually made by those who persist. This normally means that small groups of political elites govern most major decisions because only they invest the necessary time in the process.

Colleges and universities, like most other social organizations, are *fragmented into interest groups* with different goals and values ... When resources are plentiful and the environment congenial, these interest groups engage in only minimal conflict. They mobilize and fight to influence decisions, however, when resources are tight, outside pressure groups attack, or other internal groups try to take over their goals.

Conflict is normal. In a fragmented, dynamic social system, conflict is natural and not necessarily a symptom of breakdown in the academic community. In fact, conflict is a significant factor in promoting healthy organizational change.

Authority is limited. In universities, the formal authority prescribed in a bureaucratic system is severely limited by the political pressure that groups can exert. Decisions are not simply bureaucratic orders, but are often negotiated compromises between competing groups. Officials are not free simply to issue a decision; instead they must jockey between interest groups hoping to build viable positions between powerful blocks.

External interest groups are important. Academic decision making does not occur in a campus-bound vacuum. External interest groups exert a great deal of influence over the policy-making process. And external pressures and formal control by outside agencies — especially in public institutions — are powerful shapers of internal governance processes.

Such a political interpretation of academic governance draws attention to issues which are critical for anyone contemplating, or seeking to understand, how innovations — such as the establishment of new structures to promote university-community interaction — are brought about. Quoting Baldridge *et al* (1978) again:

Why is a given decision made at all? Why is it made at a particular time? The political model insists that interest groups, powerful individuals, and bureaucratic processes are critical in drawing attention to some decisions rather than to others.

Who has the right to make the decision? In a loosely co-ordinated system, we must ask the question: Why is Dean Smith making the decision instead of Dean Jones, or why is the University Senate dealing with the problem instead of the central administration? ... The crucial point is that often the issue of *who* makes the decision has already limited, structured, and pre-formed *how* it will be made.

What is the role of the committee system? As a result of the fragmentation of the university, decision making is rarely located in one official; instead it is dependent upon the advice and authority of numerous people. The importance of the committee system is evident. It ... is the legitimate reflection of the need for professional influence to intermingle with bureaucratic influence. The decision process, then, is taken out of the hands of individuals (although there are still many who are powerful) and placed into a network that allows a *cumulative buildup* of expertise and advice. When the very life of the organization clusters around expertise, *decision making is likely to be diffuse, segmentalized, and decentralized.*

Attitudes and orientations of academics

If effective power is so widely dispersed throughout the university, what are the attitudes of the staff involved in decision making? Our knowledge of academics has been much improved by a number of sociological studies undertaken in Britain and North America and, more recently, in some other countries. One of the first such studies was that undertaken by Halsey and Trow (1971), which drew heavily upon the results of a nationwide survey of British university staff which they conducted in 1965. They characterized British academics as sharing a cluster of characteristics, such as 'scrupulous honesty in intellectual life, a dedication to the highest academic standards, and a strong sense of responsibility to their students'. But in 1965, in the wake of the Report of the Robbins Committee, British university teachers were divided in their views about the future development of the universities. Halsey and Trow characterized four types of orientation, which were based on:

☐ elitist views, as opposed to the views of those who favoured considerable expansion of the university system;
☐ views which laid greater stress on the importance of teaching than on the importance of research, and vice versa.

While present-day political realities preclude further large-scale expansions of our university systems, the set of orientations which Halsey and Trow characterized still has validity. These are:

1. *Elitist researchers.* The members of this group give greatest importance to intellectual brilliance and creativity, which they take to be largely genetically given and statistically rare. The function of the education system, in this view, is to identify the small minority of very able and gifted people and to create the intellectual environment in which full promise can be developed and realized. This orientation is concerned more with brilliance of achievement than with character and ascribed status; it had been the progressive, reformist force from the middle of the nineteenth century to the middle of the twentieth century in British universities; but faced with the expansion in the 1960s it formed, in the words of Halsey and Trow, 'the most formidable bulwark of conservatism in British university life'.

2. *Elitist teachers.* This group is concerned less with brilliance and creativity and more with the development of students with sound personal qualities and commitment to social leadership. These aims are similar to those which govern the leading independent schools, to train an elite able to take responsibility for society at large. Halsey and Trow claimed, in 1971, that this was still probably the

most widely held of the four types of orientation among British university staff, but was increasingly difficult to defend in an egalitarian age.

3. *Expansionist researchers.* The outlook of this group has provided the characteristic drive behind the development of the large American graduate schools. Their view is that 'the essential function of the university is that of the intellectual spearhead for economic growth'. Academics with this orientation tend to identify the growth of knowledge with the growth of research resources, organization and number of people. They are also more likely than those of the other two groups we have considered to accept a larger, direct social role for the universities.

4. *Expansionist teachers.* The antecedents for the orientation of this group include the extramural and extension movements, and this is clearly the outlook which sustained the foundation of the Open University in the United Kingdom. 'The primary concern of expansionist teachers is with the fundamental problem of transforming a socially restricted cultural heritage into a common culture.' The stress in this view is on the popular functions of education, providing opportunities for all to achieve their highest potential, and in raising the level of knowledge and skill of the whole population. Halsey and Trow stated in 1971 that the expansionist teacher orientation, while represented throughout British universities, 'appears to have very little weight in current discussions of the future of the universities'.

Halsey and Trow made the point that these stark polarities do less than justice to the complex views and attitudes held by individual university teachers. They fail to catch the nuances of thought and feeling by which individuals manage to maintain conceptions of the universities, and of their own academic role, which reflect both expansionist *and* elitist values, and which accept both teaching *and* research as legitimate and complementary functions of the university. Nevertheless, the data of the 1965 survey, and those of more recent surveys in Britain (Williams *et al*, 1974; Halsey, 1979), the United States (Trow, 1975; Roizen *et al*, 1978) and Australia (Williams Report, 1979), show that staff differ in the emphases they place on these values. It is the relative emphasis of values and orientations that is important and which will tend to determine the degree of support which any proposals for innovation, including those designed to promote a greater degree of university involvement in its community, will receive.

External factors: universities in the aftermath of expansion

By comparing the results of surveys conducted in 1964 and 1975, Halsey (1979) concludes that the attitudes and approaches of British academics to questions of teaching, research, promotion, university governance and relations with students changed little over that 11-year period, and indeed remained basically similar to those which had been built up at the turn of the nineteenth and twentieth centuries. He points out that such conservatism was not necessarily to have been expected, since the British university system, like those of many other countries, experienced massive growth during the 1960s.

Such periods of expansion are not without their parallels in the long history of universities, from their origins in Italy and France and their subsequent spread throughout medieval Europe to their establishment in Latin America in the sixteenth century, and in North America in the seventeenth. More recent times have witnessed the foundation of universities in many parts of the world, with periods of rapid growth alternating with those of little change.[6]

But the most recent phase of expansion, from the mid-50s to the mid-70s, was larger in scale than any which had gone before. It is bringing in its wake profound changes in the relationship between the universities on the one hand and governments and peoples on the other. To put the size of the expansion into international perspective, New Zealand, a country whose total population is a mere three million, now has over 3000 university teachers — a comparable number to that of Australia in 1960 or Britain in 1945. Such expansion, of staff and student numbers, of buildings and equipment, was only made possible by large infusions of funds. During the years of expansion, not only did the real value of the budgets of university systems increase markedly, but increasing proportions of these ever larger budgets were provided by governments. The justification for this high degree of public support rests on what universities are seen to do.

If one were to seek an account of what universities do from some of their prominent members, one might conclude that the governments which funded the expansion of universities were surprisingly altruistic. A perspective commonly expressed by academics is neatly summarized by Sir David Derham (1979): 'The purposes of a university are . . . to acquire, to preserve, and to disseminate knowledge. The first involves research, and the second and third involve teaching.' Derham recognizes that other institutions can also claim these aims; what in his view distinguishes a university is the nature of the knowledge to be pursued together with the purposes of the dissemination of knowledge. He asserts the primacy of the international dimension:

> The primary commitments [of a university] with respect to the pursuit and dissemination of knowledge must be to the world, and not just to the community which gave it birth or which supports it . . . a university must be committed to the acquisition and dissemination of knowledge beyond mere reference to the needs of particular times and places.

Another vice-chancellor, Sir Charles Wilson (1979), also refers to teaching and research as the 'first-order' roles of the universities. But, more significantly, he observes that in the performance of these first-order functions, the universities are also cast in a second-order, social role.

This is to act 'as agents for the recruitment and certification of a main proportion of those who are to take up the higher employment of a society'. It is this social role which is of the greatest importance to governments and to the general public, for it is seen as implying:

☐ the provision of opportunities for individuals to advance educationally on merit, and to be rewarded by access to higher economic and social status;

☐ the provision of trained and certified manpower, which is seen as a necessary prerequisite of economic and social advance in societies in which specialized knowledge is increasingly important.

The performance by the universities of these social roles has been the prime reason for the allocation of the funds which made possible their recent expansion. The twin concepts of social demand and of manpower planning underpinned the major reports (such as the Parry Report [1959] in New Zealand, the Robbins Report [1963] in the United Kingdom) which preceded expansion, or which in some cases served to put the seal of approval on an expansion which was already taking place. From the perspective of university functions held by many academics, it is as if the universities have received public largesse for a by-product of their fundamental activities. [7]

The mid-70s saw a discontinuity in the rapid growth of universities which had characterized the previous 20 years. In many countries the number of students has since continued to increase, but at a slower rate. More significantly, the political will to continue the wholehearted commitment of public funds to universities has waned. Other areas of public expenditure, notably on health and welfare, have also come under increasing scrutiny, as has expenditure on other levels and forms of education.

There has been some criticism of and hostility towards the universities. As universities are seen, increasingly, as one further tier of the public education system — rather than as the private concern of a small minority of the population, as had been the case in university systems fashioned in the English tradition — they receive their share of those criticisms that are directed at the education system as a whole. For critics of a neo-Marxist persuasion the education system is itself part of the bourgeois apparatus of class, racial and sexual oppression. For larger numbers of educators and social reformers, who in the 1950s and 1960s put their faith in the education system as a mechanism for righting society's ills, there is disillusionment at the lack of progress towards their goals. The writings of those advocating radical non-institutionalized alternatives, such as Illich and Freire, have been much in vogue.

Then there are the criticisms of the products of universities. Criticisms of the older professions, particularly in North America, have reflected upon the institutions in which their members are trained. Similarly, concern over the cost in human and environmental terms of technological change has drastically lowered the public esteem in which the sciences are held. The expansion of higher education has produced, as was intended, a higher proportion of the population with degrees;[8] but the corollary of this is that possession of a degree is no longer the open sesame to the limited number of top jobs. While the facts of graduate unemployment are often less alarming than the publicity which attends them, the questioning of the value of a degree, in career terms, has lessened public support.

Universities have also been subject to direct criticism. The student unrest of the late 1960s shook public confidence in the institutions themselves and did lasting damage to the student image. Questions of accountability with respect to public funds were raised, have since gathered momentum, and have progressively reduced the freedom of action of university authorities. As Stephens (1977) remarked: 'The allocation of resources to universities largely determines what happens in such institutions. If a government decides it wants more engineering graduates and fewer sociology graduates it will be remarkable if in ten years universities do not mirror such ebb and flow priorities.' Another example is given in Chapter 9 of this volume; Spikins draws to our attention the fact that between 1965 and 1970 three-quarters of the university institutions in the United Kingdom established some formal activity to co-ordinate and increase the amount of work for industry undertaken in universities and notes that during this period there was 'considerable pressure from industry and government' for universities to do so, and put to use the 'substantial resources that had been built up during the 1960s'.

Changing the balance: recurrent education and other university-community links

Throughout the 1980s there will be increasing pressure on universities to use their existing resources in new ways. Where the policy of governments is to stabilize and reduce higher education budgets, it is more difficult to meet new needs, or old needs which have assumed greater priority, by creating new institutions, thus bypassing those already in existence — as was done, for example, in 1969 with the foundation of the UK Open University. The reallocation of resources within existing universities in a period of financial retrenchment and immobile and ageing staff is posing great difficulties for these institutions; but it is clearly in their own interests to adjust to changing priorities. Indeed some of the larger of the Australian universities, whose student numbers were stabilized in the early 1970s, have evolved useful mechanisms of internal resource reallocation.

Given that new developments will take place, which should have priority? Clearly a major contender for reallocated resources is recurrent education, a concept which came of age in the 1970s[9] and which will need to become a reality for increasing numbers of people as the twentieth century draws to a close. Of course, some university institutions, such as

23

Birkbeck College, London, have a long tradition of meeting the needs of adults for university education. Indeed the foundation oration to mark the start of Birkbeck's 150th academic year comprised a closely argued and persuasive statement of why the needs of adult learners should have high priority (Berrill, 1972). Most British universities, however, took little heed and Stephens and Roderick (1972), among others, are highly critical of the fact that universities continue to channel such a high proportion of their resources into 'providing what often appears to be an educational finishing school for those in late adolescence'.

In Australian universities, however, increasing numbers of mature age students are being enrolled (Hore and West, 1980). In their account in Chapter 2 of this volume of one Australian university's attempts to cater for the needs of an unusually high proportion of adult students on regular credit courses, McDonald and Knights observe that 'long held institutional prejudices against mature students' are being broken down. However, not all adults who may wish to study at university, and who are capable of profiting from such study, can readily do so. Even in a country such as New Zealand, which has a traditional policy of open entry to the general faculties of its universities, there is resentment at the rigidity of the apparatus of formal regulations and at what is perceived as the inadequacy of the response of universities to the needs of those adult learners who have to balance the demands of study against those of adult life — such as being a spouse, a parent, and earning a living.

Some of the practical difficulties faced by adult learners are being overcome by the use of appropriate technologies. As Broadbent comments in Chapter 7, it is often the availability of technology which determines whether an educational programme can be mounted at all. This theme is explored in Chapters 5, 6 and 7, which are accounts of structures established to offer educational programmes to adults at a distance from their university campuses. The three structures described started by using the technologies of postal communications, telephone, and radio, respectively; but all three have developed towards a multi-media mix. All now offer both credit and non-credit courses, though in different proportions.

In all three accounts not only is there adaptation to the needs of adult learners in that technology is used to overcome the constraints of distance and of time, but there is also evidence of the adaptation, to varying degrees, of the contents of the educational programmes to the characteristics of adults as learners.[10] Adaptation of educational programmes, both in the content and methodology of individual courses and in the types of course offered, to the characteristics of adult learners, has always been necessary for the success of centres for university extension or continuing education, as Kulich demonstrates in Chapter 4 with an account of the development of one such centre in a large Canadian university. But it is intriguing to discover, in Chapter 3, that similar adaptations have been found successful in coping with the needs of new students of a variety of ages on the campus of an 'urban community university', to use the phrase coined by Eric Robinson to describe the British polytechnics. This theme, of the creative adaptation of educational programmes to the needs of learners, recurs in several of the contributions to this volume, and gives grounds for hope that the increasing involvement of universities in recurrent education may bring about a dynamic for reappraisal and renewal of their mainstream teaching activities.

Although greater involvement in recurrent education, helped by the application of appropriate technology, is of high priority, it is by no means the only way in which universities can broaden the community base of their activities. Chapters 8-11 comprise case studies of innovations which provide services to the community and which rely on university strengths in research and consultancy. Thomas's account in Chapter 8 leads naturally from the earlier chapters, for it concerns the recent establishment of a centre designed to promote and support research into the education of adults, with the ultimate aim of ensuring that 'the best that a university can offer [in adult education] is made available to the community, and that the methods of doing this are the best that can be devised'. (The context of the research centre, a large department of adult education in an English university, can usefully be compared with the Canadian centre described in Chapter 4.)

Chapters 9 and 10 are concerned with making university resources more readily accessible to the industrial and business communities respectively. But the innovations they describe are in very different settings. Loughborough, in the English Midlands, was founded as a college at the end of the first world war and received its charter as a university of technology in 1965. Otago, whose New Zealand context is described by Rossell on p. 15, was founded as a university by a provincial ordinance of 1869. Despite their differences, both case studies demonstrate the possibilities inherent in building on the strengths of the institution and matching these with the accurately assessed needs of the communities they seek to serve.

Chapter 11 shows how services of direct value to the public can arise from a university's 'first-order' commitment to teaching. The establishment of courses of postgraduate training for educational psychologists at Otago University led to the setting up, in the University's Department of Education, of a special classroom for children under threat of expulsion from the public school system. Two teaching clinics, one based in the university itself and one located at a community health centre in a nearby town, were also developed, bringing to seven the total number of clinics operated by that university in health and health-related areas.

The final case study, in Chapter 12, defies easy categorization. Conceived as a large-scale experiment to test hypotheses concerning medieval drama, it involved the collaboration of some 800 people from the University and city of Leeds — 500 of them in the role of actors — in the presentation of a two-day performance which well over 4000 people came to watch. Although a case study of an event of limited duration, it provides an excellent example of the sharing of resources, of the use of the complementary skills of groups within and without the university, to their mutual benefit. In the words of the authors: 'it proved that academic leadership of the community can work in practical terms and that artistic collaboration between town and gown may be achieved with very little cost and to lasting mutual benefit'.

A note on national differences

Implicit in the current concern for universities to respond to community needs is the belief that in the 1980s, in response to external pressures and, to a lesser extent, to internal pressures also, universities in many countries will shift a higher proportion of their resources towards direct forms of community service. This they will do in a variety of ways, but one important element will be to increase their provision for recurrent education; this will itself imply changes in the traditional patterns of teaching and will foster closer community links.

In some universities there is now a desire to begin making such adjustments, but uncertainty about how best to proceed. In others there is still doubt as to whether universities should take on a larger community service role and concern that this might imply not only some dilution of the university's existing and widely accepted roles in teaching and research but also that aspects of direct community service might conflict with the performance of those teaching and research roles. Thus, for example, it can be argued that there is something inconsistent about becoming too involved with client relationships while trying to think objectively about problems and solutions inherent in a particular situation, or while conceptualizing relationships as part of the educational process.

To many North American readers such fears may appear insubstantial. Since the foundation of the land grant colleges (authorized by the US Congress in 1862) universities in North America have developed a much broader concept of the community service role appropriate to a university than have those in most other western countries. In the words of Clark Kerr (1972):

> The land grant movement came in response to the rapid industrial and agricultural development of the United States that attained such momentum in the middle of the last century. Universities were to assist this development through training that went beyond the creation of 'gentlemen', and of teachers, preachers, lawyers and doctors; through research related to the technical advance of farming and manufacturing; through service to many and ultimately to almost all of the economic and political segments of society . . . This was a dramatic break with earlier American traditions in higher education. It created a new social force in world history. Nowhere before had universities been so closely linked with the daily life of so much of their societies. The university campus came to be one of the most heavily travelled crossroads in America — an intersection traversed by farmers, businessmen, politicians, students from almost every corner of almost every state.

The universities founded contemporaneously with the American land grant colleges, in the industrial cities of England, in continental Europe, and in what were then the colonial possessions of European states, lacked the concept of service to the community as an autonomous function, ie as a function exercised concurrently with the functions of teaching and research but not necessarily through them. Thus it was not altogether surprising that, a century later, the writers of the report *Relationships between Higher Education and the Community* (OECD/ CERI, 1978) observed, from data collected from over 150 universities and equivalent institutions in OECD member countries, that there was a very deep division 'between institutions in the United States, Canada and to a lesser degree Portugal and Yugoslavia, where the "service" concept seemed self-evident, and the other cases where it appears almost scandalous'.

There are signs, however, that this dichotomy is beginning to be narrowed; as Clark Kerr prophesied in 1963, 'the imperatives that have molded the American university are at work around the world'. This is the case, for example, in the universities of Australia and New Zealand which, although established in the English or Scottish traditions, have had to adapt to the context of their pioneering and comparatively egalitarian societies; they are adopting aspects of North American practice to an increasing extent. It is timely, therefore, to be able to demonstrate through the case studies in this volume that a wide range of community service functions is already being undertaken by universities outside North America; it is also useful to be able to place these Australasian and British case studies in perspective by indicating, in Chapters 4 and 6, the magnitude of the community service provisions made by some of their North American counterparts.

NOTES

1. There will, of course, be some differences of opinion as to which disciplines qualify as 'fundamental'. Bissell (1968) supplies an illustrative list when he refers to physics, chemistry, biology, mathematics, political science, economics, literature, history and philosphy as occupying 'a special place because they are the sources to which all divisions of the university must regularly return'.

2. 'The integration of higher education in the local/regional community does not necessarily imply that the institutions will become "service stations" to carry out orders, but *centres for the analysis of the problems* and needs of the community . . .' (OECD/CERI, 1978)

3. Various concepts of 'community' are explored in the Report, *Relationships Between Higher Education and the Community* (OECD/CERI, 1978). One definition is as follows: 'Traditionally and realistically, the region and those persons in closest physical proximity to the campus proper comprise the community of most immediate relevance and concern to a university . . . Cognizant, however, of the varying constituencies upon which the university depends . . . and to which the university might reasonably be expected to be responsive . . . The Committee recognises also a "community of interest" to the university which is not restricted by static political or geographic boundaries. The concept of community, then, must

be viewed as a function of the changing needs, interests and compositions of constituencies which we extend to the university campus itself.'

5. Bissell (1968) maintained that one of the characteristics of a 'great' university is that 'it will be selective about what it does in the area of immediate social pressure, and it will insist upon responding in ways that draw upon its own strength'.

5. Two conflicting views of authority were neatly encapsulated in an exchange, earlier this century, between a Dean of Medicine and a university treasurer. The treasurer had referred to members of the academic staff of the university as 'employees of the Council', whereupon the Dean protested that 'the teaching staff is the university, and the Council merely a regrettable excrescence on its head' (Hunter, 1975).

6. In England as recently as 1937, the Principal of University College, Leicester was saying that the prime need of the College was to attract more students. The number of full-time students reading for degrees, 16 years after the College was founded, was still only 75 (Ashby, 1966).

7. Universities may also claim, often with some justification, to carry out other important functions. They are said 'to transmit high culture to each generation' (Annan, 1975), and to fulfil 'the vital function of social criticism and investigation' (Wheelwright, 1977). For such functions, their importance notwithstanding, the universities generally receive varying degrees of public support.

8. In Australia, for example, at the 1971 census there were about 177,000 graduates; in 1979 there were about 315,000 and in the year 2000 there will be approximately 1.3 million. This shift from graduates making up 4 per cent of the Australian population now to about 12 per cent in 20 years' time will occur even if the universities remain, throughout the intervening period, at roughly their present size (Williams Report, 1979).

9. The theme of 'recurrent', 'continuing' or 'lifelong' education was central to major national and international educational reports of the 1970s, such as Ontario's report of the Commission on Post-Secondary Education, *The Learning Society* (1972) and Unesco's *Learning to Be* (1972). See also *Recurrent Education: A Strategy for Lifelong Learning* (OECD/CERI, 1973) and subsequent reports in the series *Recurrent Education: Policy and Developments in OECD Member Countries,* also published by OECD/CERI.

10. Knowles, in the most recent (1980) edition of his classic work *The Modern Practice of Education*, differentiates adult and pre-adult learners on the basis of four criteria: 'as individuals mature: (1) their self-concept moves from one of being a dependent personality towards being a self-directed human being; (2) they accumulate a growing reservoir of experience that becomes an increasingly rich resource for learning; (3) their readiness to learn becomes oriented increasingly to the developmental tasks of their social roles; (4) their time perspective changes from one of postponed application of knowledge to immediacy of application, and accordingly, their orientation toward learning shifts from one of subject-centredness to one of performance-centredness.'

REFERENCES AND BIBLIOGRAPHY

Annan, Lord (1975) The university in Britain, in Stephens, M D and Roderick, G W (eds) *Universities for a Changing World: The Role of the University in the Later Twentieth Century*, pp 19-33, David and Charles, Newton Abbot

Ashby, E (1966) *Universities: British, Indian, African: A Study in the Ecology of Higher Education*, 572 pp, Weidenfeld and Nicolson, London

Baldridge, J V, Curtis, D V, Ecker, G and Riley, G L (1978) *Policy Making and Effective Leadership: A National Study in Academic Management*, 290 pp, Jossey-Bass, San Francisco

Benezet, L T and Magnusson, F W (1979) Building bridges to the public, *New Directions for Higher Education No 27*, 128 pp, Jossey-Bass, San Francisco

Berrill, Sir K (1972) *Lifetime Education — The Outlook in Britain*, 14 pp, Birkbeck College, London

Bissell, C T (1968) *The Strength of the University*, 251 pp, University of Toronto Press, Toronto

Boshier, R (1980) *Towards a Learning Society: New Zealand Adult Education in Transition*, 300 pp, Learningpress, Vancouver

Derham, Sir D (1979) Mobility of students and staff internationally, in Craig, T (ed) *Pressures and Priorities: Report of Proceedings of the 12th Congress of the Universities of the Commonwealth*, pp 359-65, Association of Commonwealth Universities, London

Halsey, A H (1979) Are the British universities capable of change? *New Universities Quarterly*, 33 (4), 402-16

Halsey, A H and Trow, M A (1971) *The British Academics*, 560 pp, Faber and Faber, London

Hore, T and West, L H T (1980) *Mature Age Students in Australian Higher Education*, 184 pp, Higher Education Advisory and Research Unit, Monash University, Melbourne

Hunter, J D (1975) *The History of the University of Otago Medical School*, 16mm film, University of Otago, Dunedin

Kerr, C (1972) *The Uses of the University: with a 'postscript — 1972'*, 176 pp, Harvard University Press, Cambridge, Mass

Knowles, M S (1980) *The Modern Practice of Adult Education: From Pedagogy to Andragogy*, 400 pp, Association Press, Chicago

Long, J (1968) Universities and the general public, *Educational Review Occasional Publications No 3*, 128 pp, University of Birmingham

Moodie, G C and Eustace, R (1974) *Power and Authority in British Universities*, 254 pp, George Allen and Unwin, London

OECD/CERI (1973) *Recurrent Education: A Strategy for Lifelong Learning*, 92 pp, Centre for Educational Research and Innovation, Organization for Economic Co-operation and Development, Paris

OECD/CERI (1977) *Health, Higher Education and the Community: Towards a Regional Health University*, 350 pp, Centre for Educational Research and Innovation, Organization for Economic Co-operation and Development, Paris

OECD/CERI (1978) *Relationships Between Higher Education and the Community: General Report*, 216 pp (mimeo), Centre for Educational Research and Innovation, Organization for Economic Co-operation and Development, Paris

OECD/CERI (1980) *Higher Education and the Community: New Partnerships and Interaction*, Conference Papers (mimeo), Centre for Educational Research and Innovation, Organization for Economic Co-operation and Development, Paris

Parry Report (1959) *Report of the Committee on New Zealand Universities, chaired by Sir David Hughes Parry, to the Minister of Education*, 130 pp, Government Printer, Wellington

Robbins Report (1963) *Higher Education: Report of the Committee appointed by the Prime Minister, chaired by Lord Robbins, 1961-63*, 336 pp + appendices, Cmd 2154, HMSO, London

Roizen, J, Fulton, O and Trow, M (1978) *Technical Report: 1975 Carnegie Council National Surveys of Higher Education*, 242 pp, Center for Studies in Higher Education, University of California, Berkeley

Rossell, P E (1974) *Memorandum of 19th June to the Deans of Faculties*, 3 pp (mimeo), University of Otago, Dunedin

Stephens, M D (1977) Some national trends, in Thornton, A H and Stephens, M D (eds) *The University in its Region: The Extra-Mural Contribution*, pp 181-9, Department of Adult Education, University of Nottingham

Stephens, M and Roderick, G (1972) Adult education and the community university, *Adult Education*, 45 (3), 138-42

Trow, M (ed) (1975) *Teachers and Students: Aspects of American Higher Education*, 420 pp, McGraw-Hill, New York

Wheelwright, E L (1978) Political economy and higher education, in Powell, J P (ed) *Higher Education in a Steady State: Proceedings of the 3rd Annual Conference of HERDSA*, pp 8-16, Higher Education Research and Development Society of Australasia, Sydney

Williams, G, Blackstone, T and Metcalf, D (1974) *The Academic Labour Market: Economic and Social Aspects of a Profession*, 566 pp, Elsevier, Amsterdam

Williams Report (1979) *Education, Training and Employment: Report of the Committee of Enquiry into Education and Training, chaired by B R Williams, to the Prime Minister*, Volume 2, Appendix N, pp 573-631, *National Educational Survey, 1977 and National Survey of Post-Secondary Teaching Staff, 1977*, Australian Government Publishing Service, Canberra

Wilson, Sir C (1979) Reconciling national, international and local roles of universities with the essential character of a university, in Craig, T (ed) *Pressures and Priorities: Report of Proceedings of the 12th Congress of the Universities of the Commonwealth*, pp 19-26, Association of Commonwealth Universities, London

Part 2:
Adapting to new clientele on campus

2. Experiences of adult students at Murdoch University

Rod McDonald and Susan Knights

Introduction

Australian universities have a long tradition of allowing applicants who meet the normal entry requirements to enrol as part-time students. As long ago as 1961, 20 per cent of students entering Australian universities were enrolled part-time (AVCC, 1971). In some cases this provision was extended to students living in remote areas who were offered the option of external enrolment with courses conducted by correspondence. Such provision allowed adult students to undertake degree courses without undue detriment to work and family commitments. This relatively open access to higher education was one of the factors which led to the recommendation that Australia should not establish an equivalent to the UK Open University (Karmel, 1975). But although the existing provision of part-time and external study met the needs of some older students, applicants were still required to have the normal entry qualification, ie school-leaving examinations, sometimes somewhat abbreviated in the form of adult matriculation.

Since the early 1970s universities throughout Australia have been relaxing their entry requirements to enable adult students (variously defined) to enter some courses without having to overcome the hurdles of school-leaving examinations. This change might be interpreted by the cynical as a reaction to the decreased number of 'normal' applicants — a result of the large increase in the number of tertiary institutions without a commensurate increase in the participation rate of school-leavers — and the projected decline in the absolute numbers of 18-year-olds in the population. Indeed an account of one such scheme at another university openly states:

> the Programme was started in haste when it became apparent that the first year Arts quota was not going to be filled by 'normal' students. (Isaacs, 1979)

However, it is important to note that although such motives may have played a part in breaking down long held institutional prejudices against mature students, the subsequent academic achievements of mature students, by now extensively documented (Eaton and West, 1978; Hore and West, 1980), should make them desirable applicants in their own right. For whatever reason, the percentage of adult students in

Australian universities and in other sectors of higher education has risen steadily throughout the last decade. As an indication of the level of interest, a very well attended conference devoted entirely to this topic was held in Sydney in 1978 (McDonald and Knights, 1979).

Murdoch University's flexible admissions policy

Murdoch University, located in Perth, Western Australia, was formally established in 1973 and took its first students in 1975. When the university was formally established it was anticipated that like other Australian universities it would grow quickly and have a student body of approximately 5000 by 1985. Changes in federal government policy, and the cessation of growth in the university sector overall, have resulted in a much slower growth rate than anticipated, and by 1985 (ten years after taking its first students) Murdoch University will have approximately 3000 students.

Early discussions of the Planning Board referred to the need to provide an opening for adults to enrol without necessarily having to go back to school first, and the appropriate University statute allows for the admission of any student who satisfies the University that 'notwithstanding any lack of formal educational qualifications and background, from whatever cause, he is capable of pursuing studies to degree level over a reasonable period'. Without belittling the value of providing an education for school-leavers (high school graduates), those planning the University envisaged admitting a proportion of mature students, and one of the University's stated aims is: 'to provide a liberal and relevant education for a varied range of students . . . drawn from a wide range of age groups and from many walks of life.'

This is reinforced to some extent in the papers delivered at a major conference of the foundation professors and senior administrative staff 18 months before the University took its first students. Two professors made particular reference to mature students:

> Murdoch has a unique chance to do something for special groups of people. Three groups in particular come to mind: mature-age students, students from remote areas and women.

> Let us make a strong bid for the mature-age student. The most exciting period at the University of Western Australia was said to be 1945-49 with the Reconstruction Student.[1] Our admissions procedure should be very flexible for these people.

In view of the experience of other universities, in which staff in the humanities and social sciences are generally the first to extol the benefits of admitting mature students, it is interesting that the above statements were made by foundation professors in science-based schools.

Although some of those responsible for Murdoch's attitude to mature students were probably influenced by their own previous educational experiences (either as teachers or students) or committed to the principle of lifelong learning, the following factors appear to have been the most significant:

34

1. Murdoch University was charged with the responsibility of providing educational opportunities for people living throughout the one million square miles of Western Australia. This brought with it a commitment to distance teaching and the certainty that a high proportion of these students would be mature-age.
2. Some of the foundation staff felt that Murdoch should be an alternative university, providing opportunities which would complement those offered by the earlier established university in the same city. There was also some feeling that Murdoch should be more closely linked with the community than universities have been in the past. Both these factors suggested opening the university to mature students.
3. At the time that the admission policies were formulated, the idea that mature students were 'a good thing' was gaining acceptance throughout Australia, and some universities were establishing trial schemes under which they admitted a few mature students without the usual qualifications. Undoubtedly this played some part in the decisions made at Murdoch.

The commitment to mature students was made public with advertisements like the one shown in Figure 2.1, and the University proceeded to admit mature students and school-leavers in approximately equal numbers.

A major difficulty faced by the Admissions Committee was how to devise criteria for the admission of mature-age applicants which embodied the spirit of the University's policy. The approach adopted was to ask students to provide the following information:

☐ a fairly detailed curriculum vitae, covering your school history (mention any public examinations taken, with dates, subjects passed and grades if known); details of jobs held since leaving school (with dates and descriptions) and an indication of any studies undertaken since leaving school (with dates, subjects and any qualifications gained);

☐ a brief statement of your interests and spare-time occupations, of how you plan to support yourself at university, of any alternative courses of study you might have considered or commenced and your reasons for doing so and of your future career plans;

☐ an essay of about 500-700 words describing your reasons for wanting to come to university and what you hope to get out of a university education; and

☐ any other information about yourself that you think will be relevant to a decision on your application.

Assessors from each area of study then assessed the applications.

Further developments

In the five years that the University has been taking students, two main developments have occurred. First, although mature students have become a valued and established part of many faculties, in others there has been some feeling that the proportion of mature students (between

murdoch university

has places in 1978 for

★ **MATURE-AGE STUDENTS whose personal achievements and experience compensate for the absence of formal educational qualifications**

★ **MATURE-AGE STUDENTS who wish to add to existing qualifications or resume after an absence from studies**

★ **SCHOOL-LEAVERS with a suitable school record**

★ **EXTERNAL STUDENTS**

Places are available in the following degree programmes. Those marked with an asterisk (*) may be completed externally.

ARTS
Chinese Studies
*Economics
*General Studies
*History
Psychology
*Population and
  World Resources
Social and Political Theory
*Southeast Asian Studies
*World Literature and
  Literary Theory

EDUCATION
*Teacher Education
  •Primary
  •Secondary
  •Certificate Conversion

SCIENCE
Biology
Chemistry
Environmental Science
*Mathematics
*Mineral Science
*Physics
Veterinary Biology

A limited number of places will also be available for students who do not intend to complete a degree but wish to enrol for individual courses.

 Staff of the University will be pleased to answer any inquiry. For information about Murdoch University and its admission procedures, programmes and courses, please telephone, call or write to the Admissions Office, Murdoch University, Murdoch, Western Australia 6153 (telephone 332 2211).

Applications for admission to degree programmes at Murdoch University should be made immediately to: The Tertiary Institutions Service Centre, P.O. Box 55, Nedlands 6009, (telephone 386 2466).
Applications for individual course enrolment should be made to the Admissions Office at Murdoch University.

Figure 2.1. *Press advertisement for mature-age students*

40 and 50 per cent) is unduly large. However, the expansion of universities and colleges of advanced education in Australia has resulted in an element of competition between institutions for able students. This is as true of Murdoch as it is of other universities, and accordingly even those who are not necessarily committed to a philosophy of lifelong learning are none the less committed to attracting students of the highest quality, whether they be school-leavers or mature age.

The second development has arisen out of a concern that the University might be rejecting able mature applicants who were not able to find ways of demonstrating that they had a good chance of success, and a desire of many mature applicants to be given a clearer idea of what was expected of them. Accordingly, the request for an essay has been replaced by more precise questions, relating to the reasons for selecting a given degree programme and any preparation undertaken for university study.

The University has also collaborated with some higher education institutions in Perth in offering a scholastic aptitude test to any mature applicants who wish to avail themselves of it. It is not compulsory, and is offered so that it can be used by those who feel that their applications will be strengthened by this sort of empirical information.

Study of mature students

Up to now studies of mature students in higher education have only concerned traditional institutions where they are in a small minority (Challis, 1976; Nisbet and Welsh, 1972) or unique institutions such as the UK Open University. The position at Murdoch offers the opportunity of studying such students at university without the educational aspects of their experience being overwhelmed by the social aspects of being a member of a small and easily identified minority group. Such a study was carried out at Murdoch in 1977-78 by the Educational Services and Teaching Resources Unit and although its initial aim was to assess how far that University was meeting the needs of its high proportion of mature students the outcomes of the study are wider than this.

The main questions that the study set out to answer were:

☐ How and why do mature students choose to study at university?
☐ What is the experience of mature students at university?

It was first necessary to arrive at a working definition of a mature student. Even using the criterion of age alone, there is considerable disagreement between universities. For example, the age from which special entry schemes for mature applicants operate varies from 17 years at East Anglia to 27 years for certain degrees at Strathclyde (CVCP, 1976). But age is not the only determining factor in the eyes of those who teach them. The term 'mature student' has also come to be associated with students who are attending university after a significant gap in their formal education (see for example Elton, 1975). For this study, we took students who were 25 years and older when they entered the University, as this ensured that our sample would be comprised of students who were both mature in age and who had had a significant break in their formal education.

The two questions above were discussed initially with members of the teaching staff and administration of the University, to ensure that all relevant aspects of each question were explored. Discussions were then held with groups of volunteers from among the mature student population, to ensure that the concerns of mature students were reflected in the design of the study. Those discussions were conducted using the nominal group technique[2] asking the question: 'Is there anything that prevents you from getting as much as you would like out of studying at Murdoch?' Although the answers to this question followed fairly predictable lines ('lack of time', 'access to the library' and so on) this exercise enabled us to proceed with the study in the knowledge that no aspects which students felt were important were being ignored. It also became apparent at this stage that although the students experienced some difficulties, they did not see themselves as having noteworthy problems — a fact which became increasingly obvious as the study progressed.

The next stage of the study was to conduct structured interviews with a sample of 65 mature students proportionately stratified according to age, sex, type of course and whether they were studying part-time or full-time. The interviews took between half an hour and an hour and the provision of several open-ended questions towards the end of each interview allowed for the expression of opinion on any matters of particular interest to the student concerned.

At this stage two seminars were held on the subject of adult learners. These were part of a continuing series of discussions organized by the Educational Services and Teaching Resources Unit on aspects of teaching and learning, and attracted staff from throughout the University. The seminars enabled staff to be told of some of the preliminary results of the study, and gave them an opportunity to comment.

The final stage of the study was a postal questionnaire sent to all students aged 25 and over who were registered as internal (on-campus) students, whether part-time or full-time. 340 students answered the postal questionnaire — a response rate of 70 per cent.

Results of the Study

Reasons for coming to the University as an adult[3]

One of the reasons most frequently put forward for adults undertaking university degrees is the fact that an increasing number of career avenues are now blocked for those without degrees. Career-related motivations were mentioned by almost half of the students interviewed and 79 per cent of the respondents said that a degree was either 'essential' (36 per cent) or 'probably helpful' (43 per cent) in a career they wished to pursue. Some of these students, many of them teachers, needed degrees in order to obtain promotion in their current occupation or felt that the current cutbacks in employment posed a potential threat for non-graduate staff; however, there were others who felt that a degree might not lead to career advancement within their present occupation. For example, one student was already working in marine archaeology but needed a degree in order to organize his own expeditions. Another was a technically qualified acoustic engineer who felt that his suggestions and research projects did not receive the attention they deserved because he did not have a degree. A third response in this category came from a minister of the Church who had already published two books and wanted to write more but felt that 'People don't listen to you unless they can see that you have done something.' In this case having a degree was seen as the required demonstration of 'having done something'.

A different kind of career-related motive was expressed by a third of the students interviewed who said that they needed a degree to qualify them for a change of career. A few of these students already had degrees in different subjects but most were people whose career expectations had outstripped their initial level of education. Although the sample of students interviewed contained almost equal numbers of men and women, this particular motive was mentioned by almost three times as many women as men — not surprising, considering the low emphasis placed on careers for women when most of these students left school.

Apart from those students who linked a university degree with their career aspirations, the combined results of the interviews and questionnaire indicate that between one third and one half come for reasons more closely associated with personal satisfaction or challenge.[4] Almost a fifth of the interview responses contained phrases like:

> It's something I always wanted to do
>
> I have always wanted to go to university but came from a large family and so had to go to work after school
>
> I always wanted to study maths but my father thought girls didn't need university education.

Others who spoke in terms of the need for intellectual stimulation made comments such as:

> I was fed up with four walls, kids and coffee parties
>
> I need study to keep my brain cells active.

A relatively small proportion of students indicated that they were motivated by interest in a particular subject. Only one out of the 65 students interviewed answered the question 'Why did you decide to take a university course?' in terms of subject interest and few others mentioned interest in a particular subject whilst discussing career motivations or the personal challenge presented by university. However, when asked to indicate the comparative importance of various reasons for choosing Murdoch University, the fact that it offers courses not available elsewhere was rated higher than any other reason by the largest percentage of respondents. This would suggest that the decision 'to go to university' precedes subject selection for most adult students although once the decision has been made choice of subject can have an important influence on the choice of university.

About a fifth of the students interviewed linked their decision to come to university with a change in their circumstances — either something which had already happened or something they were anticipating. The most frequently mentioned of these was a change in occupation; for example:

> After leaving school I took up professional golf. I became intensely dissatisfied with this after five years and was looking for an alternative.

Other changes mentioned were divorce,

> Following my divorce I was free from responsibilities for what seemed like the first time ever and decided to do something *I* wanted for a change

39

retirement,

> After a lifetime career in business I wanted to prepare for retirement and do something completely unrelated to profit motive

and illness,

> I have a heart complaint and am on a pension; I got sick of not doing anything.

Advantages and disadvantages of studying as a mature student

Although the traditional attitude of institutions of higher education towards adult students, especially those without the usual entry qualifications, has been negative and restrictive with the implication that such students present a problem to the system, the students in our study certainly did not see themselves as 'problem' students. They were extremely positive about the advantages of studying as a mature student despite various constraints which did not apply to younger students, especially the problem of competing demands for their time. They stressed the value of the sense of commitment they felt to their studies:

> You know what you want, why you are doing the course
>
> I *know* that this is what I really want

and often compared this with the lack of certainty they noticed in younger students:

> Younger students have too much living to do; they are just starting to spread their wings.

Apart from the sense of purpose, many students mentioned the knowledge they had gained from their work experience as another advantage:

> I can see the application of some things because of my work experience
>
> You can relate what you learn to life much better
>
> I find I can make most of my studying relevant to the real situation because I know what that is.

Another advantage of work experience is practice in dealing with organizations and people:

> Mature students are often prepared to confront the lecturer — they are more confident and assured
>
> It's easier to approach staff
>
> More familiar with organizations, complaining and getting things changed. I can be more in control of learning and dealing with people.

The experience which these students see as giving them a definite advantage over school-leavers has only been gained at the expense of formal study, and this latter aspect causes some problems. Students have initial anxieties about settling down to studying again and not being up-to-date in areas such as mathematics and science which have changed a great deal since many of these students left school. Many of the students interviewed had anticipated problems in beginning academic work but confidence seemed to be established as the first semester progressed.[5] In an attempt to see whether any particular aspect of studying caused special problems the postal questionnaire asked them to indicate their level of concern about several areas. The aspect which caused problems for the greatest number of students was knowing what standard was expected in assignments: 46 per cent of the students felt this was a problem.

Previous studies have shown that one source of difficulty for adult students in higher education has been relating to younger students and a system designed for them:

> The older adult who previously obtained a certain security from operating within his own age group must now enter a culture which is highly youth orientated. (Glass and Harshberger, 1974)

However, the results of our study indicated that although there were some mature students who felt quite distant from school-leavers, this did not concern them because they had the alternative contact with other mature students. Several respondents also made the point that older students had already established their social contacts before coming to university and did not expect the campus to supply them with a social life. The majority of students interviewed were positive about their relationship with younger students:

> They are more tolerant of the age differences than they would be in the outside world. Sharing the same demands really helps, it works both ways.

In the light of our evidence we would suggest that the feelings of isolation reported in previous studies arise not because younger students dislike mature students, but because previous studies related to mature students who were a small minority group.

Many junior members of staff at Murdoch are younger than some of the students they teach, but although one or two mature students felt that some of the staff expected them to be unduly rigid and conservative the general impression was one of mutual respect and friendliness. If any difference was observed between staff attitudes towards school-leavers and mature students it was usually seen to be to the advantage of the mature students — 'Some staff are more prepared to explain things to mature students and they are very patient.'

Implications for institutions

A question which seems likely to take on increasing importance as the number of adult students in university courses continues to grow is the extent to which the needs of adult students differ from those of school-leavers. Among adult educators, particularly in Europe and North America, various attempts have been made to differentiate between learning in adulthood and childhood. Proponents of a critical distinction between the two have even gone so far as to suggest the term 'andragogy' to describe the teaching of adults as opposed to the more familiar 'pedagogy' which they feel should be confined to the teaching of children (Knowles, 1970).

In no case is there a suggestion that teaching methods should change overnight once a student reaches a certain age, but that increasing maturity tends to be associated with an increasing desire and capability to take responsibility for learning. This view is supported most convincingly by Tough's research into informal learning projects undertaken independently by adults without any institutional support or direction (Tough, 1971). Just as teaching methods are sometimes categorized along a continuum from teacher-centred to student-centred so, it is suggested, students' preferred learning styles may be located along a continuum from teacher-directed to self-directed (Knowles, 1973). If this is true, it might be expected that mature students would tend to occupy a place further towards the self-directed end of the continuum than those who had just left school. The study pointed to the underlying competence of mature students and their ability to take a good deal of responsibility for their own learning on the one hand, and their initial anxieties and lack of certain specific skills on the other. In this section, therefore, we outline some of the teaching strategies which mature students felt were particularly appropriate to them as learners.[6]

Independent study
The results of the interviews and to a lesser extent the questionnaire responses indicate clearly that mature students place great emphasis on the value of their own life experiences and ability to take responsibility for themselves. The option of taking independent study contracts in place of formal courses was mentioned many times as an aspect of Murdoch which made this university particularly suitable for mature students.

The independent study contract scheme allows a student to study a topic or subject of personal interest which is not otherwise available as a formal course, and to obtain credit for this towards his or her degree. It differs from formal courses in that it relies on private self-directed study rather than arranged classes, and in that the initiative to choose the topic and organize the contract must come from the student. The essence of an independent study contract is that it is based on the student pursuing his or her studies independently (and meeting periodically with the supervisor) and fulfilling the assessment procedure as specified in the contract and approved by the University (Marshall and Bain, 1978).

This option is not restricted to mature students but it does accord very well with their wish for independence. It also recognizes the needs of those who wish to study an aspect of their daily work in greater depth or to follow up topics in which they have developed a deep interest over the years since they left school — for example, research on marine archaeology was undertaken by a student mentioned earlier who was an experienced diver and who had worked in a maritime museum, and a project on psychological aspects of industrial accidents was carried out by a student who was manager of an accident prevention bureau.

Given this, it is not surprising that mature students enrol for independent study contracts in greater numbers than younger students, as shown in Table 2.1.

As Bradbury *et al* point out in Chapter 3, the replacement of entire courses by independent study contracts is an innovation which has significant institutional implications. From our experience, independent study provision on this scale is very demanding for both staff and students, and does not suit all; we would never suggest that such a system should be introduced universally. However, there are many ways of enabling students to take more responsibility for the organization of their learning without changing traditional course structures: project work and even conventional essay assignments can be organized on a contract basis which requires the student to set the objectives, identify resources, state criteria for evaluation and negotiate an acceptable method of assessment (see for example Adderley *et al*, 1975).

	Education	Social Sciences	Sciences
Percentage of courses taken by *mature students* in the form of independent study contracts	2.0%	1.8%	1.1%
Percentage of courses taken by *younger students* in the form of independent study contracts	0.7%	1.0%	0.7%

(Students at Murdoch University take 24 courses in their degree; so a figure such as 2 per cent (= 1 in 50) means that, *on average*, one person in two will undertake one course as an independent study contract.)

Table 2.1. *Independent study contracts as a percentage of courses at Murdoch University*

Flexibility of assessment
Many of the students in the study also appreciated the flexible assessment system available in many courses. Anxiety about written examinations has previously been mentioned as a characteristic of mature students (Challis, 1976). The opportunity to take courses with continuous assessment or project-based assessment instead of unseen examinations was therefore welcome — in fact some students deliberately avoided courses where written examinations were required and chose courses which offered an option between a written examination and a project. The quotation below is from a 59-year-old ex-nurse who was indignant at having been told by a professor that examinations were a fact of life and she ought to get used to them:

> At the age of fifty-nine I feel quite able to decide for myself what are and what are not the facts of life.

Developing learning skills

We have already mentioned that many mature students initially felt
anxious about their ability to cope with the rudiments of university study.
For the benefit of both mature students and school-leavers, the
Educational Services and Teaching Resources Unit co-ordinates an
extensive learning skills programme to help all students — both mature
students and school-leavers — develop their learning skills. Each of the
foundation ('trunk') courses has as one of its aims the development of
the learning skills necessary for university study. The learning skills
programme is carried out within each foundation course, with certain
activities being addressed to the development of study skills within the
context of the students' overall studies. In addition, students may enrol
in a series of tutorials designed to improve specific learning skills.

Amongst the students we interviewed, some of the problems of
retrieving mathematical and essay-writing skills seem to have been
overcome within a relatively short time, and a number of students left
the tutorials as 'satisfied customers' after only a few weeks. Others,
however, stayed on, gaining not only confidence but help in a variety of
areas. More details about this programme are given elsewhere (Knights
and McDonald, 1981), but it is worth noting that the fact that these
activities were part of official university policy seemed to validate the
programme in the eyes of many mature students, who felt that it was
therefore quite 'respectable'.

Obviously some mature students need initial help with some very basic
skills — like organizing their time — and some not-so-basic ones such as
interpreting what is expected in an assignment. But if they are to be
helped in an effective and appropriate way they need to be offered more
than an initial 'patching up' at an isolated referral centre.

Other aspects

The existence of an informal and helpful relationship between staff and
students was mentioned more often than anything else as one reason
which made the university particularly suitable for mature students.
This was mentioned particularly in relation to initial anxieties about
performance in comparison with that of school-leavers and also to the
understanding extended to the time problems connected with work and
home responsibilities. It seems logical that adults who are often removing
themselves from an established position and to some extent putting
themselves at risk by returning to the dependence of being a student
are likely to feel particularly vulnerable to patronizing or authoritarian
attitudes on the part of teaching staff and to be especially relieved to find
that they are treated with respect.

Conclusion

In Australia there is no tradition of establishing separate institutions to
provide for the higher education of adult students — there is for example

no Birkbeck College or University without Walls. Instead, as noted earlier, adults have traditionally been accommodated on a part-time basis alongside school-leavers. Since the present political situation makes it certain that no new institutions of any kind will be created in the foreseeable future, it is encouraging to see from the outcome of this study that large numbers of adult students can enter a university and learn in a way appropriate to their needs without distorting the system to the detriment of school-leavers. None of the aspects of Murdoch University which were particularly appreciated by the mature students in our study were specifically designed for them: independent study contracts, assessment options and help in developing and improving learning skills are equally available to school-leavers and are used by them as well. It may well be that changes within the school system (such as the Humanities Curriculum Project and MACOS)[7] will gradually alter the expectations of school-leavers and make them, like many adults, wish for less of the traditional didactic approach.

The ways in which adult students differ most clearly from school-leavers are connected with their work and family responsibilities. The opportunity for adults to benefit from university study depends not only on the provision of an appropriate teaching system, but perhaps even more on practical aspects. Some of these (for example the opportunity to study part-time or externally and the provision of child care facilities) are within the control of the universities, but many are not: for example the need for financial support, educational leave, and career opportunities for older graduates. All these are problems with wider social implications than the introduction of a more flexible approach to admission and teaching, but they will need to be tackled if higher education is ever to become truly available to the mature adult.

ACKNOWLEDGEMENTS

We are grateful to Professor Stephen Griew for support which enabled this project to start, and to Richard MacWilliam for his considerable help in documenting the development of Murdoch University's admissions policy.

BASIC REFERENCE DATA (1980)

I. The host institution

Name: Murdoch University
Date founded: Founded in 1973; first students enrolled in 1975
Internal organization: Comprised of six Schools of Study (faculties): Education, Environmental and Life Sciences, Mathematical and Physical Sciences, Social Inquiry, Human Communication, Veterinary Studies
Number of academic staff: 200
Number of students: 2500
Catchment area: Western Australia
Designated responsibility for off-campus activities: Responsible for external university education throughout Western Australia. Approximately a third of the University's students are enrolled wholly or mainly in externally offered courses.
Income: $A15 million from the Australian Government

II. The innovation/system being studied

Name: Flexible admissions policy
Date founded: 1975

NOTES

1. Under the Commonwealth Reconstruction Training Scheme, introduced by the Australian government at the end of the second world war, places were made available for ex-servicemen (who by then were 'mature' students) to enter universities without necessarily meeting normal admission criteria.

2. The nominal group technique has been designed by Delbecq *et al* (1975) and used in several studies at Murdoch University. It derives its names from the fact that although group discussion takes place in some stages of the meeting, members of the group write down their suggestions and indicate their relative importance privately — so the group is only 'nominally' a group for part of the time. The technique thus combines the illuminative value of the contribution of ideas from members of a group in a non-threatening atmosphere, followed by a group discussion, with the benefit of members being able to indicate their considered preferences privately.

3. Some of the results in this section have previously been briefly outlined at the Annual Conference of the Society for Research into Higher Education, University of Surrey, 1977 (Knights and McDonald, 1978).

4. Although 79 per cent of the students stated in the questionnaire that obtaining a degree was related to their career plans, the interviews showed that a large proportion of these had, as their *prime* reason for attending university, reasons more closely associated with personal satisfaction or challenge.

5. This comment, and indeed this whole study, refers to the experience of students who were attending the University and who had therefore survived in the system for a period at least. Work is under way at present on the experiences of mature students who discontinue their studies.

6. In another paper we have considered how some of the outcomes of this study relate to the characteristics of adult learners as identified in less formal learning situations (Knights and McDonald, 1978).

7. An acronym for: 'Man — A Course of Study'.

REFERENCES AND BIBLIOGRAPHY

Adderley, K *et al* (1975) *Project Methods in Higher Education*, 93 pp, Society for Research into Higher Education, London.

Australian Vice-Chancellors' Committee (1971) (with Department of Education and Science), *The 1961 Study*, 297 pp, Australian Government Publishing Service, Canberra

Challis, R (1976) The experience of mature students, *Studies in Higher Education*, 1 (2), 209-22

Committee of Vice-Chancellors and Principals of Universities in the UK (1976) *The Compendium of University Entrance Requirements for First Degree Courses in the UK*, pp 316-17, Association of Commonwealth Universities, London

Delbecq, A, Van der Ven, A H and Gustafson, D H (1975) *Group Techniques for Program Planning: A Guide to Nominal Group and Delphi Processes*, 174 pp, Scott Foresman and Co, Glenview, Illinois

Eaton, E and West, L H T (1978) *The Academic Performance of Mature Age Students: A Survey of the Literature*, 10 pp, Higher Education Advisory and Research Unit, Monash University, Melbourne

Elton, L R B (1975) Mature students: OU and non-OU, in Evans, L and Leedham, J (eds) *Aspects of Educational Technology*, 9, 64-73

Glass, J C and Harshberger, R F (1974) The full-time, middle-aged adult student in higher education, *Journal of Higher Education*, 45, 211-18

Hore, T and West, L H T (eds) (1980) *Mature Age Students in Australian Higher Education*, 184 pp, Higher Education Advisory and Research Unit, Monash University, Melbourne

Isaacs, G (1979) *Mature Age Entry to the Faculty of Arts 1977*, 122 pp, Tertiary Education Institute, University of Queensland, Brisbane

Karmel, P (Chairman) (1975) *Open Tertiary Education in Australia*, 114 pp, Final Report of the Committee on Open University to the Universities Commission, Australian Government Publishing Service, Canberra

Knights, S and McDonald, R (1978) Adult students in university courses, in Billing, D (ed) *Course Design and Student Learning*, pp 15-18, Society for Research into Higher Education, Guildford

Knights, S and McDonald, R (1981) *Adult Learners in Higher Education: Their Study Problems and Some Solutions* (in press)

Knowles, M (1970) *The Modern Practice of Adult Education: Andragogy vs Pedagogy*, 384 pp, Association Press, New York

Knowles, M (1973) *The Adult Learner: A Neglected Species*, 198 pp, Gulf Publications, Houston

Marshall, L and Bain, A (1978) *Taking an Independent Study Contract*, 21 pp, Murdoch University, Perth

McDonald, R and Knights, S (1979) Returning to study: the mature age student, *Programmed Learning and Educational Technology*, 16 (2), 101-05

Nisbet, J and Welsh, J (1972) The mature student, *Educational Research*, 14, 204-07

Tough, A (1971) *The Adults' Learning Projects*, 191 pp, Ontario Institute for Studies in Education, Toronto

3. Innovations in independent study at North East London Polytechnic

Phil Bradbury, Eunice Hinds, Maggie Humm and Derek Robbins

In 1968 Eric Robinson produced a book, *The New Polytechnics*, in which he discussed the challenge posed by the proposed introduction of about 30 new higher education institutions in the UK. He argued:

> It is unlikely that universities and polytechnics will exist side by side permanently. The essential issue at stake is 'What type of universities will this country have in the future?' One of the essential components of this question is 'What type of student and what type of course of study will the universities provide?' One might interpret the polytechnic policy as an attempt to change the concept of the British university and in particular to replace the concept of the boarding school university by that of the urban community university. The essential feature of the polytechnic as an urban community university, as a people's university, must be its responsibility and responsiveness to democracy rather than its insulation from it. (Robinson, 1968)

Eric Robinson became Deputy Director of NELP (North East London Polytechnic) at its inception in 1970 and it is clear that it was his intention that the whole institution should become a 'community university'.

A Course Development Unit was established within the institution to assist staff in the task of developing new courses and, more important, to ensure that courses proposed by staff were in accord with the ideological orientation for the polytechnic prescribed by the Deputy Director. A 'systems approach' to course design was enforced whereby the proposed 'output' from courses was to be characterized by student capacity to do more than to know. The names of new departments reflected this emphasis — departments of Applied Biology, Applied Economics and, even, Applied Philosophy.

Meanwhile, at a national level, a committee under the chairmanship of Lord James of Rusholme was appointed by the then Secretary of State for Education and Science, Mrs Margaret Thatcher, to carry out an intensive study of the education, training and probation of teachers. The committee, which reported in December 1971, suggested:

> It is possible and desirable to divide the education and training of teachers into three consecutive stages: the first, personal education; the second, preservice training and induction; and the third, inservice education and training. The term 'cycles' has been chosen for these stages. (James Report, 1972)

For the first cycle the report recommended 'that there should be a two-year course leading to a new award, to be called the Diploma in Higher Education'. The report specified that this course 'would be broad in scope and would include, for all students, a substantial element of general studies, occupying about a third of the time, combined with rigorous study of normally two special subjects, one of which might or might not be related to educational studies, chosen by the students from a range of options'. The report also argued that the course, 'although designed with the needs of teachers in mind, should be widely acceptable to prospective students and employers alike'. It was felt that the course would attract students who were not committed to a career in education, and that diplomates, as generalists, would attract the interest of employers.

A Government White Paper in December 1972 accepted the recommendation of the James Committee that there should be a new award, but significantly widened its potential:

> The Government believes that a range of intellectually demanding two-year courses will be a critical element in achieving greater flexibility in higher education. They welcome the James Committee's recognition of the potential of two-year courses, but the proposals which follow are designed to serve a wider purpose than that envisaged in their Report. (White Paper, 1972)

There is a suggestion here of a wider context of thinking about the needs of higher education in the 1970s. The OECD (Organization for Economic Co-operation and Development) had already organized a meeting on Short-Cycle Higher Education in November 1971, the proceedings of which were published in 1973 under the title *Short-Cycle Higher Education: A Search for Identity*. In the introduction to that publication, it was pointed out:

> The majority of OECD member countries are envisaging, as one of their main strategies, a wider diversification of their post-secondary systems, the development of a variety of extra or non-university institutions and programmes originally created to provide terminal and, for the most part, vocationally oriented post-secondary education. For want of a better term, they are referred to in this volume as short-cycle institutions (SCIs) or short-cycle higher education (SCHE). (OECD, 1973)

The DipHE (Diploma in Higher Education)
Even before the appearance of the Government White Paper, Eric Robinson had established an *ad hoc* working party on the DipHE at NELP. The working party produced an interim report in October 1972 in which it argued:

> An important principle of NELP policy is to design courses to cater for the needs of prospective students rather than to seek students to fit courses that NELP would like to run. Having defined the DipHE concept the working party, in accordance with this policy, then sought to identify, for planning purposes, types of potential students for whom the programme was intended so that their estimated needs would form the basis of detailed planning. (NELP, 1972)

In 1973 the working party was extended, and a DipHE Development Unit was established for the academic year 1973-74 by the Academic Board and Governors with the brief of preparing proposals for a DipHE course that could commence in 1974. Eric Robinson left NELP in the spring of 1973 and Tyrrell Burgess was made Head of the Development

Unit and, subsequently, of the School for Independent Study which was established in 1974 to run one of the first two DipHE courses in the UK.

The context of the innovation in the School for Independent Study at NELP can, therefore, be summarized briefly as follows. The innovation occurred in the early days of an institution which was itself established with an innovating intention. The first Deputy Director saw polytechnics as potential change agents in UK higher education, moving the whole system towards greater flexibility and community involvement. Equally he seized the opportunity of a new national award to establish within NELP a course which would sustain the innovating momentum of the new institution. Many members of staff within NELP did not share the Deputy Director's perception of the function of polytechnics and, therefore, resented the development of a course which might enforce that perception. The difficulties in the development of the School for Independent Study are, therefore, a direct result of the ambitious and reforming intentions which were alive in the context from which it emerged.

Finally, it should be pointed out that the NELP DipHE scheme is not the only one, nor is NELP the only institution to offer independent study. Many colleges and polytechnics now run two-year courses leading to a DipHE. These are sometimes self-sufficient integrated courses (as for example at Bulmershe College, Bradford College and Middlesex Polytechnic) and sometimes are simply the first two years of an existing modular degree course (such as at City of London Polytechnic).

There are also other independent study schemes, such as those at Lancaster University (Percy and Ramsden, 1980) and at Murdoch University in Western Australia (Chapter 2), and the 'contract learning' schemes in the United States (Knowles, 1970, 1975, 1978, and Berte, 1975). In these cases, however, independent study is often only a part of wider schemes; nor is the community orientation, which is central to the arguments of this chapter, usually so explicit as with the NELP scheme.

Aims of the innovations

The DipHE and the subsequent Degree by Independent Study (discussed later in this chapter) have wide-ranging aims which all relate more or less directly to a new concept of education in what was seen as an institution attempting to model itself as a 'community university'. The essential aim uniting these schemes, however, was a desire to sustain momentum towards mass higher education by introducing short-cycle flexibility into the system. An emphasis on local intake was part of this wider perspective. The Polytechnic lies in an area of London where there is very little tradition of higher education and one of the declared aims of the Polytechnic is to increase the educational opportunities for local people.

The DipHE and local recruitment
When the DipHE was being planned it was consistently declared and argued that the programme should be such as to attract people from the local area.

The local area was seen implicitly as an important part of the wider community because of its very low recruitment into higher education. It was noted that in 1972, the Polytechnic's own local education authority areas (the London Boroughs of Newham, Barking and Waltham Forest) had the lowest take-up rates of university places in the Greater London area. Two of them had less than a third of the Greater London average.

Scrutiny of DES (Department of Education and Science) 'Statistics of Education' reveals a similar dismal pattern for the whole decade 1968-78. Nor is this the case only for take-up rate into universities. The take-up rate into advanced further education (degree and diploma courses in polytechnics, colleges of higher education, etc) is very similar. Over the same decade, Barking had the lowest take-up rate into advanced further education each year, Newham the second lowest take-up rate for all but one year, and Waltham Forest, variably, the third, fourth and fifth lowest.

The DipHE planning team observed that this state of affairs was more related to traditional attitudes to education than to any inability of the young to benefit from higher education. It would, therefore, be inappropriate for the programme to require of all students evidence of achievements atypical of the area they sought to serve. The team also opposed the notion that knowledge is cumulative, and argued that this further removed any need for prior knowledge qualifications in entrants. Accordingly, passes in the GCE (General Certificate of Education) at A (advanced) level, the usual matriculation requirements for entry to higher education, were played down. Indeed the planning team was strongly committed to open entry but was obliged, at least initially, to compromise on this key issue. More explicitly, as regards the local community, it was laid down that where applicants exceeded the number of places available, preference would be given to applicants from the local London boroughs.

The wider aims of independent study

As regards the programme of independent study itself, the DipHE aimed to start at a point appropriate to each student, not at some predetermined point. It aimed to allow the students to decide for themselves what their interests were, what they needed to study and what would be the best method of going about it. It was thought that employment or other life experiences might have presented people with problems which they thought education could help them solve. Students were also expected to try to work out what they wanted to be able to do at the end of the course. Implicit in these aims was the idea that students should constantly be referring to the outside world, to the wider community, as an integral part of their studies. In particular, they would be encouraged to have placements with appropriate outside agencies, and to undertake project work on problems directly affecting the local community.

The criterion for admission to the DipHE was to be whether the student was likely to benefit from the course. Consideration would obviously be given to the students' ability to cope and to motivation. Because the course was unique it was important to ensure that students clearly understood its structure.

The DipHE's aim was to enable people to become educated without necessarily having to accept an established body of knowledge. It was felt that a student's expert knowledge in one field should be balanced by an ability to work in other areas. The planning team became increasingly aware that employment opportunities change so there is a need to adapt and modify skills. The notion of 'general competence' developed and it became an aim of the course to ensure that all students had what came to be termed 'transferable skills'.

In order to allow students to work on acquiring skills which would be transferable to different situations, not just relevant to their special interest, the idea of central studies developed. The aim of the central studies component was to allow students to learn appropriate transferable skills and knowledge (ranging from the technical, such as typewriting and use of video, to the more abstract such as methods of inquiry and criticism of theory) through workshops and similar activities, and further to learn to use these skills by working with peers. Thus developed the notion of group project work, where groups of students themselves identify problems and then work on solving them. The aim of transferability was carried further by asking students to work with peers who had different individual interests. Collaboration with others, therefore, came to be seen as an aim of the DipHE, and it was hoped the students would develop interpersonal skills.

Methods by which the innovation became established

Once the aims of the DipHE had been established it was necessary to write a submission to the CNAA (Council for National Academic Awards), the national agency which approves schemes for non-university degrees and other qualifications in the UK. This submission stated that students should plan their own course during the first few weeks of the programme, writing a 'statement' of intent (the proformae for proposals for DipHE and degrees by independent study are shown in Appendices 3.1 and 3.2). The course would be in two sections:

□ *Individual work*, where a student would follow a programme of study planned with the help of an individual work tutor (an appropriate member of the lecturing staff from one of the Polytechnic's various faculties), who would supervise the work;
□ *Central studies*, where the student could study basic skills and do group project work. The student would identify which skills he or she required.

The 'statement' would go to a Validating Board of people who had achieved recognition in their own fields. (The first chairman of this board was Lord James.) The task of the Validating Board would be to endorse the judgement of the staff of the school as to what was a valid programme of study to second year degree level. Once students' programmes were validated these would form the bases of their courses in the Polytechnic; students would be assessed according to the criteria indicated in their statements. Any changes to statements could be submitted to subsequent meetings of the Validating Board (which in fact meets three times a year).

Students were to be assessed both on their individual work and on their general competence. The latter was to be assessed by what was to be known as the 'set situation'. This was a group project lasting approximately five weeks in the final term of the course, but upon which there were six criteria to be imposed, namely that the problem, which forms the basis of the set situation project, should:

☐ enable each individual to demonstrate his/her achievement of his/her own agreed objectives within the group activity
☐ be capable of a solution in the form of a group product within the stated time scale (normally about six weeks)
☐ have its origins and/or relevance within the local community around the Polytechnic
☐ be demonstrated to be socially useful
☐ involve a technical/scientific perspective
☐ be capable of requiring students to search for, collect, and analyse data from library and field sources.

The third and fourth of these criteria may be seen as a way of trying to institutionalize the kind of relationship the programme was intended to have with the wider community.

The CNAA lacked clear criteria as to what the DipHE should be, but was prepared to accept this as a framework for study. There was, of course, no set syllabus, although there was an elaborate 'file' of learning materials which would be available to students to use if they so wished. It may well have been that this 'file' was a prominent factor in the CNAA's original approval of the scheme, although it was in fact never much used and is not used at all by present students.

A major sticking point for the CNAA was entry criteria. It could never really come to terms with the idea of a course not based on accumulated knowledge and pressed strongly for conventional entry criteria instead of the open entry equally strongly favoured by the planning team. The compromise agreed was that the Polytechnic should aim to achieve a balance between A level entry and mature entry (over 21) and have a maximum of 10 per cent 'special' entry (under 21 and without qualifications).

Once CNAA approval had been secured, the next step was to secure the support of individual work tutors throughout the Polytechnic. This was achieved by circulating details of the scheme to all academic staff (some 700) in the Polytechnic and building a card index of those staff who indicated their interest in participating. Also, a system of faculty linkmen was established. These linkmen introduce the School's students to the different faculties, find appropriate tutors for students and offer general advice.

To ensure that staff are not unduly overburdened, an administrative structure was established for crediting faculties with additional staff and resources according to the number of students supervised. Unfortunately, however, contact hours can only be credited to tutorial staff *after* students have chosen their topics and this inhibits staff participation since they may find existing teaching commitments already too heavy. It is not, then, solely the timetabling allowance which motivates individual work tutors. Interviews among such staff reported elsewhere (NELP, 1979) indicate other benefits such as broadening perspectives, being able to see a particular project or piece of study all the way through and actually learning from students' work.

The School for Independent Study was established as an entity independent of other faculties with Tyrrell Burgess as Head and a staff of 12 tutors drawn from different disciplines. The first intake of 73 students was in 1974. These students had been attracted by a considerable amount of press publicity, some of which was from advertising but most of which was generated by interest in the DipHE in general and in the unusual nature of the DipHE by Independent Study in particular.

Development of the innovation

Early plans that the School should expand to have an annual intake of 300 students have not so far come to fruition, and the intake has remained at around 100 students. The School's development has been, therefore, more in its methods and theoretical stance than in size or formal status within the Polytechnic. The School has grown in three basic ways: first it developed key characteristics of independent work; then it developed innovations such as the part-time DipHE and one-year degree programme, and finally it developed strategies to cope with the problems of working and teaching independently.

Key characteristics
One key characteristic of independent study is that it develops students' consciousness of their own needs and helps them successfully to pursue their own aims. By devising courses which mix theoretical and community ideas, and by emphasizing the acquisition of transferable skills and knowledge based on real-life problems rather than those defined by disciplines, the School reduced the importance attached to subject-based education and could appeal to a broader range of students.

'Community' has come to be seen both as a resource to, and as a provider of, students for the School. What is interesting is the way students from all our courses concentrate on a basic epistemelogical problem: 'How does knowledge relate to experience?' They do not try to 'earn' intellect cumulatively, but develop their ability to 'know' alternatives by working empirically on cases. So work, whether from DipHE or degree courses, looks very similar. Students have investigated intentional communities (adolescent gangs), the communities of place (rented housing), communities of race (Chinese-speaking nursery children) or communities of the past (a Yiddish East End life).

Another key characteristic relates to the distance of the School from the Polytechnic. The School has been isolated geographically for five years on its own precinct, but the distance is rather one of *difference* from other students. This is almost certainly why the principle of voluntarism, which the School has evolved as a substitute for bureaucratic courses, can exist. The School depends for its existence on the involvement of staff across the Polytechnic to tutor students on a part-time basis. 'Voluntarism' exists best precisely in rebellion against an overwhelming presence of 'established fact'. Our students have supported and exploited the implicit needs of Polytechnic staff to extend expertise in areas outside their regular courses.

The degree and part-time DipHE

The impetus for a *degree* by independent study came from two directions. One was the Deputy Director's interest in self-directed adult education. He saw a potential degree in the context of a whole range of post-diploma possibilities, and as an umbrella organization for students within, and outside, the Polytechnic. The other direction was the need to provide a 'second cycle' course for holders of the DipHE. The DipHE was to take students from dependency through stages of diminishing dependency, so by the time they gained their diplomas they should be self-reliant. The degree aimed to build on this foundation. The double aim ensured planning for the degree would be done by staff within the School since they had already taken a test of likely degree interests among the 1974 intake of DipHE students: Art/Design 14, Arts 22, Business 3, Human Science 13, Science 5, Management 4, Others 6. One of the senior staff of the School co-ordinated and initiated various planning committees to prepare a degree submission for the CNAA.

There were two possibilities. One was to develop access to existing Polytechnic degrees. For adults this might mean several kinds of preparatory courses or evidence of external study. For the DipHE students it would mean probably only a short course which would be a reorientation rather than preparation. The other possibility was for the School to mount its own degree course open to DipHE and other students, which would be based in the School. That this latter possibility became policy resulted from the crucial timing of the submission. Other faculties were uninterested, or very dilatory, in themselves providing either bridging courses to existing degrees or faculty-based one-year degree courses. This inertia combined with the specific needs of the first students completing their DipHE in July 1976 ensured that the School itself would organize the degree. An account of the basis of the degree course and of the way in which it developed has been given elsewhere (Robbins, 1977).

The School duly prepared a submission by January 1976 which went to the CNAA in February 1976 and was approved, in co-ordination with a one-term pre-course (preparatory course), to run from September 1976.

The degree is awarded with honours and requires a one-year programme of study, equivalent to the third year of undergraduate education, which can be taken by students who have successfully completed the DipHE. The course is divided into two: *central* tutorials common to all students run by the School and equivalent to 0.2 of each student's weekly timetable; and *special* research supervised by an appropriate faculty tutor for the rest of each week. A programme of study is devised by each student during the pre-course and the degree offers the student the opportunity to design and justify his/her own completely individual course which, at one extreme, is analogous to postgraduate research and, at the other, takes the form of individually devised combinations of options forming a personalized course. Faculty agreement was co-ordinated via the Polytechnic Academic Board. No proposal is accepted by the Registration Board (meeting at the end of the pre-course) unless the student has a coherent proposal, a volunteer tutor and the agreement of the appropriate faculty to resource him or her. The staff teaching the DipHE courses also run, teach and maintain the degree and pre-course within the School for Independent Study.

The part-time DipHE has been another development in the School which offers potential means for making closer links between the Polytechnic and the community. It was felt that this mode of study (which requires a minimum of three years for qualification), offered extra flexibility and placed more emphasis on the local population. Obviously, if people were studying part-time, they would need to live within reasonable travelling distance of the Polytechnic.

Further, because the students would be studying part-time, they could carry on with their jobs and their study could be closely related to their jobs. The very fact of being able to continue in employment would make higher education possible for people who could not afford to give up their salary for a student's grant. The possibility of career change would therefore be enhanced for the middle-aged. The course was made flexible by having only one evening for 'core' meetings at which students need attend. The other meetings (personal tutor groups and meetings with individual work tutors) would be flexible and fit in with the time students had available. One group of people it was hoped might particularly benefit from this flexibility was young mothers hoping to enhance job prospects when their children were old enough for them to return to work.

Problems of teaching and learning
Some problems of independent study have, ironically, come from the 'community' orientation of the course. Overall, there has been an improvement in drop-out rates because staff and students have become much clearer about the nature of independent study and have created a less ambiguous programme. But this clarity has been gained by a narrowing

down of the uses of 'community'. Whereas community-based projects were at one time seen as an end in themselves, there has been a movement towards seeing project work as an institutionally controlled pedagogic device for inculcating skills (for further discussion see pp. 63-4).

This has had two consequences. The first is a student bias towards arts and social science, both in the DipHE and in the degree, and a subsequent academic resistance to scientific and technological fields. The difficulty for students, particularly when transferring from the DipHE to the degree, is to move from developing their practical experience to tackling general structural questions.

Many students are content with existing definitions of social needs and fail to find a method which can analyse that quantitative abstraction. They are not helped by the conflict in the School between those staff who teach self-awareness and those who aim to develop skills. The move, in the School, from spontaneity to a more overt structure and common practice has tended to position staff with radically different philosophies on to different courses in the School rather than allowing their differences to generate more exciting academic exchanges within each course.

The second consequence has been to make assessment aims and procedures more restricted. By using, in the DipHE, 'social relevance' as one of the devices for assessing a student's contribution to the final group project (the set situation) the course may very well encourage in students a limited concept of community. Naturally they often choose projects which can produce attractive visual material rather than projects which rigorously treat social relations. Staff find difficulty assessing an explicit level or standard of work except in narrow technical terms (eg information retrieval). It is particularly difficult to assess each student in isolation in the case of degree work.

However, the innovations in teaching methods and course planning developed by the School show that independent study is more far-reaching than the usual schemes for projects, related studies, or 'minor units' in courses. The general characteristics of the School already described are no longer experimental. In approving the full-time DipHE for a five-year period, and in accepting the degree and part-time DipHE, the CNAA has acknowledged the innovations developed by the School.

The principle of voluntarism is the most important development. Staff, whether within or outside the School, work with students on a problem or area of knowledge in which both have an interest. The role of the tutor is, then, different from that which is usual in higher education. Tutors are more responsive, aiming, through a more informal interaction with students, to create confidence rather than instil subject knowledge *per se*.

The School has transferred responsibility for the choice of study and the method of learning and assessment to the individual student. This transfer has been made easier by the development of the crucial first stage in the DipHE programme — the planning period. Here students practise group work, have a trial attachment to a specialist tutor and are introduced to the theory and range of transferable skills and research methods. By the end of the planning period the students have designed their own programmes of study, setting out details of the skills, knowledge and qualities that they intend to develop by the end of the course and which will form the basis of their assessment. It helps the broader range of student intake to come to terms with their own educational strengths and weaknesses and provides a supportive environment where they can improve basic competence, if necessary, in numeracy and literacy.

Similarly, for the degree, students take a part-time, once weekly, pre-course lasting for one year (normally concurrently with DipHE second year) where they design their course programme for the degree year. The pre-course has now developed as an alternative educational structure which strives to bridge disciplinary, departmental and other specialized boundaries of inquiry and knowledge to develop a fully ecological view of society. It borrows theoretical models from any discipline that can contribute to cultural explanation (a functional model from sociology, a systems model from environmental studies, a paradigm from science, an artistic model, and so on). Students evolve their own general proposition about culture which becomes a working hypothesis to examine in their degree year.

The development of flexible assessment procedures continues. Despite the enforced stringencies of the set situation an open attitude to assessment still prevails on the DipHE programme. Assessment is not confined to the presentation of written material. Students often mount their work for display and frequently include video, exhibitions, presentations, dramatizations and tapes. Since the structure of assessment usually defines for students their course possibilities the emphasis on visual, not just verbal, presentation has been crucial to the continuation of more open-ended project work.

Similarly, although the degree students have been required by the CNAA to take individual written examinations, they can choose that their value in the assessment be as low as 15 per cent. Degree students have written novels, made physiological measurements of the effect of yoga and constructed portable windmills. The dissertation or final product (a film or novel) has a special role; it is much longer than is traditional in first degrees. Because of the standard and scope of most dissertations, students can study their topic in greater detail than is permitted to regular undergraduates.

Evaluation of the innovation

The philosophy underpinning the independent study schemes thus demands a particular kind of intended relationship with the wider community. It is a two-way relationship: on the one hand providing access to higher education for sections of the community (especially in this case, the local community) who otherwise would not have it, and on the other hand engaging students in practical activities which are an integral part of their studies and which involve the wider community.

Independent study and local recruitment

The scheme has clearly been successful in attracting students from the local community. If the number of students who had resided in the local area (ie the London Boroughs of Newham, Barking and Waltham Forest) prior to embarking on the DipHE is compared with the total intake to the course, a quite remarkable trend emerges, shown in Table 3.1.

Session	Total intake	Local intake	% local intake
1974-75	73	4	5.5%
1975-76	98	13	13.3%
1976-77	89	17	19.1%
1977-78	92	14	15.2%
1978-79	101	24	23.8%
1979-80	102	30	29.4%

* 'Local' in Tables 3.1 - 3.6 means resident in one of the London Boroughs of Barking, Newham, or Waltham Forest at the time of application.

Table 3.1. *Local* intake to full-time DipHE 1974-79*

We see a steady increase in the number of students entering the scheme from the local area, from one student in 20 in 1974 to one student in three in 1979. To set these figures in context, a number of other questions need to be examined. For example, how do these figures compare with the Polytechnic as a whole? Further, do the local students coming on to the course do as well as others? (Ie does the course in any real sense satisfy their educational needs?)

On the first matter, comparable figures for the rest of the Polytechnic are, unfortunately, not available at the time of writing. However, information is available for the last three years on both the number of local applicants across the Polytechnic and on the number of firm and provisional offers which have been made to them. These data are shown in Tables 3.2 and 3.3.

The equivalent figures for the DipHE are shown in Tables 3.4 and 3.5.

By comparing Tables 3.2 with 3.4, and 3.3 with 3.5, it can be seen that both the number of local applicants and the number of offers made to local applicants are comparatively higher for the DipHE than for the average course across the Polytechnic; in 1979 these differences are particularly marked. Furthermore, it is known that the proportion of places offered which are finally taken up is slightly higher in the case of local applicants for the DipHE than it is for other DipHE applicants. If this pattern of higher local uptake of places offered, observed for the DipHE, applies across the Polytechnic as a whole, then it can be deduced that the actual proportion of local students in the Polytechnic is between 10 and 12 per cent. Referring back to Table 3.1, with these overall percentages of local

Faculty	1977-78	1978-79	1979-80
Humanities*	14.8%	12.4%	12.2%
Business	8.6%	8.5%	7.4%
Engineering	7.0%	6.2%	7.0%
Environmental Studies	4.8%	4.2%	3.4%
Human Science	8.8%	6.3%	8.6%
Science	7.2%	6.5%	7.0%
Art and Design	5.7%	4.7%	5.4%
Management	7.0%	8.9%	9.4%
Polytechnic	8.0%	7.2%	7.3%

*Data for the Faculty of Humanities include those for School
for Independent Study.

Table 3.2. *Percentage of local applications to NELP, by faculty, 1977-79*

Faculty	1977-78	1978-79	1979-80
Humanities*	14.2%	16.4%	17.9%
Business	11.5%	10.7%	10.7%
Engineering	7.1%	8.1%	7.9%
Environmental Studies	5.8%	7.3%	5.0%
Human Science	12.1%	9.1%	13.4%
Science	6.6%	8.9%	11.0%
Art and Design	5.7%	9.6%	12.2%
Management	7.2%	4.9%	7.4%
Polytechnic	9.4%	10.7%	10.6%

*Data for the Faculty of Humanities include those for School
for Independent Study.

Table 3.3. *Percentage of provisional and firm offers made by NELP
to local applicants, by faculty, 1977-79*

Session	Total applicants	Local applicants	% local applicants
1977-78	249	33	13%
1978-79	254	42	17%
1979-80	278	61	22%

Table 3.4. *Percentage of local applicants to full-time DipHE, 1977-79*

Session	Total offers	Local offers	% local offers
1977-78	134	18	13%
1978-79	129	26	20%
1979-80	144	38	26%

Table 3.5. *Percentage of provisional and firm offers made to local applicants to full-time DipHE, 1977-79*

Year	All students			Local students		
	Intake	Awarded DipHE	% success	Intake	Awarded DipHE	% success
1974-76	73	43	59%	4	2	50%
1975-77	98	44	45%	13	7	54%
1976-78	89	42	47%	17	9	53%
1977-79	92	47	51%	14	10	71%
1978-80	101	55	54%	24	15	63%

*For definition of success rate, see note on page 67.

Table 3.6. *Relative success rate* *of local students on full-time DipHE, 1974-78*

students in mind, it appears that whereas in 1974 the proportion of local students on the DipHE was low in comparison with the proportion of local students in the Polytechnic as a whole, between 1975 and 1979 the proportion of local students on the DipHE rapidly grew to exceed the proportion in the Polytechnic as a whole.

How well do the local DipHE students fare? At the time of writing five cohorts of students have completed the full two-year cycle of the DipHE. The success rate[1] of local students, as compared with all students, is as shown in Table 3.6.

Perhaps the figures given in Table 3.6 are too small to draw firm conclusions, but they do suggest that the local students fare at least as well as, and in some cases rather better than ($p = 0.08$, χ^2 test), other students.

The quantitative data above offer a very general indication of how the DipHE by Independent Study provides a means of access to higher education for the local community. The trouble with these as with all such raw numerical data is that they convey little about the actual people who lie behind them and can even sometimes be quite misleading. If, for example, the increasing number of local entrants were all people who would have gone on to higher education anyway but preferred either the style of the programme or to study closer to home, then this would be rather different a situation from where the entrants would simply not otherwise have gone on to higher education at all.

The following pen portraits will convey something of the people behind the numbers. They have been selected not necessarily because they are representative of all others, but because they indicate the nature and variety of local intake.

☐ Jane was a housewife living with her family close by the Polytechnic. She went to a local grammar school, leaving at the age of 16 with passes at GCE ordinary (O) level in two of the five subjects she had sat — Art and French. She was 35 when she came on to the course. She had had a number of different clerical/secretarial jobs; immediately prior to joining the course she worked as a cashier with a local bookmaker. On the course her special interest was organizations and their development. She obtained her DipHE in two years and is now working on the administrative staff of the local education authority.

☐ Vera was 40 when she joined the course and she also had a family. She was born and brought up in Dominica but came to the UK over 20 years previously and lived most of her life in Newham. She studied for (and failed) GCE A levels on a part-time basis. Her special interest was community relations, especially race relations. She failed to satisfy her assessment requirements the first time round but re-submitted her work to a later Assessment Board and was successful. She now works in the area as an education welfare officer.

☐ Barry was a 'special entry' applicant. He was 18 and had left a local comprehensive school at 16 with one O level. He had then gone to the local technical college where he gained three more O levels, then worked as a library assistant for a year. He was keenly interested and involved in the labour and trade union movement, and his special interest was in industrial safety. He gained his DipHE in two years and is at present a civil servant in the Department of Employment.

☐ Barbara, aged 24, was a housewife, married to a teacher and with two young children. She had left school at 15 with no qualifications and had a number of jobs as typist, receptionist, etc. Her special interest was education and, in particular, the teaching of art. She left the course at the beginning of the second year having found the difficulties of raising two children too much to cope with whilst doing the course.

☐ Monica, aged 38, came from the Midlands where she had been to a secondary modern school, leaving at age 15. She had subsequently trained and worked as a nurse, eventually moving to Newham where she had lived for a number of years. Her special interest was delinquency. She gained her DipHE in two years, now works as a health visitor in the local area and is training as a fieldwork teacher.

☐ Simon, aged 20, lived locally and had been to a fee-paying high school. He had left at 16 without qualifications and subsequently held a number of clerical jobs. His special interest was music, but whilst he completed the two years, he failed to satisfy his assessment requirements.

☐ Steven, aged 26, was brought up in the local area by adoptive parents. He left school at 16 without any qualifications and held a wide range of jobs from bookseller to welfare assistant. His special interest was adolescence, and he gained his DipHE in two years, continuing the following year to get an upper second class honours degree by independent study. He is now working as a part-time research assistant.

☐ Antony, in his early thirties, was born and educated in the West Indies, immigrating to the UK when in his late teens. He lives locally with his wife and two sons, and is a production line worker at a local Ford Motor Company plant. He was in the first cohort of students to enrol on the part-time DipHE and was one of the first students to gain the DipHE by this mode of study. His special interest was a study of the role of social workers in contemporary society, and he is now proposing to undertake a trainee social work programme with one of the local authorities.

A note needs to be added here concerning the part-time DipHE scheme. The full- and part-time courses share aims concerning the wider community but, as has been noted, the part-time course was felt to have particular importance for the local population. In fact, over 60 per cent of students enrolling on the part-time DipHE live in one of the three local London boroughs. In another sense, however, the reality has been different from expectations. It was thought that this was a course for which there would be a great demand. Pursuing the policy of flexibility, termly intakes (ie three per year) of 50 part-time students were the target. For the first intake there was a door-to-door delivery of literature throughout the local area and an open evening, but only 35 students enrolled. Since then the target of 50 has consistently failed to be met, and has had to be reduced to 25.

Many forms of advertising have been tried, eg posters in libraries, talks to local organizations, approaching employers, radio talks, newspaper articles and open evenings. Existing part-time students say they are sure there is a need, but the School is simply failing to attract the students.

Group projects, individual placements and other activities
in the local community
Despite the problems with the part-time course, the indicators seem clearly to suggest that the School is providing a means of access to higher education which had not previously been available for members of the local community. However, the success of group project work in contributing towards the notion of a community university has been rather more questionable. Staff attitudes have themselves been ambivalent and changing. The fundamental conflict between group work as providing a service to the community and group work as a teaching device has never

63

been properly resolved within the School. Because of this, and because of the inevitable conflicts of interest which arise within project groups, students have found it one of the more difficult components of the scheme. This in turn has led to increasingly tight controls with rigid timetables, deadlines for submission of plans, completion dates and presentation dates. Inevitably, this control renders group project work less able to meet needs which the wider community may have. It is a very happy coincidence indeed when an institutionally determined timetable matches precisely that required by a felt community need. The effects of this problem are becoming more visible within the School, with increasing numbers of students proposing alternatives to group work and the set situation (as they are permitted in the regulations in an attempt to sustain an ideology of 'independence').

The relationship between students' individual work and the wider community seems to work more successfully. There is greater flexibility here, with students more able to match their own educational needs with the needs of the community. The activities range from placements, sometimes arranged by the student's tutor, more often negotiated by the students themselves, to field studies. The following examples might serve to indicate the specific nature of some of these activities.

☐ Mary spends one day each week working in a local school. She assists with various classroom duties, but specifically is teaching a 'backward' boy to learn to read. She thus contributes to the work of the school whilst herself learning about the development and education of young children. The placement was arranged by her tutor.

☐ Matilda spends one day a week at a local refuge for battered wives. She, whilst contributing to the needs of the refuge, is able to conduct her own study, at first hand, of the causes and social origins of this particular problem. She arranged the placement herself with the support of her tutor.

☐ Keith spends his holidays working on oil rigs in the North Sea. His special interest is underwater technology. His tutor helped him to arrange this work.

☐ Linda is conducting a study of library misuse. She currently spends a great deal of time discussing this with librarians in the area. Her work, which has elicited considerable interest, will culminate in a report which will be made available to the librarians. She arranges the interviews herself.

A community orientation clearly emerges as an important component of the School's activities. The stance of the School is that its relationship with the community is two-way and it has explicitly chosen to see the community as including that very large number of people for whom and to whom higher education is a distant and unapproachable mystery. It has had varying degrees of success in fulfilling the role it has set itself but seems clearly to have had some success.

Finally, the School has also tried to develop a position for its activities within higher education. It organized a three-day conference in April 1979 and helped set up ACID (the Association for Colleges Implementing DipHE), a national group of DipHE teachers with its own periodical. There are specific publications on the work of the School, some of which are included in the bibliography (Burgess, 1977; Burgess and Adams, 1980; Percy and Ramsden, 1980). This chapter, we hope, will contribute to the development of that position.

APPENDIX 3.1 DipHE STATEMENT PROFORMA

NORTH EAST LONDON POLYTECHNIC
School for Independent Study

Full-time/part-time DipHE

Proposed statement by .... (student's name)
of a programme of study leading to the award of the Diploma of Higher Education in the context of his/her present position and intentions.

APPENDIX A	*Experience* I present here a critical appraisal of my educational and other experiences.
APPENDIX B	*Present position* I am able to identify the following areas of knowledge, skills and experiences which I indicate as strengths/weaknesses and regard as potentially relevant to the development of my programme of study.
APPENDIX C	*Intentions* I am able to identify the following intentions, personal, academic and vocational on gaining the Diploma.
APPENDIX D	*Knowledge, skills and experience needed* Consistent with my stated intentions I am currently able to identify that by the end of my programme of study I will need to have acquired the following areas of knowledge, skills and experience.
APPENDIX E	*Proposed programme of study* In order to acquire the above areas of knowledge, skills and experience I have formulated the following plans for individual work and central studies.
APPENDIX F	*Assessment* In order to demonstrate that I have achieved my targets I propose the following form of assessment.

Signature of student ....
Signature of Personal Tutor. ....
Signature of Individual Work Tutor ....
Approved YES/NO. Date of approval/rejection ....
Signature of Clerk to the Validating Board ....

APPENDIX 3.2. DEGREE PROPOSAL PROFORMA

NORTH EAST LONDON POLYTECHNIC
Student . . . .
School for Independent Study
PreCourse tutor . . . . . .
Faculty of Humanities
PreCourse year . . . . . .

BA/BSc(Hons)(CNAA) by Independent Study
An interim/final proposal for a programme of study leading to the award of
BA/BSc(Hons)(CNAA) by Independent Study.

Section 1 A statement of the proposed programme of study

Section 2 A statement indicating competence to undertake the proposed
programme of study

Section 3 A statement indicating the proposed modes of study

Section 4 A statement indicating the location of the proposed programme of
study within and/or in relation to the Polytechnic

Section 5 A statement providing an explicit justification for the proposed
programme of study

Section 6 A statement indicating the modes of assessment for the proposed
programme of study

Signature of student . . . .
Date of proposed entry to degree programme . . . .

BASIC REFERENCE DATA (1980)

I. The host institution

Name: North East London Polytechnic
Date founded: 1970
Internal organization: Eight faculties (see Table 3.2) though currently being
reorganized into six. Each faculty has its own internal organization.
Number of academic staff: Approx 750
Number of students: Approx 7000 (full-time equivalent)
Catchment area: The Polytechnic serves no particular catchment area, and has an
international student population.
Designated responsibility for off-campus activities: None in particular
Income: Approx £Stg 20 million

II. The innovation/system being studied

Name: School for Independent Study
Date founded: 1974
Nature: Polytechnic School, initially located outside faculty structure, but since
1978, located for administrative purposes in the Faculty of Humanities.
Responsible for NELP's independent study programmes.
Internal organization: Three courses, each with a course leader and various
cross-course activity groups (eg assessment, admissions, development, etc)
together with a research section.
Number of academic staff: 19 (full-time equivalent)
Number of non-academic staff: 5 full-time (including 1 technician) and 5 part-time
Number of students: 190 (full-time equivalent)
Income: Not available, but approximately pro-rata for the size of the School
Income as proportion of institution's total income: See above

NOTE
1. A note of caution needs to be sounded here concerning the notion of 'success'. In the sense used here it means those students gaining their DipHE in the minimum time available (ie two years). This definition is a limited one. Many students who do not 'succeed' in this sense have left during the two-year course and most of these do so for positive reasons, rather than simply 'dropping out' in the traditional sense. By way of example, a submission to the CNAA on the first two years of operation of the diploma reveals that 27 students out of 98 in the 1975 cohort had left the course by the beginning of the second year. Their reasons were as follows:

14 transferred to alternative courses
5 left for personal reasons
2 took a year's leave to return the following session
1 took up employment
1 died
4 found the course unsuitable.

The breakdown of which of these students were local is not available, but the point being made here is that, even by the most rigid definition of 'success', local students seem to do at least as well as, if not better than, others.

REFERENCES AND BIBLIOGRAPHY

Baudrillard, J (1975) *The Mirror of Production*, 167 pp, Telos Press, St Louis
Benjamin, J (1980) *In Search of Education*, 160 pp, North East London Polytechnic, London
Berte, N R (1975) *Individualising Education through Contract Learning*, University of Alabama Press
Burgess, T (1977) *Education after School*, 256 pp, Penguin, London
Burgess, T (1979) New ways to learn, *Journal of the Association of Colleges Implementing DipHE Programmes*, 2(2), 39-48
Burgess, T and Adams, E (1980) *Outcomes of Education*, 181 pp, Macmillan, London
Cavalcanti, P and Piccone, P (1975) *History, Philosophy and Culture in the Young Gramsci*, 158 pp, Telos Press, St Louis
Duberman, M (1974) *Black Mountain*, 527 pp, Wildwood, London
Durkheim, E (1956) *Education and Sociology*, Free Press, New York
Eley, V (1980) The DipHE at NELP, *Journal of the Association of Colleges Implementing DipHE Programmes*, 3(1), 5-9
Freire, P (1972) *Pedagogy of the Oppressed*, 156 pp, Penguin, London
Gray, S (1977) The first DipHE at NELP, *Journal of the Association of Colleges Implementing DipHE Programmes*, 1(1), 47
Gray, S (1979) Creating independent study, *Journal of the Association of Colleges Implementing DipHE Programmes*, 2(1), 18-21
Gray, S (1980) Alternative criteria for course entry: a case study, *Evaluation Newsletter*, 4(1), 13-22
Halsey, A H (1972) *Educational Priority*, HMSO, London
Illich, I (1973) *Deschooling Society*, 116 pp, Penguin, London
James Report (1972) *Teacher Education and Training: Report of the Committee appointed by the Secretary of State for Education and Science, chaired by Lord James of Rusholme*, 128 pp, HMSO, London
Knowles, M S (1970) *The Modern Practice of Adult Education: Andragogy vs Pedagogy*, 384 pp, Association Press, New York
Knowles, M S (1975) *Self-directed Learning: A Guide for Learners and Teachers*, Association Press, Chicago
Knowles, M S (1978) *The Adult Learner: A Neglected Species* (second edition), Gulf Publications, Houston
NELP (1972) *Interim Report of Working Party on the Diploma of Higher Education*, 12 pp, North East London Polytechnic, London

NELP (1979) *The NELP Experience of Independent Study*, North East London Polytechnic, London

OECD (1973) *Short-Cycle Higher Education: A Search for Identity*, OECD, Paris

Open University (1976) *Report of the Committee on Continuing Education, chaired by Sir Peter Venables*, 128 pp, Open University, Milton Keynes

Percy, K and Ramsden, P (1980) *Independent Study*, 80 pp, Society for Research into Higher Education, Guildford

Popper, K (1959) *The Logic of Scientific Discovery*, Hutchinson, London

Ramsden, P (1979) Freedom to learn? Problems of co-operation and choice in independent study, in Cox, R (ed) *Co-operation and Choice in Higher Education*, London

Robbins, D (1977) A degree by independent study, *Higher Education Review*, 9(3), 35-52

Robinson, E E (1968) *The New Polytechnics*, 264 pp, Penguin, London

Roszak, T (1960) On academic delinquency, in Roszak, T (ed) *The Dissenting Academy*, pp 11-45, Penguin, London

White Paper (1972) *Education: A Framework for Expansion*, 50 pp, Cmnd 5174, HMSO, London

Young, M F D (ed) (1971) *Knowledge and Control*, 289 pp, Collier Macmillan, London

4. Continuing education at the University of British Columbia

Jindra Kulich

The beginnings of university extension activities in Canada go back to the mid-1800s when McGill College (later McGill University) in Montreal started to offer public evening courses. Most Canadian extension activities started with *ad hoc* public lectures, moved on to courses for specific publics such as farmers, teachers, fishermen, and finally led to the establishment of formal extension departments (Kidd, 1956; Corbett, 1952). Queen's University in Kingston, Ontario formally established extension in 1889, after some 12 years of actual programmes. Other early extension departments were established at the University of Saskatchewan in 1910 (this was a Department of Agricultural Extension; general education programmes were added first in 1938); University of Alberta in 1912; University of Toronto in 1920; McGill University in 1927; St Francis Xavier University in Antigonish, Nova Scotia on the Atlantic coast in 1928; and at the University of British Columbia on the Pacific coast in 1936 (after some 20 years of extension activities) (Kidd, 1956; Selman, 1966).

Extension work of the Canadian universities started to develop at an accelerated rate in the 1950s, especially in its non-credit general education aspect. Development of continuing education programmes in the professions was a feature of the 1960s. The hallmarks of the 1970s were increasing attention to degree credit programmes for part-time students, gradual recognition of the importance of continuing education by university administrations in the late 70s, and an explosion of enrolment in all types of university continuing education.

Enrolment in non-credit university continuing education in Canada increased by 93 per cent between 1971 and 1977. Universities with full-time enrolments of 10,000+ students provided the largest non-credit programmes; in 1976-77 these universities accounted for 63 per cent of courses offered and 66 per cent of total non-credit university continuing education enrolments. In 1970-71 (when the collection of statistics on continuing education in the universities was started by Statistics Canada) there were 156,528 registrations and 117,690 participants in all of Canada; by 1976-77 (when the collection of these statistics unfortunately ended) the comparable figures were 301,865 and 226,966 respectively. The participation rate of the population aged 15 years and over not in full-time attendance at an educational institution was 8.9 in 1970-71 and 15.3 in 1976-77. In terms of registrations, in 1970-71 Ontario had the most with 55,567, Alberta was second with 26,248, and British Columbia was third with 23,259, while Prince Edward Island was lowest of all the provinces with only 323 registrations. In 1976-77, the order remained the same, although registrations increased significantly for Ontario, Alberta and British Columbia. In terms of participation rate, however, in 1970-71 Alberta was highest with 20.6, British Columbia second with 12.6, Saskatchewan third with 10.7, and Ontario only fourth with 7.8, while Newfoundland was lowest with 1.4. By 1976-77 Alberta was still highest with 34.5, Saskatchewan moved to second place with 22.0, British Columbia dropped down to third place with 20.9, and Ontario remained fourth with 14.0, while Newfoundland was replaced by Prince Edward Island as last with 3.2 (Newfoundland shot up to 11.4, an increase of 740 per cent!) (Statistics Canada, 1978). Unfortunately, comparable statistics are not available from 1977 on.

The University of British Columbia and university extension

British Columbia is the westernmost of the ten provinces of Canada, located on the Pacific coast. It has a population of almost 2.5 million in an area of 893,000 sq km (some 75 per cent of this population is concentrated in approximately 5 per cent of the territory in the south-west corner of BC). The economy consists mainly of forestry, mining, agriculture and fisheries, while tourism, manufacturing and transportation also play an important role.

Recent Ministry of Education figures show that from a population of 1.6 million persons aged 20 or over, some 390,000 participate in adult education programmes sponsored by one of several public education institutions. Among these institutions are three universities, several post-secondary (primarily vocational) institutes, 14 regional community colleges, and a number of local school districts. The three universities account for just over one-quarter of the 390,000 participants in adult education, with the University of British Columbia alone accounting for some 80,000 (approximately one-fifth).

The University of British Columbia

The University of British Columbia was incorporated by an act of the Provincial Legislature in 1908, but did not open until the autumn of 1915, in Vancouver. It remained the only public university in British Columbia until 1963, when the Provincial Legislature created the University of Victoria on Vancouver Island (formerly Victoria College of the University of British Columbia) and the new Simon Fraser University, built in Burnaby, on the outskirts of Vancouver.

The University of British Columbia remained the largest and most comprehensive of the three universities. Today it has 12 faculties (Agricultural Sciences, Applied Science, Arts, Commerce and Business Administration, Dentistry, Education, Forestry, Graduate Studies, Law, Medicine, Pharmaceutical Sciences and Science). In addition the University also has nine schools (Architecture, Audiology and Speech Sciences, Community and Regional Planning, Home Economics, Librarianship,

Nursing, Physical Education and Recreation, Rehabilitation Medicine, and Social Work). UBC continuing education is carried out by the Centre for Continuing Education, the Executive Programs Division of the Faculty of Commerce and Business Administration, the Continuing Education Division in the Health Sciences, and the Field Services Office of the Faculty of Education. Part-time degree credit programmes (primarily in the Faculties of Arts, Education and Science) are administered by the Office of Extra-Sessional Studies. The degree credit enrolment in the University reached 25,697 students in 1979-80, while non-credit continuing education programmes accounted for almost 80,000 registrations.

The University of British Columbia is governed by a Board of Governors which is responsible for financial matters and by a Senate which is the highest authority in academic matters. The Director of the Centre for Continuing Education is a statutory member of Senate and Senate has a Standing Committee on Continuing Education. The chief executive officer of the University is the President, who has four Vice Presidents reporting to him (Academic Development, Faculty and Student Affairs, Finance, and Administration). All the deans of the 12 faculties of the University, as well as the Director of the Centre for Continuing Education and the Director of the Office of Extra-Sessional Studies, report to the Vice President, Academic Development. (University officers in charge of programmes in the other above mentioned continuing education units report to the appropriate dean.)

UBC University Extension 1915-1970
Almost from its inception, the University of British Columbia was involved in extension activities, at the outset primarily in vocational rehabilitation of first world war veterans and in agriculture. These early activities were the result of social and government pressures at that time, as well as of the vision and commitment of the first two University Presidents, Dr F F Wesbrook and Dr L S Klinck. This activity had ceased by 1933 due to a financial crisis in which the University found itself. In 1934 the Carnegie Corporation made a grant of $50,000 to the University of British Columbia; it is a credit to the University community of that day that $30,000 of the grant was allocated to restore its service to the larger community. In 1936 the University established a university-wide Department of University Extension (Selman, 1966).

During its existence from 1936 to 1970 the Department of University Extension changed scope and emphasis several times in response to the changing needs of society and individuals in British Columbia, changing climate and priorities within the University, and emergence of other providers of adult education (for history of the Department see Selman, 1966 and 1975; Kulich, 1976).

Throughout its early years the Department built up a considerable non-credit programme and services which extended throughout the Province. The major thrust was in general education, arts and cultural services, and rural leadership; technical programmes for fishermen and farmers formed an important part of the programme. Extension specialists employed by the Department travelled to remote communities and gave lectures in their specialities.

During the second half of the 1950s the Department changed from a unit heavily involved in teaching to one whose primary responsibility was the planning and organization of adult education programmes, leaving the teaching to regular faculty members. The other significant shift was in the transfer of a number of programmes from the University to other sponsors in the community and an increased emphasis on building up continuing education programmes in the professions and general education programmes offered at an academic level appropriate to a university.

In the early 1960s the priorities of the University changed significantly towards strengthening its graduate work and de-emphasizing extension activities. As a result parts of the general education extension programme were phased out, and most of the province-wide programmes were discontinued in the mid-60s. This decade was a difficult time for the Extension Department, hard on the morale and enthusiasm of its committed staff (Selman, 1975). While the second half of the 1960s was a period of retrenchment for the general continuing education programme and services which up to that point were among the best and most comprehensive in Canada, a new positive climate for continuing education was growing in the professions and the leadership of the Extension Department realized clearly this new need and opportunity. As a result a new impetus was given to the Department through the expansion of existing and the establishment of new continuing education programmes in the professions.

In 1968 the Senate set up a Committee on Continuing Education to examine University policy on continuing education. The Committee's report was accepted by Senate in June 1970, and the Department of University Extension became the Centre for Continuing Education.

The UBC Centre for Continuing Education

Genesis
In the Extension Department's darkest hour, a President's Committee on Academic Goals in its report *Guideposts to Innovation* (UBC, 1964), having stated that the Committee regarded continuing education as a direct reponsibility of the University, recommended that 'the Department of University Extension be replaced by a Faculty of Continuing Education'. This recommendation, however, was not acted upon by the University. A proposal from the Extension Department to Senate in 1966 which recommended that the Extension Department become a Centre for Continuing Education and its Director become a dean was rejected by the Faculties in 1967.

The climate within the University, both in the President's Office and in Senate, which in the mid-60s was detrimental to the work of the

Extension Department and to the community service tasks of the University, changed gradually in the late 1960s towards renewed acceptance of the need for and importance of continuing education. The factors which influenced this shift included developments in society and in the professions, changing attitudes of academic staff, personnel changes in the President's Office, and the improving economic climate.

After the defeat of the Extension Department proposal in 1967, Senate set up in 1968 a Committee on Continuing Education. The Committee's report and recommendations were approved by Senate in June 1970. The report reiterated the University's commitment to continuing education, recommended a change in organization of the Department of University Extension, gave the professional faculties the right to conduct their own continuing education programmes if they so chose, and recommended the establishment of a President's Co-ordinating Committee on Continuing Education which would deal with University-wide concerns related to continuing education. With the approval of the report, the Department of University Extension became the Centre for Continuing Education. Significantly, the recommendation for a more adequate financing of continuing education was not accepted by the Board of Governors.

The mandate of the Centre for Continuing Education
In terms of legislation, which in Canada is very scanty in this area, the Centre for Continuing Education (as well as the other administrative units for continuing education at UBC) operates within the terms of the BC Universities Act of 1974 (British Columbia, 1974) which states:

> Each university shall, so far as and to the full extent which its resources from time to time permit . . . provide a programme of continuing education in all academic and cultural fields throughout the Province.

There is no legislation for financial support of university continuing education and no direct line item subsidy from the Government to the University for this part of its activities.

The University of British Columbia in 1979 issued a mission statement (UBC, 1979c) which included a statement on the University's role in continuing education. The following excerpt from the statement signifies the University commitment:

> The University of British Columbia, like the other universities and provincial institutes, has a province-wide mandate and responsibility for providing credit and non-credit continuing education and professional development, both full and part-time. This responsibility is particularly marked in professions in which only UBC has professional Faculties or Schools and in areas where UBC has special expertise. It should use its unique resources to provide continuing education, to provide leadership and to experiment in the broad field of continuing education, to cooperate with other institutions in broadening the scope of continuing education, and to provide professional training and research in continuing education.

The Centre for Continuing Education at its establishment in 1970 was given exclusive mandate for 'general programmes carrying no credit towards degrees, though of a level appropriate for University instruction, and dealing with liberal and scientific studies, public affairs and community projects' (UBC Senate, 1970).

Until 1976 the Centre also administered on behalf of the appropriate academic departments evening credit courses (this function was given over to a new Office of Extra-Sessional Studies established in 1976); the Centre, in co-operation with academic departments, is still responsible for development and administration of a credit distance education programme.

In the area of education for the professions, by 1970 the Faculties of Dentistry, Medicine and Pharmacy and the School of Nursing already had their own programmes in continuing education, co-operating in a Division for Continuing Education in the Health Sciences independent of the Department of University Extension. The Faculty of Commerce was also operating its own programme. The Faculties of Agriculture, Applied Science, Education, Forestry, and Law, and the Schools of Architecture, Community Planning, Home Economics and Social Work exercised their option to have the Centre carry out their professional continuing education programmes. In 1973 the programme of the School of Social Work separated from the Centre, while in 1976 the School of Librarianship asked the Centre to co-operate in establishing its programme of continuing education. In 1979 the Faculties of Agriculture and Education exercised their option to take over their continuing education programmes.

The Centre for Continuing Education is the only administrative unit of the University whose *sole* responsibility is non-credit continuing education and community service. Within its mandate its responsibility is University-wide and province-wide.

The role and goals of the Centre for Continuing Education
Gordon Selman, former Director of the Centre, states in his analysis (Selman, 1975) that the Centre for Continuing Education was created from the Department of University Extension in a move to rationalize and to give direction to UBC's efforts in continuing education:

> The significance of the change of terminology from 'extension' to 'continuing education' was that the committee [the Senate Committee on Continuing Education] felt that in view of the presence by then of the college system in the Province, the University could and should restrict itself to more advanced work; it should be concerned with 'continuing' the education beyond an already considerable level of attainment of its graduates and others at that same general level.

In the late 1970s a new interpretation of 'continuing education' as different from 'extension' ('extension' understood as being able to extend only that which already exists in the academic departments), espoused by the Director of the Centre and for a long time not substantially challenged by the academic departments, allowed the Centre to venture into new areas of programming and community service, to break new ground, and to staff a considerable proportion of its programmes with non-faculty.

In order to make its position clear, to consolidate current practice, and to prepare for renewed discussion within the University of its role and goals, the Centre prepared a statement, accepted unanimously by its professional staff in February of 1979 (UBC Centre for Continuing Education, 1979). After an outline of the context in which continuing education operates in British Columbia and of the mandate and responsibility for continuing education given to the University by the BC Universities Act and the policy adopted by UBC Senate in 1970, the Centre defined its role as follows:

> Within the context of adult learning in British Columbia, the Centre for Continuing Education strives to create a continuing education programme which will make effective use of UBC resources (academic, organizational and service) and, where appropriate, also of resources found in other post-secondary institutions and in the community. It channels these resources to serve the educational needs of the people throughout British Columbia. Some of the more important ways the Centre serves these needs are outlined below.
> 1. Through innovative and creative programmes, services and delivery systems, the Centre applies knowledge and skills and creates receptive attitudes . . .
> 2. The Centre for Continuing Education, with its professional staff of adult educators, also sees itself playing a leadership role in the advancement of continuing education as an important function of the University . . .
> 3. The Centre's third role is that of an important communicative link between the University and the community.
> 4. Finally, the Centre's professional staff is providing leadership in the broad field of adult education in British Columbia, Canada and abroad.

Governance of Centre programmes and services
A Council for the Centre for Continuing Education was established in 1970 so that the Centre would operate with the Council's advice and consent. The Council comprised representatives of the faculties which work through the Centre, representatives of faculty members who teach in Centre programmes, representatives of the community, and representatives of the Centre's professional staff. Through the Council the Centre reported to Senate, the highest academic authority of the University (UBC Senate, 1970). The intention was to give the Centre for Continuing Education a mechanism similar to the faculty councils governing each of the 12 faculties. However, the community representatives, who expected that the Council would enable the Centre to move faster and serve the community better, became frustrated by what they perceived as blocking on the part of the faculty members on the Council. A number of faculty on the Council, on their part, became dissatisfied with what seemed to them naive or unrealistic demands on the University on the part of the community representatives (often seen as aided and abetted by representatives of Centre professional staff). The Council, which at the outset was seen by everyone, in his or her own way, as a useful and helpful tool, turned, in spite of valiant efforts of the Director of the Centre to make it work, into another burdensome structure and after five years of existence ceased to function.

The other mechanism created in 1970 — the President's Coordinating

Committee on Continuing Education (renamed in 1976 the President's Permanent Committee on University Extension and Continuing Studies), with the task of assisting the President in matters of the interface between the separate continuing education units, their mandates, and possible jurisdictional conflicts — is still functioning well.

Since the discontinuation of the Council for the Centre for Continuing Education, the Centre reports to Senate through the Senate Standing Committee on Continuing Education. Administratively the Centre is responsible through its Director to the Vice President of Academic Development, the second-highest ranking officer in the University administration. (Ever since the establishment of the Department of University Extension in 1936, its Director reported directly to the President; with the growth of the University administration this shifted in the 1970s to reporting to the Deputy President, and in 1976 to the Vice President, Academic Development. Thus the Extension Department and later on the Centre always had direct access to the President's Office.)

The Centre is responsible to Senate and the University administration for its programmes and community services. In liberal arts and science the Programme Directors who are in charge of planning and administration of programmes and services in these areas liaise with appropriate academic departments, individual faculty, and groups and individuals in the community, while they alone are responsible to the Director of the Centre for their programme areas. In 1980 the Centre established an Advisory Committee to the Director on General Non-Credit Continuing Education Programmes. The Committee, appointed by the Director of the Centre, is comprised of six faculty members from the Faculties of Arts and Science, two community representatives, the Associate Director and the Director of the Centre. In the professional areas, the programme directors work closely with advisory or policy committees comprised of faculty representatives and representatives from the professions; the composition, relative strength of the faculty and professions, and powers of these committees vary from profession to profession. The programme directors in these areas are responsible for academic matters to the dean of the appropriate faculty or to their policy committee, and to the Director of the Centre for all other matters.

Staffing

As is common current practice in non-credit continuing education in North America but unlike the established pattern in many other Commonwealth countries, the Centre for Continuing Education does not employ any full-time teaching staff; its professional staff is charged with responsibility for programme planning, organization, administration and evaluation, and only occasionally is this staff engaged in teaching the programmes offered by the Centre.

Currently the Centre has a staff of 30 professionals — three in the Director's Office (Director, Associate Director — Programme Coordination, Assistant Director — Finance and Administration) and 27 Programme

Directors in charge of 28 programme and service areas, as well as 50 secretarial and support staff.

Most of the Programme Directors have postgraduate degrees in the subject matter or professional areas in which they programme; a number also have postgraduate degrees in adult education. All the professional staff are members of the Faculty Association, although none has a faculty rank (at this time none has a cross-appointment to an academic department, although there were such cases a few years ago). As of 1979, the Programme Directors have confirmed appointments which are equivalent to faculty tenure. They qualify for the same benefits as faculty (including a form of sabbatical leave) and the salaries are comparable.

Instructors in the programmes are employed by the Centre on a programme to programme basis, subject to enrolment, on a professional services contract. UBC faculty teaching in the Centre programmes do so on an 'overload' basis, not as part of their normal academic load. The Centre is not restricted to engage only UBC faculty to teach in its programmes, but contracts with faculty from other post-secondary institutions in British Columbia and further afield, professionals in the field, and other qualified instructors in the community. The Programme Directors are responsible for assessing the qualifications of the non-UBC personnel engaged to teach in the Centre programmes; they do this in consultation with the appropriate academic departments and outside sources.

The secretarial and support staff are members of the University-wide clerical trade union and their hiring and working conditions are governed by the union contract between the University and the union.

Programmes and services
During the last ten years the Centre for Continuing Education has recovered most of the ground lost in the cutbacks in the mid-60s, particularly in the creative arts. New general education programmes have been added and continuing education in the professions has expanded steadily. In the late 1970s the Centre was able to start moving some of its programmes back to locations in the Interior. The major and most significant community project of the Centre during the last few years is the Women's Resources Centre, established on campus in 1973 and moved in 1974 to a downtown location.

The Centre's activities can be divided into programmes and services. Programmes again can be subdivided into general continuing education programmes and continuing education in the professions. Guided Independent Study (credit and non-credit distance education) combines both programmes and services. The total statistics of the Centre's activities in 1979-80 show 52,526 registrations.

General continuing education programmes use the resources of the University to popularize research results in the humanities, social sciences and sciences, apply the insights and skills residing in a university to solve individual and social problems, enrich the quality of cultural life, and foster positive attitudes to the development of human potential and lifelong learning. In concert with the learning needs of adults many of the programmes offered are not single-discipline-oriented but rather are inter- and multi-disciplinary. Although there is close co-operation and some overlap among several of the programme areas, the following areas have been designated for organizational purposes: Creative Arts, Daytime Programme, Educational Travel and Overseas Programmes, Conservation and Energy Management, Humanities and Sciences, Languages, Pre-retirement Programme, Senior Citizens Programme, Public Affairs, Social Sciences, Summer Programme, and Women's Programmes and Lifestyles. The enrolment in the general continuing education programme in 1979-80 reached 21,857 registrations (13,072 in courses, 5261 in single lectures, 2842 in short courses, 587 in field trips and 95 in educational travel and overseas programmes).

Continuing education in the professions is designed to enlarge the knowledge and skills of the practising professional, both through showing him or her innovative approaches and opening new horizons, and by refreshing or updating knowledge and skills obtained in preparatory training. Inter-professional programmes bring together several professions to deal with the many problems and challenges which are beyond the expertise of any one profession. Professional programme areas organized through the Centre for Continuing Education are: Architecture, Adult Education Training, Community and Regional Planning, Computer Science, Education of Young Children, Engineering, Gerontology, Home Economics, Instructor's Diploma Programme, Legal Education, Librarianship, Local Government Programmes, and Women in Management and Career Development. Programmes in these areas show, in 1979-80, 18,188 registrations (4966 in courses, 2749 in single lectures, 10,467 in short courses, and six in educational travel).

The two services organized by the Centre for Continuing Education are the Reading, Writing and Study Skills Centre which enrolled 1128 university students and adults in the service programmes, and the Women's Resources Centre which served 9796 women in information and counselling interviews. The Women's Resources Centre, located physically in the downtown community, provides counselling services to women on educational opportunities, careers, and lifestyles, as well as offering psychological testing; it is separate from and has a different function from the UBC Student Services Department which deals primarily with regular credit students at the University.

Guided Independent Study is responsible for all individual distance education by correspondence, audiotapes and television. It co-operates closely with the appropriate academic departments in developing new credit courses and servicing courses offered. GIS staff have capabilities in course design and editing and provide support services to course writers and tutors. Forty-six credit courses (40 in the Faculty of Arts, and two each in the Faculties of Commerce, Education and Science) are available to students. The Centre is currently co-operating with the Faculty of

Forestry on the development of six GIS credit courses. Most of the credit courses still rely exclusively on the correspondence mode, while a few courses use audiocassettes. Only one experimental television course was developed and tested; the Forestry courses will rely heavily on videotapes. The Centre offers a correspondence Criminology Certificate Programme for police and correction officers, and several of the courses in the Certificate in Education of Young Children are available on audiotapes. A Study Assistance Programme is also available on audiotapes. The total enrolment in Guided Independent Study in 1979-80 reached 1557 (1353 credit students, 129 certificate students, and 75 students in the non-credit and service courses). The future development of Guided Independent Study from 1980 will concentrate on courses in the professional faculties.

Centre programmes are offered in the evenings, during daytime, on weekends, and in short courses of from one to five days' duration. They are held on the University campus, in several downtown locations, and in the suburbs. Although most of the programmes are still located in Greater Vancouver, since 1976 the University has again supported the Centre in expanding its general and professional programmes to areas throughout the Province. By 1979-80 4760 participants were enrolled in programmes offered outside the immediate area around Vancouver; to this must be added 960 participants in Guided Independent Study who resided outside this area. This represents almost 11 per cent of total registration.

Links with the University community

The governance pattern of the Centre for Continuing Education within the University structure was outlined earlier. Through it, the Centre has formal links with the University administrative and management structure. The Programme Directors are in continual liaison with academic departments and individual faculty members on matters of programme planning, development and evaluation.

Since the President's Permanent Committee on University Extension and Continuing Studies meets only infrequently and on specific issues, and the Senate Standing Committee on Continuing Education only has one representative from each of the University continuing education units, the Centre has attempted over the last few years to set up informal meetings for all professional staff and faculty at the University engaged in the organization of continuing education, but staff of the other units seemingly do not have a strong enough need to associate with colleagues who work in continuing education in other parts of the University. Liaison between the various continuing education units is therefore restricted to specific matters; with the increasing need to co-operate on inter-professional programmes, this primarily functional contact may lead to more informal association in the future.

Professional staff of the Centre also participate in the activities of the University by serving on a number of faculty and University-wide committees such as Faculty Councils of Agriculture, Arts, and Education, Departmental Committee on Adult Education, President's Committee on

Gerontology, Senate Standing Committee on Continuing Education, Senate Standing Committee on Liaison with Post-secondary Institutions, University Lectures Committee, Faculty Association Executive and others.

Links with the larger community
University extension activities cannot be organized solely from the university enclave, without contact with the potential clientele outside. The vitality and success of any university extension programme depends on a reasonably favourable university climate, the imagination and creativity of the programming staff, availability and suitability of faculty and other resources, and close liaison with existing and potential clientele.

In the case of the Centre for Continuing Education, professional staff are in continual liaison with participants in Centre programmes (by attending a number of the programmes and talking to participants, evaluations, and participant surveys); have memberships (and often hold offices) in relevant professional and community associations; participate in the social, political and cultural life of the community; and in other ways keep in close touch with developments in the professions and the community. The degree of success of individual Programme Directors and their programme areas can almost be predicted by measuring their efforts at maintaining a close relationship with the appropriate segment of society.

Finance
The Centre for Continuing Education is an integral part of the University and as such its budget is part of the University budget. The University provides the Centre with offices, use of classrooms, light, heat and janitorial services. Until the mid-60s the University also provided all the salaries of approved programme organizing and support staff and the Extension Department was responsible for raising from fees only the direct costs of mounting its programmes and services (costs of publicity, instructor salaries, instructional supplies). Since 1966 the Extension Department, and later the Centre, had to meet the cost of a considerable number of the staff salaries as well as the direct programme costs. Approximately 75 per cent of the funds required by the Centre now come from fees and other revenue and 25 per cent from the central University budget. Although the amount of the budget provided by the University rose from just over $C300,000 in the early 1970s to almost $C1,000,000 in 1980, the relative share between University budget and revenue from fees remained the same as the Centre's programme (and with it revenue and expenditures) increased more than threefold during the decade.

The fact that the Centre has to meet three-quarters of its required expenditure budget from revenue it raises has been a considerable burden which has prevented the Centre from developing some of the services and programmes needed in the community for which it could not charge fees. Since the Centre is free to switch funds among its programmes and services, it does support some of these services and programmes from 'excess' revenues raised by other programme areas on the principle of 'robbing Peter to pay Paul'. This can be considered as a hidden tax on participants in some programmes to support other programmes; the participants have no say as to which programmes will be supported from fees they pay.

On the other hand, having only one-quarter of its expenditures tied to the University two-year budgeting cycle, the Centre enjoys fiscal freedom not given to any other academic unit of the University, the only responsibility being that it may not require funds from the central University budget over and above the allocated amount. Thus the Centre can respond quickly to new programming needs (and to service needs) and employ additional staff as required when it expects to generate surplus funds or expects to recover the additional cost from new revenue. Sometimes this means living dangerously, but it has allowed the Centre to grow in times of limited University budgets coupled with increasing interest in continuing education and growing enrolment. As long as there is sufficiently widespread ability among the potential participants to pay the fees the Centre has to charge in this 'pay as you go' market economy approach, and as long as the Centre will retain its ability to support programmes and services from suplus revenue in other programmes, the current financial set-up is functional.

Problems and challenges
The development of human potential, individual fulfilment, and the development of society as a whole, are of prime importance. Lifelong, continuous learning is one of the main forces in this development. In modern society, individual and societal learning needs are inextricably intertwined and all must be met if the individuals and the society are to grow. Continuing education must reflect all the learning needs of both individuals and society.

Those of us who have a commitment to continuing education not only must be, but also must be perceived to be, responsive, responsible and accountable — to the participants and potential participants, to our own institutions, to the government and to society at large. Yet in being responsive, responsible and accountable to all these, at times, conflicting demands and disparate needs, we cannot be like a straw in the wind. We have to bring our own professional expertise to bear on the formation of our programme and we have to maintain our integrity. As professional adult educators serving the needs of individuals and society, we must employ judgement but we cannot sit in judgement. All these pressures do not make our work easy, but they do make it interesting, challenging and fulfilling. We learn to work and to thrive in a climate of creative tension.

The greatest challenge facing the Centre for Continuing Education relates to the differences of view as to its role in general and liberal education. The academic departments and many individual faculty naturally view general education from the perspective of their own academic discipline. The adults in the community, on the other hand, naturally look towards the Centre and the University for assistance in solving problems and concerns they and society face in daily life. Such problems and concerns usually cannot easily be solved with expertise applied from one academic discipline but rather require an inter-disciplinary or cross-disciplinary approach. In designing programmes in response to the needs of the adult population, the programme directors in the Centre often have to try to combine disciplines and approaches which seem strange bedfellows to many faculty, and work in innovative ways which do not easily portend their academic level. This makes the general and liberal education programme of the Centre often open to questioning and challenge by faculty and academic departments. Thus far this tension has worked mainly in creative ways, but it could become a real problem for the ability of the Centre staff to respond to needs and for their creativity and vitality.

The programme challenges facing the Centre for Continuing Education in the near future are: response to important public issues such as conservation, lifestyle counselling, and development of human potential. In the professional areas the challenge is the expansion of inter-professional programmes dealing with involved social and human problems, and the greater infusion of liberal education into comprehensive continuing professional education programmes.

Among other challenges facing the Centre are: finding more formalized ways of input from participants into future planning; working towards changes in the internal reward system of the University towards increasing weight for continuing education teaching; and heading off any further decentralization of continuing professional education into the professional faculties and schools.

The considerable support, both moral and practical, from the President's Office which the Centre has enjoyed over the last five years is a manifestation of the University administration's commitment to continuing education as an important function of the University of British Columbia.

Conclusion

Many Canadian universities have a long record of making their human and material resources available to the community in various ways beyond the usual education and training of young people. The scope and intensity of this contribution to society at large evolved in tune with the changing social, economic and political conditions and the changing climate within the universities. At one time, in most of Canada, the universities were the main providers of publicly funded adult education. With the expansion of adult education programmes under the local school authorities in the early 1960s and with the advent of the community colleges, university adult education has undergone significant changes in programme scope, level and the territory covered. For some universities, unfortunately, the public school and community college programmes were an excuse for drastic cutbacks or even discontinuation of the provision. For others, the new programmes of other institutions meant release of scarce university resources to meet newly arising needs and demands for continuing education programmes such as continuing education in the professions and expansion of part-time degree programmes.

The University of British Columbia has been involved in a cyclical development of its provision of adult (continuing) education to the citizens of British Columbia. It moved from the early, strongly vocationally oriented service, to a comprehensive, province-wide provision of a very broad general non-credit education programme and on to the drastic cutbacks and programme curtailment, only to find and respond to new needs and demands in continuing education in the professions, new expansion of the general education programme, services to major segments of society (counselling and programmes for women), and considerable expansion of provision for the part-time degree student. UBC is entering the 1980s with a very broad and comprehensive continuing education programme, but of a much greater magnitude than in the earlier period.

In terms of organization, the University of British Columbia has gone through the developmental stages of extension work organization (Gordon, 1980; Pedersen and Fleming, 1979; Selman, 1973). The early beginnings of this work were *ad hoc* programmes organized by various academic departments and faculties. This led to the establishment of a centralized unit, the Department of University Extension. With the advent of continuing education in the professions, some faculties established their programmes outside the Extension Department (this trend was started in the health sciences, a pattern which is true of North American development of continuing education in the professions). This development eventually led at UBC to what might be termed decentralized centralization.

The organizational pattern of continuing education at UBC is a hybrid between centralization and decentralization. Some of the proponents of centralization (Pedersen and Fleming, 1979) see the continuing education function as too important to be left largely unco-ordinated; they also predict an unprecedented increase in interest in continuing education throughout the university and thus increasing influence by the university administration over the extension programmes. Others see the need for centralization in an extension or continuing education division as a prime necessity and the only assurance of survival of continuing education in the university (Gordon, 1980), or in the necessity for co-ordination and effective use of resources (Houle, 1980). On the other hand, there are examples of decentralization of the responsibility for continuing education into the academic departments (one such attempt, too young yet to be adequately evaluated, is the continuing education programme of Simon Fraser University in British Columbia). Developments across North America seem to indicate that the smaller universities will opt for a centralized model, while large, comprehensive universities will yield

83

to the pressure from professional schools to decentralize.

The University of British Columbia model of decentralized centralization is a viable and functional alternative for major, comprehensive universities. In this model, the closely related and interacting continuing education programmes in dentistry, medicine, nursing and pharmacy are centralized in the Division of Continuing Education in the Health Sciences. The varied business and management programmes are centralized in the Faculty of Commerce and Business Administration. The Faculties of Agricultural Sciences and Education and the School of Social Work operate their own programmes. The part-time degree credit courses are centralized in the Office of Extra-Sessional Studies. All non-credit general education programmes, as well as continuing education programmes in many of the professional schools and faculties are centralized in the Centre for Continuing Education, which remains the major continuing education unit at UBC.

The Centre for Continuing Education, as the only unit of the University whose sole mandate is continuing education, plays an important role in keeping the University community aware of the need for continuing education and in serving as a link between the University and the community at large. The UBC model satisfies the need of many of the professional faculties to be directly and intimately involved in the provision of continuing education in their profession, while at the same time, through the Centre for Continuing Education, it satisfies the need for one designated unit to be responsible for fostering the awareness in the University about the University's responsibility for and mission in the provision of continuing education. This decentralized centralization model can be applicable to other major comprehensive universities in their efforts at providing appropriate continuing education service to their communities.

BASIC REFERENCE DATA (1979-80)

I. The host institution

Name: The University of British Columbia
Date founded: 1908
Internal organization: Comprehensive multiversity. Twelve faculties: Agricultural Sciences, Applied Science, Arts, Commerce and Business Administration, Dentistry, Education, Forestry, Graduate Studies, Law, Medicine, Pharmaceutical Sciences, and Science.
Number of academic staff: 1889
Number of students: 25,697 students in regular (Winter) Session; 3015 students in Spring Session; 3917 students in Summer Session.
Catchment area: Students in core faculties come predominantly from British Columbia; students in professional faculties and graduate studies come from all of Canada and abroad.
Designated responsibility for off-campus activities: Responsible for university continuing education throughout British Columbia.
Income: $C190 million

II. The innovation/system being studied

Name: Centre for Continuing Education (formerly Department of University Extension)

Date founded: 1970 (1936)

Nature: A unit responsible for general non-credit continuing education, credit and non-credit guided independent study, and approximately half of the activities offered by the University in professional continuing education.

Internal organization: Divided into 28 programme areas along profession or discipline lines, but with many links and inter-disciplinary and inter-professional programmes.

Number of academic staff: 30 full-time (all non-teaching)

Number of non-academic staff: 50 full-time

Income: $C3.5 million of which 25 per cent was from general university funds, 75 per cent from fees and other sources.

Income as proportion of institution's total income: 1.8 per cent

REFERENCES AND BIBLIOGRAPHY

British Columbia (1974) *Universities Act (1974)*, 28 pp, Queen's Printer, Victoria

Coady, M M (1939) *Masters of their Own Destiny*, 170 pp, Harper and Brothers Publishers, New York

Corbett, E A (1952) *University Extension in Canada*, 63 pp, Canadian Association for Adult Education, Toronto

Gordon, M (1980) The management of continuing education: centralized and decentralized forms and functions, in Alford, H J (ed) *Power and Conflict in Continuing Education*, pp 170-87, Wadsworth Publishing Co, Belmont

Harrington, F H (1977) *The Future of Adult Education — New Responsibilities of Colleges and Universities*, 238 pp, Jossey-Bass, San Francisco and London

Hesburgh, T M, Miller, P A and Wharton, C R (1973) *Patterns for Lifelong Learning*, 135 pp, Jossey-Bass, San Francisco and London

Houle, C O (1980) *Continuing Learning in the Professions*, 390 pp, Jossey-Bass, San Francisco and London

Kidd, J R (1956) *Adult Education in the Canadian University*, 137 pp, Canadian Association for Adult Education, Toronto

Kidd, J R and Selman, G R (eds) (1978) *Coming of Age: Canadian Adult Education in the 1960s,* 410 pp, Canadian Association for Adult Education, Toronto

Kulich, J (ed) (1976) *Former UBC Extension Directors Reminisce: 1936-1976*, 50 pp, Centre for Continuing Education, University of British Columbia, Vancouver

Laidlaw, A F (1961) *The Campus and the Community: The Global Impact of the Antigonish Movement*, 173 pp, Harvest House Limited, Montreal

Niblett, W R and Butts, R F (eds) (1972) *Universities Facing the Future*, 400 pp, Jossey-Bass, San Francisco and London

Pedersen, K G and Fleming, T (1979) Continuing education divisions and the crisis of success, *Canadian Journal of University Continuing Education*, 5(2), 5-11

Pike, R M (1980) Open access in Canadian higher education during the seventies, *Canadian Journal of University Continuing Education*, 7(1), 4-7

Selman, G R (1966) *A History of Fifty Years of Extension Service by The University of British Columbia 1915 to 1965*, 60 pp, Canadian Association for Adult Education, Toronto

Selman, G R (1973) What future for university continuing education units? *Dialogue*, 1(2), 35-49

Selman, G R (1975) *A Decade of Transition: The Extension Department of The University of British Columbia 1960 to 1970*, 37 pp, Centre for Continuing Education, University of British Columbia, Vancouver

Shannon, T J and Schoenfeld, C A (1965) *University Extension*, 115 pp, Center for Applied Research in Education, New York

Stager, A A (1972) Economics of continuing education in the universities, in Ostry, S (ed) *Canadian Higher Education in the Seventies*, pp 265-89, Economic Council of Canada, Ottawa

Statistics Canada (1978) *Continuing Education: Universities 1976-77*, 54 pp, Statistics Canada, Ottawa

Stern, M R (1980) Universities in continuing education, in Alford, H J (ed) *Power and Conflict in Continuing Education*, pp 4-24, Wadsworth Publishing Co, Belmont

UBC (1962) *A Symposium on Continuing Education in the Professions*, 62 pp, University of British Columbia, Vancouver

UBC (1978) *Continuing Education Activities of The University of British Columbia 1976-77*, 38 pp, University of British Columbia, Vancouver

UBC (1979a) *Continuing Education Activities of The University of British Columbia 1977-78*, 50 pp, University of British Columbia, Vancouver

UBC (1979b) *Continuing Education Activities of The University of British Columbia 1978-79*, 72 pp, University of British Columbia, Vancouver

UBC (1979c) *The Mission of The University of British Columbia*, 77 pp, University of British Columbia, Vancouver

UBC Centre for Continuing Education (1979) *Statement of Role and Goals,* 7 pp, Centre for Continuing Education, University of British Columbia, Vancouver

UBC President's Committee on Academic Goals (1964) *Guideposts to Innovation: Report of a President's Committee on Academic Goals*, 67 pp, University of British Columbia, Vancouver

UBC Senate (1970) Meeting Minutes, June 10, 1970, pp 5284-90, University of British Columbia, Vancouver

Whale, W B (1976) University extension units are in danger of winning their battle, *Canadian Journal of University Continuing Education*, 3(1), 44-50

Part 3:
Meeting course needs off campus through appropriate technology

5. Correspondence as the core: the Centre for University Extramural Studies, Massey University

Donald Bewley

New and old directions

Although the 1970s, when the UK Open University first flourished, may have seemed 'the decade of distance education', there already existed many worthwhile ventures in teaching at a distance, mainly dependent on correspondence, which had long and reputable histories. Most venerable was London University whose external degrees (Duke, 1967) originated in 1858; London ceased most of its external operation in the mid-70s, having served many young universities throughout the Commonwealth and many aspiring tertiary institutions in Britain. On the other side of the world Queensland University's 'external studies' programme pre-dated the first world war; in New Zealand the Correspondence School was founded years before the depression of the 1930s (Rayner, 1949). By 1970, the number of institutions teaching off-campus, post-secondary students ran into hundreds around the world. Some distance teaching institutions — in countries of such different character as the USSR and New Zealand — provided systems of primary, secondary and tertiary opportunity that were counterparts to the conventional schools.

In the 1970s, however, development was spectacular. Exciting technology, confident marketing and some fresh academic attitudes gave impetus to many new institutions in countries which had previously had little positive interest in students who could not attend classes. Television brought education into the homes of millions while computers or telecommunication satellites enhanced distance education's contemporaneity. 'Open education', which such devices promise — ready access for all who feel the need — became a social catch-cry (MacKenzie, Postgate and Scupham, 1975; Unesco, 1978). Universities were able to regain public esteem after the disenchantment of campus rebellions in the late 1960s by taking on new roles and responsibilities, teaching adults in mid-career, offering continuing education to professional people whose skills were becoming obsolete. In scale of operation, in the visibility of their teaching, in their sophisticated centralized management, in their high public profile and in their high capital cost, these new ventures in distance education differed markedly from their predecessors.

This worldwide interest in university education at a distance, which was stimulated especially by the UK Open University (Perry, 1976) also increased awareness nationally and internationally of existing systems (Holmberg, 1977 and 1981). Although a few wilted into plaintive envy, other established correspondence systems adopted unfamiliar technologies in order to catch up. Some, however, have reconciled themselves to uncomfortable comparison with their glamorous colleagues, have re-examined the qualities and creditable activities from which they still take pride and others perhaps can take example, and have based fresh development on those existing foundations. So it has been in New Zealand (Bewley, 1981).

Extramural university study in New Zealand

That New Zealand has for many years had 'open' university education — in two senses of 'openness', wide public access and off-campus enrolment — may come as no surprise. Its sparse population, its intense concern for equality of educational opportunity, its renowned correspondence school for children in remote areas, would suggest the existence of some similar tertiary provision. And those familiar with New Zealand education would guess that its distance education would be sound rather than glamorous, unobtrusively available rather than intensively marketed, parsimonious rather than expensive. These are indeed some of the attributes of 'extramural studies' provided by Massey University. Closer examination, however, brings some surprises. In size the roll of extramural students (7700 in 1981) may not seem large compared with some institutions, but Massey reaches twice the proportion of New Zealand's national population that the Open University does in Britain. Extramural study has a long history; although the present tuition programme at Massey has existed for only 20 years, the opportunity to enrol at a distance, study privately, and present oneself for examination has existed for more than a century — almost since the inception of university education in New Zealand (Beaglehole, 1937: 129). Because of these origins, the Massey tuition system, which would later win national and international regard as valuable and innovative, had an inauspicious start, in marked contrast to the eager hopes and high ambitions of the UK Open University and its offspring a decade later.

In 1959 the New Zealand university system underwent structural change from a single federal institution to four separate universities — Auckland, Victoria University of Wellington, Canterbury and Otago — and two agricultural colleges, Lincoln and Massey. This reorganization gave scope to reconsider the opportunities which the dissolving University of New Zealand had hitherto provided for 'extramural' students (Parton, 1979: 189-91). Students distant from the four cities where the university colleges were situated had been allowed to enrol, follow the published prescriptions of courses, take the same final examinations as internal students and gain credits towards a degree in arts or commerce or, to some extent, science. Those who surfaced at the examinations — and many who enrolled sank without trace — offered scripts varying widely in quality; many fell to the sacrificial knife of failure. Even such brief encounters with students who were absent and anonymous exacerbated the doubts felt by academics about their profession in New Zealand. For years their teaching had been subjected to external assessment. Most of their classes for arts and commerce were for evening part-time students. The federal system allowed arts, science and commerce students to move mid-course from college to college. While a few staff gave help to extramural students, and offered to assess occasional assignments, many others complained fiercely about the system of exempting students from attending classes that 'provided a degree but not a university education'.

Yet the responsibility of the University towards its extramural students was socially inescapable. To deprive the teacher, minister or other professional person who worked among the settlers in the backblocks of the country of his chance to study independently and earn the same qualifications as his city-based colleagues ran counter to deeply held egalitarian beliefs among pioneer New Zealanders (Bewley, 1970).

As separation and autonomy approached, the universities hoped to abandon extramural study, reinforcing thereby other pressures to increase internal attendance. At the last moment, however, there was a reprieve (Parton, 1979: 212-14). A shortage of teachers prompted the suggestion that exemption be retained but be supported by correspondence tuition; and that the branch of Victoria University, set up alongside Palmerston North Teachers College to provide its students with some degree teaching, reproduce its courses for extramural students in correspondence form. Extramural study as we know it nowadays began in a mood of reluctance.

Extramural development at Massey University

The expectation was that very few courses (English, education, mathematics, history, perhaps French and geography) would be offered, none very advanced because time at the two-year teachers college would not allow. Two factors, however, strengthened and stimulated the extramural programme soon after its establishment. First, having conceded the necessity of some extramural study, all the universities not only retained the power to exempt some of their own students from lectures, but required those exempted students (their numbers increased as evening classes were reduced) to become 'registered for tuition' in the new correspondence courses. In doing so they boosted the Palmerston North branch college's enrolment. From these inflated numbers substantial departments were to grow. Secondly, Massey Agricultural College was in 1963 accorded independent status as a university incorporating the functions (including extramural tuition) of that branch college. Massey's newly acquired 'general studies' faculty began to push upwards towards full undergraduate and graduate programmes for its own degrees, and to push outwards in its range of disciplines. Since viability for a discipline was based on numbers and extramural teaching added to those numbers, each new discipline offered its courses extramurally, at least at first- and second-year level.

Before 1963 Massey College had faculties of Agricultural and

Horticultural Science, Food Science and Biotechnology, Science and Veterinary Science. Between 1963 and 1980 Massey University developed from General Studies four more faculties in Business, Education, Humanities and Social Sciences. All eight faculties have extensive internal programmes from bachelor to doctoral level and seven now offer extramural courses towards seven degrees and more than a dozen diplomas, both undergraduate and graduate. Veterinary Science is the exception. In some faculties — Business, Education, Humanities and Social Sciences — almost every undergraduate and diploma credit course has its extramural counterpart. The others offer a limited range, parts of the Agricultural Economics degree, a single mid-career diploma for food technologists, and a quota of places in a few first- and second-year science courses. The same academics who teach internally devise extramural versions of their courses, set and mark mid-course assignments and assess the final results of extramural as they do internal students. Examinations are the same for both, held at the same time and day whether on campus, or throughout New Zealand or half a world away overseas. It is the responsibility of each faculty to decide how much of its teaching will be extramural, reporting any decisions for change to the University's senior academic body, the Professorial Board.

Until 1979, a constraint on the range of courses remained; no courses that would complete the major in a degree were offered extramurally. Consequently all students were obliged to study internally for at least that advanced part of their degree; and therefore no completely extramural degree could be achieved. While the great majority of students were teachers and were eligible for transfer to university cities, for a year's leave with pay, the different merits of extramural and internal study could be combined. Many New Zealand graduates in the 1960s and 1970s had this mixture of experience. Some had begun with an internal credit or two acquired while training in a university city but at a non-university institution and some had started uneasily or immaturely as full-time university students and had suspended study for a year or two. They joined those who were not teachers, who had no previous university experience, and many of whom (a majority of these women) were second-chance students.

As Massey's extramural programme expanded and diversified, as its clientele extended and as social and economic opportunities to complete degrees contracted, the pressure from experienced and successful students grew. In 1976-77 Massey reviewed its extramural programme and *inter alia* recognized that the time had come to introduce 300-level extramural papers. After two years of debate, feasibility studies — and hesitation, while the University Grants Committee was persuaded — the programme began.

Organization and methods

The Centre for University Extramural Studies (CUES) services various faculty courses. It brings the extramural programme to public notice, counsels and enrols students, maintains their academic records, assists academic staff in the presentation of their courses in off-campus form, arranges the printing or tape recording of study materials, despatches them on whatsoever schedule the academic believes most suits his course, is the channel inwards and outwards for students' postal assignments (they are marked by academic staff in the departments), makes all accommodation arrangements when on-campus courses are held in the May and August university mid-year vacations, promotes and organizes off-campus visits by academic or counselling staff to centres near students' homes, establishes examination centres at 30 or more centres in New Zealand and as many overseas wherever the students are, ensures that the right papers are in the right places at the right time for the right candidates, receives and distributes examination scripts to departments and finally despatches results to extramural students.. The cycle of work is repeated annually, overlapping each year with the next, and increasing in volume as courses proliferate and student numbers grow. The Centre staff remains small: a Director who, as an academic, reports to his colleagues at Professorial and Faculty Boards, is assisted in implementing policy, monitoring academic quality in courses, advising students, and in maintaining relationships about extramural studies with universities and other agencies by a Resources Officer (advising on course design and teaching technology), a Research Officer (examining performance aspects of the system) and a part-time Course Adviser (counselling students, especially new ones, about their choice of courses). In administrative partnership with the Director is a Deputy Registrar (Extramural) with two or three middle-level Registry officers plus the Centre's two dozen secretarial and clerical staff.

Correspondence materials, study guides and assignments are the main teaching medium, with some face-to-face teaching at vacation schools on-campus or weekend encounters off-campus. However much an established system has evolved using printed correspondence materials, it nowadays must also consider other media and their technology — television, audio- and videocassettes, satellites, computers and the variety of devices that augment our telecommunications systems. Massey has invested substantially in the written word. A printing press, established in the late 1960s with substantial priority time assigned to production of extramural materials, has made an immediate impact on the quality of text; it has kept pace with rapidly escalating demands for varied production, and, with the addition of word processors, has extended our capability for good quality presentation. Because it is economic for relatively short runs, printing remains the basis for Massey's multiplying courses with relatively small enrolments instead of our relying on the economies of scale that could only be achieved in New Zealand's small population by offering fewer courses with large enrolments. By opting out of a requirement of long print runs we make other gains. Material can be prepared afresh for a revised run each year. And an academic can update study material until a month before despatch. However, small enrolments inhibit the use of open-broadcast, especially television: not only are large audiences required, but programmes go out on schedules that distance education students may be trying to avoid. Few New Zealand courses would provide an audience of sufficient scale, and even those where there could be 'spin-off' to a sizeable extra audience do not generate the staff and finance to make such a resource-demanding medium as television a major mode of teaching. Departments have some equipment, and the Resources Officer at CUES has established a foundation of skills and resources from which there could be take-off in video distance teaching as home videocassette recorders become common enough for programmes to reach students anywhere in New Zealand. In the meantime, we experiment jointly with the NZ Technical Correspondence Institute, with the use of the telephone as a teaching medium in order to limit travel and to be on track for advances in communications technology that may eventually affect our clienteles and our operations.

Among academic staff and students there are strong feelings that the tasks of study and teaching would be more comfortable if there was a nationwide regional network of people able to help extramural students. Most extramural students incur periods of anxiety, isolation, the need for someone to turn to when a question, even a minor one, wants a prompt and reassuring answer. A number of networks have evolved. For many year students have been encouraged to form local study circles for particular subjects: they have been sent lists of other students nearby; many vacation courses, or off-campus visits by academic staff earlier in the year, have prompted the formation of such groups. Although their function ends when the current course is complete, some members continue together and carry membership over the following year to another paper. Wider associations of local students have grown up, some linked to local community education organizations or institutions, especially the 'community colleges'. All extramural students are members of an Extramural Students Society. Three or four years ago its Palmerston North-based management committee resolved to foster local groups of members (Owen, 1981; Tripe, 1981), giving formal identity to existing groups and stimulating others where none existed, until now almost the entire country is covered by 'co-ordinating panels' (with branches also in Fiji and Western Samoa). For its part, the University has assigned faculty funds to encourage departments to operate off-campus: some departments with large first-year enrolments replicate in other centres (sometimes with local assistance) the vacation courses they hold at Massey; others appoint local tutors either with designated tutorial responsibilities or to be 'on call', these latter often being graduates who are experienced extramural students. To this variety CUES is now hoping to add its own scatter of 'co-ordinators' to unify these various extramural 'agents' and 'agencies' and gain more efficient use of their efforts.

An innovatory activity?

When extramural tuition began in 1960 it was more derivative than innovative. The opportunities it provided had existed for decades; the model of correspondence teaching it followed had been well established at Australia's University of New England several years before. It has developed little of the splendid technology of distance education foundations of the 1970s. Yet recently CUES was named one of New Zealand's innovatory centres under the Asian programme of Education Innovation for Development (AREID). This paradox can be explained in various ways. The recent vogue of distance education has perhaps bestowed the accolade of 'innovation' on all such institutions. Massey's range of extramural courses has extended into new academic territories beyond those for which the programme was originally conceived. Within the context of post-secondary education, Massey has evolved a style of operation more entrepreneurial than most other universities; more immediately responsive to emergent changes in society; more flexible in its relationships with non-university educational institutions and with the consumers of education; more aware of the personal needs of its students who undertake studies, in mid-life and in mid-career, outside the walls and sometimes the strict regulations of a university, but with aspirations that are in fact consonant with its ethos and goals. These explanations contribute to whatsoever reputation for innovation Massey's extramural studies programme has. It is not its history or its organization that earns that reputation but the way it has managed to combine sound academic principle with a perception of social needs.

The opportunistic nature of the development of Massey's extramural studies programme — and in this respect it may be typical of many of the earlier correspondence-based distance education systems — contrasts sharply with the intensely planned and programmed development of the UK Open University. The opportunities which have been grasped are the development of a wide-ranging programme to suit the needs of a rapidly diversifying population of students, encouragement to other organizations as they seek to interact with Massey, and acceptance of the initiative of students in using resources available in their communities. Such 'opportunism' has as its corollary an outlook that weighs the possibilities of new ventures as they are suggested by outside groups, submits them to the checks and constraints built into the university system, but treats them seriously as expressions of public need deserving serious and positive consideration. For many years extramural development reflected the current needs of the teaching profession and the internal needs of faculties and departments to establish their range of staff and interests to ensure academic viability. There is however a 'marketplace' where the academic consumer seeks out the wares that would satisfy his requirements; it is a marketplace controlled by mechanisms which govern whether or not a development is truly academic and whether the public purse (all New Zealand universities are government-funded) should afford

95

such provision. A university need not be reluctant to sense public expectations nor be chary of meeting such expectations if they can be measured against the criteria.

The 'market' for extramural courses has been among those professions that extend throughout the country (such as teaching, nursing, business management, social work and most recently the police) where there is common mobility as members progress within their professions, and where no one should be disadvantaged by serving away from the main centres where the universities are. The 'market' is among individuals who seek to improve their knowledge and skills but cannot wait for a move, or who are established in a location from which no transfer is imminent. The 'market' (and the economic implications of the term become strained) is among men and women, especially in recent years among women, who are dissatisfied with the opportunities they have hitherto been offered, and who sense in the university's outreach to them, a means of discovering new quality in their lives and themselves. The 'innovation' to all these consumers is that the university is conscious of the market among them for its wares.

While expansion has been considerable, in numbers, range of courses and styles of presentation, the extramural programme has remained under constraints imposed by its history: the anguish of debate whether an entire degree should be offered extramurally; parsimony in staff; limited resources for presentation and off-campus support services; the abstinence of some faculties and the absence of others. While many of the objectives, principles and procedures formulated during its initial years still pertain for extramural studies at Massey University today, there were many areas of development unimagined then which have emerged and perhaps distinguish New Zealand's from many other systems of university distance education.

One, already mentioned, is the emergence of a strong student share in the extramural enterprise. Another is its international role. Massey retains some responsibility for providing distance education among the island states of the South West Pacific with which New Zealand has traditionally had educational links, although in this CUES now takes a minor share alongside the University of the South Pacific (Bewley, 1981); its role within Unesco's regional network for Asia and the Pacific is increasing; some of its specialist qualifications attract overseas attention that envisages aid and interchange of credits. Within New Zealand other distinctive activities arise from the collaboration of CUES with other New Zealand universities, tertiary institutions and correspondence and community education organizations.

Within the New Zealand tertiary education community

Little more need be said of the relationship with other universities. All of them continue to exempt some students from attending lectures but where Massey offers an extramural course the student is usually required to 'register for tuition' for the Massey course, follow its teaching, take its examination, and credit the course to his home university as though the teaching had been provided there. Massey's expansion has given students in other universities — those who leave their degrees incomplete, or take a break before resuming internally in a later year — increasing scope to insert extramural credits in their qualifications.

The interchangeability of extramural and internal credits, and of Massey courses with those at other universities, has won confidence — albeit sometimes grudging — for Massey extramural courses from the other universities. This confidence has been reinforced by the internal performance of students proceeding from extramural to internal study. If the 'majoring' level of their chosen subject is not available extramurally, some Massey extramural students want to take a major elsewhere but credit it to a Massey degree. This can be arranged. Such arrangements smack of anomaly but also of realism and good sense and accord with the sharp respect which the agency financing the universities on behalf of the government, the University Grants Committee, has for rationalizing and economizing efforts. There is sometimes friction but there is also a sense of necessary collaboration between CUES and the programmes of other universities that is typical of the way a small country must husband expensive resources.

Also at the tertiary level, various polytechnics (some of which have regional responsibility and are called community colleges), teachers colleges, seminaries and other institutions for professional training maintain various contacts with Massey. There are parts of the programme at some teachers colleges and polytechnics for which the students enrol extramurally so that when their professional training is complete they can carry forward credit towards future degree studies (most probably extramural studies) in mid-career.

Perhaps the greatest economy that this interaction with other tertiary non-university education institutions has afforded us has been our avoidance of a binary system and a proliferation of degree-awarding institutions which we could not afford to staff and maintain. If degree credit is available to those who attend non-university institutions either within or following ordinary courses, the ambitions of those institutions for higher status are more easily dispelled. So far New Zealand has been spared (except in one instance) the very traumatic experience of institutional closure as a means of rationalizing over-extended resources.

Community education

Extramural Studies is part of a total national system of correspondence education undertaken by three complementary institutions, the Correspondence School, the Technical Correspondence Institute and Massey. Demarcation is rarely if ever a matter of dispute. It is more important that adult students seeking a 'second chance' enter the distance education system at the appropriate place. Knowledge by staff within the institutions of one another's function, appropriate redirection of prospective students, and informal, infrequent meetings among senior staff have sufficed so far. For the future there are more positive plans of developing and sharing regional support services, as a result of a recent 'working party' on adult education at a distance in New Zealand surveying current practices and purposes (NZ Department of Education, 1979).

All three distance education institutions perceive themselves as participants in the surge of 'continuing education' that has affected New Zealand recently (Boshier, 1980) as it has so many other countries. Even the Correspondence School, founded for children in remote areas, now has a large group of adults seeking renewed opportunity to upgrade or extend their schooling from former days. It is commonly acknowledged that distance learning serves well the interests of those who bypassed former opportunities of attending university and who in many cases discontinued secondary education before they had achieved their potential level of attainment. In particular many women left the formal education system achieving less than they might have done. Since the mid-70s there has been a 3 : 2 proportion of women to men among extramural students and it is perhaps not surprising that while 25 per cent of all extramural students have been admitted under regulations for underqualified mature age students, the figure for women is nearer 30 per cent.

There has been a proliferation of new agencies and institutions of continuing and community education, and for Massey extramural students this has meant new possibilities of support close to home. It has become an important sphere of activity for CUES to establish lines of contact with newly founded community colleges, or with community education 'projects', 'councils' and 'committees' that have sprung up throughout the country, to help them identify extramural students in their community. It is not a difficult task. Extramural students are vocal on their own behalf. Many are well above average in initiative and not surprisingly many of them have been active in promoting and organizing community education ventures. They work on the behalf of others, but expect the agencies to serve their own extramural interests from time to time by providing places for extramural students to meet, tutors to visit, information to be available. Little money changes hands. The exchange is more of mutual esteem, public notice of their joint positive activities and the promotion of consciousness and support.

It costs the University little either in fees paid, or energies expended, to use these resources. When time, organization, energy and resources are expended, it is in maintaining liaison, encouraging new kinds of activity, and recording achievements, none of them costly.

The individual in the system

Through the educational organizations with which Massey's Centre associates, it can respond to many educational interests current in society.

However, a system of learning which in essence provides independent study for individuals needs to be responsive to them without the intervention of other agencies. For all its network of formal and informal relationships with other educational institutions, CUES deals with each student separately and its staff achieve their greatest professional satisfaction when students report a sense of personal care, respect for their special, infinitely different, circumstances, and attention to particular problems, despite distance and ever-multiplying numbers. It is gratifying that such reports occur, and professionally satisfying that such diverse individuals can be catered for within the institutional framework of the University and become active and loyal members of the university community and protagonists for the extramural system. Such gratification and satisfaction is inevitably tempered by our recognition that not all extramural students flourish, that withdrawal (some, but not all, of which seems wastage) seems inevitable and predictable (Tremaine and Cavanagh, 1979) and that some interests cannot be as well served as they expected. Indeed it may not be within the capacity of an organization to solve these problems through greater 'efficiency' or by the academic adapting his teaching. The range of students goes beyond the customary group and while positive factors of maturity and experience increase so too do the effects of negative attributes, weaker initial school qualifications, less practised study skills, and stronger inclinations to dogmatism. Not only are the academic's stereotypes of his students challenged, his teaching responsibilities and tasks are also radically disturbed by the need for more precisely structured courses, pressure to employ the devices of educational technology, the threat of editorial intervention in his teaching material, and the general lack (but occasional intensification) of interactive situations with students face-to-face. Where his external teaching is an offshoot of simultaneous internal courses, there is the extra burden of duplicating teaching in a second mode, of aligning courses that have inherent significant differences, and balancing the respective needs of and giving due attention to both present and absent students.

Conclusion

Massey is only one of many universities around the world meeting the challenge of how an institution which draws some of its strength and status from the well defined traditions and conventions of the British and European universities can serve the particular and changing needs of its own society. It must decide not only how much it draws on the fast growing repertory of distance teaching, how much it relies on the pattern of flexibility and adaptation which has until now been its style, and how far its growth can continue without having an untoward radical effect on the national university system; but also how far it must continue to respond to new voices in the community, asking that universities serve wider social purposes.

BASIC REFERENCE DATA (1981)

I. The host institution

Name: Massey University
Date founded: As Massey Agricultural College, 1927; as Massey University, 1964
Internal organization: Eight faculties: Agricultural and Horticultural Science, Food Science and Biotechnology, Veterinary Science, Science, Humanities, Education, Social Sciences, Business; divided into 37 departments and teaching units.
Number of academic staff: 427
Number of students: 13,635 (internal 5936; extramural 7699)
Catchment area: Internal students in general faculties (eg Humanities, Business) come predominantly from lower Central North Island; students in applied science faculties come from throughout New Zealand; extramural students come from throughout New Zealand.
Designated responsibility for off-campus activities: (i) Extramural tuition throughout New Zealand; (ii) Extension responsibility for lower Central North Island but specialist faculty extension activities occur throughout New Zealand.
Income: (1980) $NZ 21 million (89.5 per cent from government grants, 4.9 per cent from student fees, 5.6 per cent from other sources)

II. The innovation/system being studied

Name: Centre for University Extramural Studies
Date founded: 1960 as part of Victoria University of Wellington's branch college; integrated with Massey University in 1964.
Nature: Provides distance education for university degrees and diplomas throughout New Zealand and South-west Pacific.
Internal organization: Administrative unit to administer enrolments, records and examinations, produce and distribute study material (devised and taught by staff of academic departments) for extramural students.
Number of academic staff: 3.5
Number of non-academic staff: 33
Income: While some separate accounts are held (eg travel, some capital items), much of the activity is part of wider university operations and funds (eg non-academic staff as part of Registry, examination costs as part of integrated operation, etc).
Income as proportion of institution's total income: Meaningful separate accounting is not therefore identifiable.

REFERENCES AND BIBLIOGRAPHY

Beaglehole, J (1937) *The University of New Zealand*, 431 pp, New Zealand Council for Educational Research, Wellington

Bewley, D R (1970) Extramural Studies at Massey University — the first decade, *Continuing Education in New Zealand*, 3(2), 11-42

Bewley, D R (1979) Massey University and the University of the South Pacific: Registration for tuition, Paper presented to the Open University Conference on the Education of Adults at a Distance, reprinted in Crump, P and Livingston, K (eds) *ASPESA Forum '81 Papers*, pp 385-90, Massey University, Palmerston North and University of the South Pacific, Suva

Bewley, D R (1981) *Massey University Extramural Studies*, Commonwealth Conference on Materials for Learning and Teaching, Wellington, 1975; revised 1981, 23 pp, Massey University, Palmerston North

Boshier, R (1980) *Towards a Learning Society: New Zealand Adult Education in Transition*, 300 pp, Learningpress, Vancouver

Duke, C (1967) *The London External Degree and The English Part-time Students*, Leeds Studies in Adult Education No 2, Leeds University Press

Holmberg, B (1977) *Distance Education: A Survey and Bibliography*, 165 pp, Kogan Page, London and Nichols Publishing Co, New York

Holmberg, B (1981) *Status and Trends in Distance Education: A Survey and Bibliography*, 200 pp, Kogan Page, London and Nichols Publishing Co, New York

MacKenzie, N, Postgate, R and Scupham, J (1975) *Open Learning: Systems and Problems in Post-secondary Education*, 498 pp, Unesco Press, Paris

New Zealand Department of Education (1979) *Learning at a Distance: Report of the Working Party on Continuing Education at a Distance, chaired by D James, to the Director-General of Education*, 137 pp, NZ Department of Education, Wellington

Owen, J (1981) The role of student bodies in distance education, in Crump, P and Livingston, K (eds) *ASPESA Forum '81 Papers*, pp 167-79, Massey University, Palmerston North and University of the South Pacific, Suva

Parton, H (1979) *The University of New Zealand*, 277 pp, Auckland University Press and Oxford University Press (for University Grants Committee, New Zealand)

Perry, W (1976) *Open University: A Personal Account by the First Vice-Chancellor*, 298 pp, Open University Press, Milton Keynes

Rayner, S A (1949) *Correspondence Education in Australia and New Zealand*, 119 pp, Australian Council for Educational Research Series No 64, Melbourne University Press

Tremaine, M G and Cavanagh, B (1979) *Why Students Withdraw*, 79 pp, Massey University Centre for University Extramural Studies, Palmerston North

Tremaine, M G and Wagner, G A (1981) *Readability: An Issue in Distance Learning*, 105 pp, Massey University Centre for University Extramural Studies, Palmerston North

Tripe, J (1981) The growth and development of the Extramural Students Society: Massey University, in Crump, P and Livingston, K (eds) *ASPESA Forum '81 Papers*, pp 181-92, Massey University, Palmerston North and University of the South Pacific, Suva

Unesco (1978) *Open Education: Experiments and Experiences in Asia and Oceania*, Bulletin of the Unesco Regional Office for Education in Asia and Oceania 19, viii, 220 pp, Unesco, Bangkok

6. Teleconferencing: a distance learning system Wisconsin style

Lorne A Parker

We live in an age that can be accurately labelled 'The Communication Revolution'. It is commonly accepted that our society was once an economy based on agrarian production of goods, which was transformed in fundamental ways with the development of industrialization. The resulting industrial society is now being transformed into an economy based on the delivery of information services. The country literally runs on information.

These cultural and economic trends have been fuelled by an exponential upward curve of communication technologies. Technological breakthroughs which are chemical, mechanical, electromechanical and electronic are announced almost weekly. The costs of these technologies are plummeting while their capabilities to generate, store, translate and transmit data are rocketing. While the economy is wracked by inflation, communication services are becoming some of the alltime bargains.

Some of these technologies are linking in character, and they produce interactive networks which permit the request, location and transfer of information. Among such networks are satellites, television broadcasting, community antenna television, information services via cable, local loop distribution, and computer-based information networks. These permit the distribution and exchange of information among a large number of people, either singly or simultaneously, depending upon the nature of the system.

Other technologies are self-contained and are not necessarily part of such networks, although most can be linked to them to provide ancillary functions. These include such technologies as videocassette, videodisc, microfiche and ultrafiche retrieval systems, microprocessor-based technologies, personal computers, computer games, self-paced instructional devices, teaching machines, and holographic data storage systems. These have the advantage of dedicated local use and full-time access, and also the disadvantage that any information to be retrieved can be made available only at the local site.

In the near future, all of these technologies will be smaller, lighter, more portable, less expensive, and will have increased capacity for storage, retrieval and transmission of data. They are also converging to interact with one another in new and sometimes unexpected ways.

These technologies hold promising prospects for the field of continuing education. They provide additional information resources, flexibility, speed and interaction. The linking technologies may facilitate learning by two-way interaction, permitting traditional question and answer methods to be used in distance learning. The availability of self-contained technologies will permit rapid random access to a wider range of information, and provide the additional benefit of individualized access at any time of day or night. Newer technologies free the user from sequence and permit random access to any part of the prepared programme material.

Obviously no single medium is adequate to resolve the communication and learning needs of all those desiring continuing education. So we need to consider the appropriate matching of user needs, medium capabilities, time constraints, programme availability, and budget.

The telephone merits a second look. At first glance it appears to be a limited medium with little potential in education. The telephone has, thus, often been ignored in favour of its more glamorous sisters — television, radio, and computerized instruction. But a second look reveals its particular advantages: the telephone is interactive, flexible, low-cost, widely available, and supported by a well-developed infrastructure. It can also offer a visual communications channel: using telewriters, graphic input devices, or slow-scan televideo systems, a telephone network lends itself to a variety of instructional formats. In short, the telephone is uniquely suited to many educational roles, one of the foremost being the delivery of programmes to adult learners.

Continuing professional education and non-vocational adult education are two of the fastest growing areas of higher learning, in the USA as elsewhere. Their rapid growth reflects both a new philosophy of education and the need for professionals to keep abreast of information. It is also the result of the simple demographic fact that the USA is becoming an older society: in the 1970s the number of 25 to 34 year olds increased 44 per cent, and this dramatic shift to an older population will continue well into the 1980s and 1990s.

Higher education has traditionally focused on full-time, on-campus youth who enrolled in formal degree programmes. However, the new post-secondary student, the adult, has a different view of education and wants learning opportunities to be available in his/her home community. These part-time learners are people of all ages and lifestyles, and they have diverse learning needs. Rather than defining education as a terminal degree programme to prepare one for future goals, the adult learner sees education as a self-directed activity that continues throughout life. Education, conceptualized as lifelong learning, is a vehicle for continual vocational development and leisure pursuits.

Aside from such personal goals, continuing education is increasingly viewed as a necessity in many fields, eg medicine and engineering. Practitioners are not only strongly encouraged but often required to enrol in continuing education programmes as a practical means of maintaining professional skills amidst rapid changes in technical information. This tendency for professional associations and licensing boards to encourage continuing education will most likely accelerate, forcing educators to revise their curricula and teaching methods.

The adult learner, who is often a distant learner, requires non-traditional delivery systems. To reach adults in their home communities, higher education, which is primarily campus-based, must implement new modes of instruction. However, the development of outreach programmes is often limited by budgetary constraints. Instructing students near their homes or places of business is usually not justified economically if an instructor must travel great distances to serve a few participants at each classroom site. What alternative, then, is most economically feasible, makes best use of teaching resources, and effectively meets the educational needs of distant adult learners?

In response to this question, many educators are turning to the telephone — one of the oldest and most effective media. Although this invention is over 100 years old, it remains the basic instrument of the new communications technology. After many small-scale experiments in the 1960s, the telephone's unique advantages are leading to a second generation of educational telephone networks in North America and Europe.

There is almost universal agreement that two-way communication is a desirable and necessary element of distance education (Holmberg, 1981). A telephone network is interactive, allowing students and instructor to exchange information, ask questions and receive immediate feedback. The process of interaction between faculty and students and among the students themselves is perhaps the most important of the educational processes. While television and radio may be appropriate for some courses, these essentially one-way systems have disadvantages when discussion and immediate feedback are required.

A television network which uses cables, microwave or broadcast channels, is also costly and cannot easily be modified to incorporate new receiving locations or shift transmission sites. A telephone network can use various combinations of dedicated and dial-up lines to minimize cost while maximizing flexibility of reception and transmission. For example, dedicated lines may interconnect any number of remote classrooms while dial-up lines allow people at additional locations to bridge into the network.

The telephone also offers instructional flexibility. Course materials can be modified easily at a reasonable cost. The latest telewriting equipment or slow-scan televideo system can display a variety of graphic or pictorial information to supplement audio instruction.

In Wisconsin, the focus has long been on the telephone. The Wisconsin Idea, that the boundaries of the campus are the boundaries of the state, provides the philosophical base for state-wide outreach programmes. The University of Wisconsin pioneered the development of general educational outreach in the USA and over the years has been a leader in dynamic programmes of adult education and public services. With the appointment of Charles R Van Hise as President in 1903, Wisconsin led public institutions of higher learning in taking this stored-up knowledge of the University to the people beyond the immediate campus (Axford, 1969). In this supportive environment, the University of Wisconsin Extension's

Educational Telephone Network (ETN) and State-wide Extension Educational Network (SEEN) have flourished. Today, these telephone networks annually attract over 36,000 students — engineers, teachers, physicians, nurses, librarians, lawyers, businesspeople, social workers and others (Parker, 1976).

Wisconsin's Educational Telephone Network (ETN)

A brief history
The University of Wisconsin has a long tradition of providing educational opportunities to students in their home communities. In 1907, UW President Charles Van Hise challenged educators to extend the 'boundaries of the campus to the boundaries of the state'. This, the Wisconsin Idea, has been applied successfully to education. It has lived and grown through the years and is the basic philosophy behind the implementation of the two interactive telecommunications systems mentioned in this chapter.

Education by telephone, not as a network, began in Wisconsin as far back as 1962, when the University of Wisconsin-Madison presented a science lecture to students in La Crosse, Wisconsin. Much earlier examples of such point-to-point use of amplified telephone messages in education could be found in other parts of the country. Actually, the idea of using the telephone for teaching was conceived in the early 1950s. Before that, attention was focused on teaching students how to use the telephone.

The Educational Telephone Network (ETN) was established in 1965 by the Department of Postgraduate Medical Education, after an unsuccessful try at using two-way radio for state-wide educational conferences for doctors. One of a physician's biggest problems is fulfilling his moral obligations to his patients to keep up with current events in medicine. There are so many demands on a doctor's time that taking a day off for education becomes an impossibility. ETN's medical programmes help provide the highest calibre of medical instruction at a low cost — incorporating topics directly applicable to clinical practice and presenting programmes on a regular basis in the physician's home communities.

The first programme consisted of a 30-minute lecture that was tape recorded in advance. The lecturer provided a written outline of the lecture, along with visual materials to be used. These visual materials were duplicated on 35mm slides. Sets of slides were loaded into carousels for projection at each of the participating hospital locations around the state. The slides and copies of the written materials were mailed to each conference location a week in advance of the programme.

The lecturer, at the appropriate time, called for the slides, which were shown at each of the conference locations. After the lecture each distant learning hospital was called in a predetermined order so that listening physicians, through a moderator, could question the lecturer or comment on the presentation. All questions and answers were heard over the entire network (Parker, 1977).

ETN was thus established to meet the continuing education needs of medical doctors in all corners of the state. It is now a four-wire dedicated telephone network that takes the form of a huge party-line. The two-way audio medium reaches into ETN learning centres, in courthouses, extension offices, University of Wisconsin campuses and centres, libraries and hospitals in each of the state's 72 counties. In all, University of Wisconsin-Extension faculty can reach into 120 different Wisconsin communities via ETN to more than 200 specific sites. More than 30,000 students enrol in programmes in a traditional academic year (Parker and Baird, 1977).

ETN station equipment
The vehicle that links all the ETN students into one large Wisconsin classroom is an amplified telephone device called Edu-Com II. Developed by Darome, Inc, Harvard, Illinois, in conjunction with the University of Wisconsin and Wisconsin Telephone Company, it is a portable, self-contained unit consisting of a large speaker and four microphones. The unit plugs into a standard telephone jack and AC power outlet. All ETN classrooms have identical equipment and no technical skill or special knowledge is required to operate it. The Darome Edu-Com units are designed for groups of up to 200 students per location. In cases where an ETN classroom is this large, the units have a built-in public address unit for easy hearing at any particular site.

Instructors may originate programmes from any state-wide ETN classroom or from ETN studios in Old Radio Hall on the University of Wisconsin-Madison campus. Participants at any ETN location simply depress and hold a bar on the base of one of the microphones and speak with the instructor or any other ETN student in the state.

ETN programming
From the 18 locations participating in the first ETN programme in 1965, the system has expanded both in listening locations and programme diversification. In addition to the original medical sessions, programmes are now offered in pharmacy, English, law, social work, library science, education, nursing, agriculture, engineering, economics, business, the arts, and many more. Most ETN programmes are non-credit, continuing education for professional adults, although there are some credit courses offered each semester. Programmes vary from one to three hours in length and include a variety of programme formats.

This year's programmes range from security guidelines for bank employees to adolescent depression and from update training for election officials to small church organists. In all, approximately 300 different credit, non-credit and public service programmes were offered to 32,305 participants during the 1979-80 academic year. This enrolment was up 793, or 2.5 per cent from the previous year. A breakdown of enrolments includes 19,548 enrolled in non-credit programmes, 12,632 in public service programmes, and 125 in credit programmes.

Among public service programmes with audiences of 600 and more were these: Cattle Feeding Day, 600; American Water Works Association Operator Training Meeting, 615; Uniform Dwelling Code, 678; and Horse Production Series, 812. The continuing education category 'health science' showed the higher numbers of enrolments in single programmes. Emergency Management Techniques enrolled 928 paramedics state-wide; medical technology seminars attracted 783; neurological disorders enrolled 659 pharmacists, physicians, nurses and allied health professionals.

In addition to course offerings, the network is also used in other ways. Messages from the University-Extension office in Madison are relayed each morning to state-wide Extension faculty, followed by agents in turn, forwarding messages to the Madison office. County faculty also confer with each other via ETN each morning either by prior arrangement or by spontaneous inquiry. State-wide departmental meetings are also regularly scheduled on ETN. Emergency agricultural information concerning early Wisconsin frost or corn blight disease, for example, is also disseminated to agents around the state via ETN.

Cost of the ETN system
Educational programming on the ETN system is an important activity of many University of Wisconsin-Extension faculty members. And, the cost is minimal — for ETN non-credit programmes, about $US 0.22 per student contact hour. This cost reflects only the telephone system rental payment for station equipment and its operation, and not course instructional materials or an instructor's time. The cost is determined by the total operating budget for Instructional Communications Systems, the unit administratively responsible for the Educational Telephone Network system.

Wisconsin's State-wide Extension Educational Network (SEEN)

The limitations of a purely audio interactive communications system were one reason for the initiation of SEEN, the State-wide Extension Educational Network. Because ETN offered only oral information, Extension engineering faculty saw drawbacks in trying to teach their courses via this system. A major portion of engineering lectures and discussions involve the use of mathematical equations or other graphic information. Even though the economies of ETN were beneficial, engineering faculty could give little serious consideration to teaching their courses over this system until technology came to the rescue.

In 1969, the electrowriter was added as an experiment to 10 ETN locations and was an immediate success. Students and their instructors liked the system and its potential. An exchange of electrowriter courses was soon developed between Wisconsin and the University of Illinois. But the scheduling of Wisconsin and Illinois courses proved to be difficult due to the number of other programmes carried over ETN. The installation of a separate electrowriter network, SEEN, became necessary.

When SEEN was initiated by Extension programming faculty in 1969, it was a programming decision and not an administrative decision. Thus, the normal administrative decision process was unnecessary. For the past 12 years, the unique capability of the SEEN system for both audio and visual programming has made it possible to deliver continuing education opportunities to engineers throughout the state, even in the most isolated communities of northern Wisconsin (Jackson *et al*, 1978).

SEEN uses leased, commercial telephone lines to transmit audio and visual materials simultaneously. Two-way audio communication allows students at any SEEN location to participate actively in the course, asking questions and exchanging information with the instructor and fellow students at all of the connected sites. Electrowriters supply the visual element. Any material that is customarily shown on a classroom chalkboard — equations, diagrams, outlines, graphs, line drawings — can be presented instantly on the electrowriter and transmitted over the telephone lines to all SEEN locations. Students view the material exactly as it is created by the instructor and may comment or ask questions at any time during the session.

The SEEN system links more than 20 locations throughout Wisconsin with approximately 3500 miles of long-distance telephone lines. These locations were selected according to population densities, educational needs of local residents, and distribution of engineers and other professionals in the state. This configuration allows the network to serve 80 per cent of Wisconsin's engineers and technicians. The classroom settings vary. Some are in county courthouses, while others are on campuses or in manufacturing firms. In addition to intra-network communication, a telephone call from anywhere in the USA can be tied into the system, providing contact with outside experts.

Programming for engineering education
Extension Engineering offers SEEN programmes in two general areas: non-credit continuing education and credit undergraduate and graduate education (Klus *et al*, 1974).

Continuing education, the largest programme area and basis of the entire teleconferencing network in Wisconsin, is directed to the practising engineer and other professionals. Engineering courses are usually conducted over a six- to eight-week period, meeting once or twice each week. They tend to be practical 'state of the art' courses tailored to the needs of professional engineers. A typical course in this category is the 'Industrial and Manufacturing Engineering Refresher' which reviews current techniques in manufacturing processes, scheduling, cost analysis, quality control, and other pertinent topics. Continuing education courses are usually offered between 16.30 and 22.00, Monday through Thursday, times that are convenient for working engineers. Participants earn Continuing Education Units (CEUs) for each programme satisfactorily completed.

Wisconsin engineers who enrol in continuing education programmes have a unique opportunity to earn a Professional Development Degree in Engineering, a post-baccalaureate degree pioneered at the University of Wisconsin. The PD degree programme is based on the special needs and personal objectives of the full-time employed engineer. Each student enrolled in the degree programme meets a faculty adviser to establish an organized plan of educational development. The plan is flexible and can be changed to reflect new learning objectives. The PD degree requires 120 CEUs. In addition to SEEN courses, units may be earned in short courses, institutes and seminars, workshops, correspondence study, videocassette courses, and individual guided study programmes.

Undergraduate and graduate credit courses are available to both off-campus and on-campus students, and are customarily conducted during the morning or afternoon hours. Continuing engineering students may also enrol and take the course at any SEEN site. Resident campus students are usually enrolled in SEEN courses that are simultaneously telecast to the 14 two-year campuses of the University of Wisconsin centre system. This arrangement is often more economical than offering separate classes at each school; it also allows flexibility in programme topics and the most effective assignment of faculty specialists from any part of the state. Basic courses in statics and dynamics for pre-engineering students, for example, originate at the centre in Wausau and are received by about 50 students in groups of four or five at other centres during a mid-morning hour. Although this time of day is not convenient for most continuing education students, several have joined this class. In many cases, the inclusion of working students who are occupationally associated with the subject matter has added much to the relevance and scope of instruction. In such subjects as products liability, welding metallurgy, and pollution control, the experienced engineer has contributed a great deal to the course and challenged the instructor to keep abreast of engineering practice.

Administration is a co-operative effort

The administration and management of the ETN and SEEN programmes involves three groups: Instructional Communications Systems, Extension's Departments and Extension agents at the local level.

Based in Madison, Instructional Communications Systems (ICS), a division of University-Extension, is responsible for the overall administration of SEEN, co-ordination of network programming, and management of the technical system. Co-ordinating functions include programme scheduling, instructional design, promotion, and evaluation. ICS also serves as a liaison between Extension Departments and the local agents. Technical management of the system involves the operation and maintenance of the telephone network, studios, classroom hook-ups, electrowriters, and audio equipment as well as the production, recording, and distribution of programmes (Parker *et al*, 1977).

The course design, faculty identification and all academic matters related to ETN and SEEN programmes are managed by the programming department. The programming department initiates courses, conducts direct mail promotion, and co-ordinates with other Extension departments and UW-campuses.

The third branch of administration is provided by the Local Programme Administrator (LPA), an Extension agent headquartered at or near an ETN or SEEN location. The LPA is the contact person at each site who is responsible for scheduling, managing, and promoting programmes at the local level. The LPA may also have a programme aide to welcome and assist students, operate the audiovisual equipment, and in general, help people obtain a positive educational experience.

The faculty

The instructional services for SEEN courses are supplied by three types of faculty:

- ☐ the professional staff of an Extension Department
- ☐ the teaching faculties of the 27 campuses in the University of Wisconsin system
- ☐ members of the community with appropriate experience and teaching expertise.

Those in the first category supply the bulk of offerings of the non-credit variety, dealing with subjects of current relevance in their areas of professional competence. These teachers are able to respond quickly to the changing aspirations of continuing education clientele. Participation in ETN-SEEN teaching is encouraged as a substantial method of professional advancement.

The ETN-SEEN courses offered for credit are generally taught by resident campus faculty, and are adapted directly from existing courses offered to students on campus. The ETN-SEEN courses offered by these faculty members are generally simulcast to the network from a class of resident students. Teachers in this category have in the past been compensated by an 'overload' payment in addition to their regular faculty salary, but they now often engage in ETN-SEEN programming as a part of their regular academic activities.

Building upon the long experience of the evening, non-credit offerings based in Milwaukee, some of the SEEN schedule is devoted to simulcast versions of these courses. The instructors may be from any of the three types of faculty. Those not on the staff of UW-Extension are usually compensated at an hourly rate. Since the network began operation in 1969, more than 100 men and women have served on the SEEN instructional staff.

The technical system

A successful educational teleconferencing system, whether made up of two or 200 locations, includes three basic technical components: the terminal or station equipment, the interconnecting transmission system, the network control centre. Many variables influence system design. Included are the number of locations; the geographic area covered; the network configuration (whether the system is a four-wire, multi-point dedicated network or a two-wire dial-up network); and the network's intended use. No two designs are likely to be the same, but several ingredients are common to successful systems:

□ An educational teleconferencing system should be able to connect participants at widely scattered locations
□ The system should provide a communication environment that duplicates (as closely as possible) the single-site discussion group
□ Terminal or station equipment should provide even sound distribution and allow easy participation
□ The system should be manageable, allowing additional locations and equipment as well as modifications to meet users' changing needs
□ A network control centre should provide a programme origination point and essential supervision of the system's technical operation
□ The transmission system should provide clear, intelligible communication between all points on the network
□ The system should be able to connect groups anywhere in the world via regular telephone service
□ Methods should be developed to recognize quickly and to clear up any technical problems interfering with service
□ Equipment should feature the latest technology and be reliable and serviceable
□ All terminal equipment, station location interfaces, and installation procedures should be standardized throughout the system.

With these general capabilities in mind, the three basic components of the SEEN system will be described in greater detail (see also Braun *et al*, 1976).

Station equipment
Each of the SEEN classrooms has identical equipment: a Darome Convener for two-way voice communication and a Victor Electrowriter[1] which either transmits or receives graphic material. Using these devices, an instructor can present both audio and visual information to students in a number of widely scattered locations.

The Darome Convener is a self-contained, portable conference set that contains four microphones and a speaker that plugs into a standard telephone jack and AC power outlet. Students simply press a bar at the base of the microphone to participate in class discussion. Each microphone has a 6 metre cord to allow easy access by students. As many as 16 microphones may be placed in a single classroom using a jack provided on the unit and audio mixers. The audio amplification system is sufficient to provide highly intelligible sound in a classroom seating up to 300 people.

Electrowriters permit the transmission, reception and projection of any visual material that is customarily shown on a classroom chalkboard. As shown in Figure 6.1, the instructor writes on the electrowriter transmitter with a special ball-point pen. Pen position and movement create tone signals that are carried over regular telephone lines to electrowriter receivers in SEEN classrooms around the state. These signals are translated by the receiver into an instantaneous and faithful reproduction of the instructor's writing. The image on the receiver is then projected on to a screen, which becomes the classroom chalkboard.

Figure 6.1. *An instructor using the Electrowriter*

The basic electrowriter system consists of a transmitter and receiver, each of which has an electronic pen, servo-mechanism, and a writing area of 112 sq cm. The SEEN electrowriters were modified by Instructional Communications Systems to double the writing and viewing area, making, in essence, a two-frame system. While one frame is being developed by the instructor, students can also see the frame which was previously discussed.

Distribution network
The SEEN system uses two dedicated, four-wire, multi-point teleconferencing networks; voice signals are transmitted over one network,

while the second network simultaneously transmits the signals from the electrowriters. The combination of two four-wire networks gives the system greater flexibility, for both audio and visual information can originate from any of the SEEN locations.

SEEN's dedicated system uses permanently installed facilities leased from the telephone company on a 24-hour basis. Because the listening centres are permanent, all the points on the system are wired to operate like a 'party-line'. On a four-wire system of dedicated lines, each message is carried on its own pair of wires, eliminating feedback on the return loop. Greater control over signal levels, signal-to-noise ratio, and signal bandpass also results in a transmission quality far exceeding that of a two-wire conference system.

The basic building block of a multi-point, dedicated network is a four-wire, six-way bridge. Using such bridges together with existing telephone lines, a network is formed in a regional building-block fashion. However, the practical size limit for any region is 20 stations because of the noise created by the multiple facilities and circuit terminations. Most of the techniques used to construct a multi-point, private line teleconferencing system are standard operating procedures within the telephone industry. Equipment is available from several manufacturers and suppliers.

An important ingredient in a successful dedicated telephone network is the ability to connect other locations to the four-wire system. By bridging a dial-up call to the private line network, SEEN's coverage is extended to any location where there is a telephone.

Studio control complex
The studio control complex consists of studios from which programmes may originate and a control room for network operation. It is located on the University of Wisconsin-Madison campus and is operated by Instructional Communications Systems. The control room and studios were designed to provide smooth, trouble-free programming and to minimize the burden on the instructor. Because all technical aspects of a programme are handled by a trained engineer, the instructor is free to concentrate on his/her material and presentation.

The control room is equipped to handle five major functions: programme control, telephone network control, studio sound control, monitoring, and network failure detection.

1. *Programme control:* The control room technician uses a console to control programme audio sources, such as tape recordings and microphones. For example, the technician loads any insert tapes on the tape machines and plays them on cue from the instructor. The technician also controls the electrowriter signals and records programmes for future reference on 'make-up' sessions.

2. *Telephone network control:* Complete control of the entire telephone network is maintained in the control room. Prior to

programme time, the technician establishes the teleconferencing network, quickly tying in the appropriate locations. The network of dedicated lines can be arranged as programmes and enrolments dictate. Participating locations can be selected for total system programming, or regional networks can be established and programmed simultaneously. Dial-up bridging controls also allow the technician to tie regular calls into the private network.

3. *Studio sound control:* Studio sound system equipment is used to control the distribution of audio programming to three areas: to the studios, so the instructor can hear the response from the network, to the control room, so all audio channels can be monitored, and to administrative offices, so staff can listen to programmes. General building paging with emergency override to all areas is also provided by the control room.

4. *Monitoring* is an important function that contributes to the overall quality of network programming. Console controls and VU meters allow the technician to cue and listen to any of the audio sources without connecting them into the network or programme. The technician is also able to monitor selectively the output levels at the distribution console and correct the level quickly, if necessary. Another monitoring feature is used to check whether transmit signals are getting through the master bridges at the telephone company. The quality of the visual presentation is monitored on an electrowriter receiver in the control room.

5. *Network failure detection:* Quick detection and resolution of network failures is vital to the success of any teleconferencing network. Within a 16-hour programming day, an average of three or four system failures may occur on Wisconsin's two educational telephone networks. Adequate monitoring and test features are, therefore, necessary to minimize network downtime and programme interruption. An experienced control engineer can isolate a problem quickly and identify the source — station equipment, transmission line, carrier system, or some other characteristic failure. For more complex failures, the problem can be reported to the telephone test board which then helps to isolate and correct it. Given the ability to isolate a region quickly, the technician can bypass the problem area and continue to operate the remaining parts of the network. A control room microphone allows the technician to talk to any point on the network.

A separate auxiliary SEEN control room serves as a back-up unit. Although not as sophisticated as the main control room, the auxiliary equipment is capable of transmitting a SEEN programme to all network locations. Adjacent to the auxiliary control room and separated from it by glass windows is the SEEN studio. The studio is equipped with an electrowriter transmitter, microphones, projection screen, and table and chairs. The electrowriter transmitter is contained in a special table that allows it to be flush with the table surface for ease of writing. The electrowriter also sits on a swivel base that can be adjusted for the most comfortable position. A microphone head-set frees the instructor's hands for writing. Eight bar-activated, table microphones allow students to interact with participants at other SEEN locations. Tables and chairs are arranged as in a classroom setting, with each table having two microphones. An electrowriter receiver in the auxiliary control room is used to project the visual presentation on to the screen in the studio as the instructor writes on the transmitter.

Programme planning

Effective use of the ETN-SEEN network depends on careful programme planning. From the inception of a topic through final production, programming is a complex process that requires close co-ordination between the instructional department, ICS staff, and local Extension agents.

Programme planning has evolved from direct experience with educational teleconferencing in Wisconsin. As new approaches proved successful, they were incorporated into a set of programming guidelines which have become standard operating procedures. These procedures delineate the steps in the programming process and specify co-ordinating functions, but they are flexible enough to accommodate diverse programme needs.

Programme planning basically involves seven stages: content selection and development, network scheduling, operational design, programme announcement, promotion, registration, and production. Standard procedures guide programmers through this process. A 20-minute videotape acquaints programmers with the many elements involved in effective programming, including support services available at ICS and other Extension departments. A brochure on planning procedures is also available to programmers.

Content selection and development
The content of ETN-SEEN engineering courses is initiated and developed by Extension faculty. For continuing education courses, departments have found that effective programming is based on an accurate determination of the educational needs of its clients. This is accomplished in several ways: questionnaire surveys; voluntary suggestions from both instructors and students; advice from persons such as industrial training directors or those serving on various continuing engineering studies advisory committees; and spontaneous 'targets of opportunity' that indicate a subject likely to be of current interest to a specific clientele. For example, close watch is kept on legislation which appears to require an increase in some technical skill or knowledge, such as a new uniform single-family housing code or a solid waste disposal law. Graduate and undergraduate courses are based on the more traditional requirements of

a degree programme as well as the willingness of an instructor to offer a course in the ETN-SEEN mode.

Scheduling of programmes

Programme time on the ETN-SEEN network is usually scheduled at an annual scheduling meeting held in January. One or two weeks before the meeting, programmers are invited to submit programming requests for the academic year. Using established procedures, these requests are sorted and pre-plotted on a master schedule so as best to use network hours and resolve conflicts before the meeting. The meeting itself gives programmers an opportunity to review the entire schedule, negotiate hours if needed, and firm up their programme times. Two weeks after the meeting, all requested network time is rechecked and confirmations are sent to the programming departments. Requests for time can also be made during the year, but it is to the advantage of the programming department to reserve network time at the annual scheduling meeting (Seaman, 1976).

Instructional design

Interactive telephone networks such as ETN-SEEN are unique instructional modes. Although they are similar in some ways to face-to-face teaching, there are important differences. Effective programming, therefore, requires that certain elements be incorporated into course content and teaching style.

The design techniques used in ETN-SEEN programmes are based on 16 years of experience with Wisconsin's educational telephone networks, and accumulated research in communications, adult education, listening and learning theory. Workshops, printed materials, and faculty consultations help ETN-SEEN instructors implement these techniques and use the networks most effectively.

Four design elements are considered essential to interactive programmes: personalizing the experience, varying the style of presentation, seeking participation from the state-wide audience, and obtaining feedback (Baird, 1976; Monson, 1977). Each design element is incorporated into a programme by using a number of practical techniques:

1. *Personalizing the experience* helps students feel comfortable in the distant learning environment by creating a congenial atmosphere and group rapport. ETN-SEEN instructors usually adopt an informal teaching manner, allowing their personalities to come through. Frequent use of names and locations identifies participants. By emphasizing common objectives and the sharing of ideas and experiences, learners scattered throughout the state feel that they are part of a group.
2. *Style of presentation* involves many elements, all of which contribute to the goal of helping the learner understand and remember the material. By co-ordinating the interplay between audio and visual information, the instructor guides the students

through the learning process. A variety of illustrations, such as drawings and graphs, presented on the electrowriter amplify ideas and underscore key points. The visual development of equations accompanied by a clear and concise verbal explanation help the learner understand the mathematical relationships. Instructors often exploit the two-frame capacity of the electrowriter by reviewing the material previously presented, which contributes to the clarification and retention of ideas. Topic outlines, bibliographies, lists of resources available for self-study, and other hand-out materials distributed before the programme help students organize the learning experience.

3. *Participation* is an integral part of interactive media such as ETN-SEEN. However, it does not occur automatically. Detailed class rosters, for example, are used to direct questions to those with specific engineering experience and training. At the beginning of a programme, many instructors converse informally with students at different locations to 'break the ice' and stimulate discussion.

4. *Feedback* enables both the student and the teacher to assess the learning experience, achieve programme objectives, and improve overall performance. Informal question-and-answer periods interspersed throughout the programme provide immediate feedback on how well the material is understood. Many instructors ask participants to send in questions and comments; others make periodic phone calls to students in their classes to find out if the programme is meeting objectives. Individual or small group projects and written responses to specific questions are other means of obtaining feedback.

Evaluation

The purpose of evaluation is to determine the strengths and weaknesses of current programmes so that improvements can be made in future programme design. Changes in programme design come about through an analysis of evaluation results by programme co-ordinators, educational specialists and individual programme lecturers. Through this exchange and analysis, the results of the evaluation can be built into the next learning experience (Parker, 1976).

Evaluation can stimulate consideration of overall goals and values in teaching. It is this stimulation that shapes the educational process and motivates improvement in educational quality. However, there are other peripheral benefits of conducting a formal evaluation. For one, it provides one additional channel of communication between the participants and the instructor. The evaluation is a tangible sign of interest in student opinion. This can be particularly meaningful for remote participants who have little contact with the home base of programme origination.

The development of the evaluation instrument

A systematic method of studying the characteristics of the adult participants and of measuring the components of educational communications has been devised. This is known as the Programme Evaluation Checklist (PEC).

The General Information part of the Programme Evaluation Checklist comprises questions on demographic information such as age, sex and educational background. The individual programme co-ordinator may specify any further information he/she may wish to obtain, such as professional experience or occupation. The data obtained are used to construct a profile of student characteristics, which gives a present and future picture of target audiences for particular programmes, and allows for a comparative analysis of various audience types' receptivity to teleconferencing programmes. Frequently, the General Information portion also asks if the audience has participated in ETN courses in the past and if they would be interested in future ETN programmes. Previous experience with ETN programmes will condition the participant's evaluation of the course, and the degree of interest shown in future courses may indicate modified reactions to the course.

The second part of the Programme Evaluation Checklist comprises questions designed to measure the components of educational communications. There are essentially five steps in the development of the checklist items. First, the critical expectations of ETN programmes are identified. These are programme objectives in the most general sense, ie the quality of student-teacher contact, scope, relevance and importance of subject matter, and the instructor's ability to tailor his/her teaching performance to an audio delivery system.

Secondly, course design must be broken down into various aspects which facilitate the ordering of data, and thirdly, the objectives must be classified into these categories. The following are the seven primary aspects and expectations with which the teleconferencing systems are concerned:

- ☐ The environment — the arrangement of the physical facilities, seating, lighting, etc
- ☐ The technical components — the functioning of the mechanical components of the programme
- ☐ The audiovisual materials — the use of auxiliary materials and equipment
- ☐ The programme aides' behaviour — the performance of the persons responsible for the individual listening stations
- ☐ The lecturer's behaviour — the delivery of course material
- ☐ The programme organization — the involvement of the participants in the presentations and discussions of programme content
- ☐ The programme influence — the impact of the educational programme upon the participants.

Fourthly, descriptor words for these categories are derived. The items as they appear on the checklist are classified in six groups: programme facilities, programme lecturer, organization, programme material, programme content, and technical operations quality.

Fifthly, with these categories and descriptors formulated, course expectations are framed into positive, affirmative statements which describe the programme from the student's point of view. These are the evaluation checklist items, for example: 'The material presented in this course can be applied to my present needs.' (This item is followed by a list of the programme material which was included in the course.) At least five of these items are asked for each of the seven programme aspects. Usually there is one item at the end of each evaluation checklist which asks for the participant's overall feelings towards the programme, and frequently there is a space left for comments.

The use of the evaluation instrument
Each of the items which comprise the Programme Evaluation Checklist is assigned a ten-point, ordinal rating scale. This rating scale is a systematic procedure for measurement for which patience and writing ability are not needed. These factors often render an open-ended evaluation format invalid. Because of the geographic dispersion of the audience, evaluation by observation is impossible. The rating scale appears on the PEC instructions which explain that zero indicates the item does not describe the course, and nine means it very definitely does. For each item, the participant is instructed to fill in the number that represents his response. The responses are then run through the computer to obtain mean responses for each item. These means are further grouped into 'subscores' for each aspect of the programme. In this way, programme strengths and weaknesses are easily pinpointed for an individual course, and the data provides a base for statistical comparison from course to course, from year to year. This method of evaluation can provide relatively reliable feedback in a very short period of time, usually prior to course completion. The PEC is also a research tool which can be repeatedly employed to test teaching techniques in the field of educational communications.

The future of the telephone in education

The telephone has served Wisconsin well in extending educational opportunities to students throughout the state. The teleconferencing networks have increasingly grown in number of enrolments, programming hours, and variety of classes offered. This expansion is expected to continue as more adults seek off-campus educational programmes for professional development and personal growth.

Supporting the Wisconsin experience are many studies that show the telephone to be an effective, inexpensive educational medium. Rao and Hicks (1972), for example, reviewed 18 experiences in teaching by telephone and concluded that students learn as much or more in telephone classes as in face-to-face discussion. Similar conclusions were drawn by

Hoyt and Frey (1972), Pellett (1970), Blackwood and Trent (1968), and many others.

The future of the telephone in education depends not only on its effectiveness as an audio medium but also on its capacity to provide quality visual information. This consideration is especially important in technical fields such as engineering where instructors often present mathematical and graphic material. New telewriting and televideo systems have recently been introduced that have great potential in education. A variety of graphic and pictorial information can be presented over regular telephone lines using improved electro-mechanical pens, graphics tablets, video writers, electronic blackboards, computer-graphics systems, or slow-scan televideo systems.

Electro-mechanical pens that write on paper-covered surfaces, such as the Victor Electrowriter, are probably the oldest of the telewriting systems, entering the market of telephone technologies in the early 1960s. Since then many improvements have been made to increase their resolution and accuracy. Their relatively low cost also makes these devices attractive for transmitting hand-drawn graphics — equations, line drawings, outlines, diagrams, graphs.

Graphics tablets, video writers, and the electronic blackboard are similar in a number of ways. Hand-generated material is accurately reproduced by writing directly onto conductive surfaces. Graphics tablets usually have electronic grids or specially coated transparent sheets that sense pen movements. To produce graphic material on a video writer, one writes directly onto a TV monitor with a light pen. Ordinary chalk is used to present information on the pressure-sensitive electronic blackboard made by Bell Laboratories. The Electronic Blackboard has been tested in continuing engineering education for a number of years at the University of Illinois at Urbana-Champaign. All of these systems digitize the information and display it on monitors at remote locations.

Computer-graphics systems are capable of showing both written material and computer-generated graphics. A graphics tablet is used for hand-drawn information. In addition, these systems are programmed to perform various computer graphics, such as constructing bar charts and diagrams. Some have programmed symbols that can be placed instantly at any point on the televised display. The symbols may be mathematical or simple figures that can be animated to show, for instance, an aeroplane flying through a cloud or a person walking. Many firms have lines of computer graphics systems or will design packages especially to meet the user's needs (Machover *et al*, 1977).

Slow-scan televideo systems add another dimension to telephone instruction — the capacity to present pictorial information as well as graphics. Any image that can be captured by a video camera can be shown on a televideo system, including views of the instructor and classroom, outdoor scenes, written and prepared material. The picture is transmitted over the telephone lines during a number of seconds and is shown as a frozen image on a remote TV monitor. Past systems were quite limited, used mainly for security-surveillance operations. However, the recent application of electronic technology has greatly improved their performance and versatility.

The new telewriting and televideo systems provide additional flexibility for visual instruction over a telephone network. Combined with its proven effectiveness as an interactive audio medium, the telephone can play a unique role in education — a role that extends teaching resources to adult learners in many distant locations.

BASIC REFERENCE DATA

I. The host institution

Name: University of Wisconsin-Extension
Date founded: 1849
Internal organization: University of Wisconsin has been involved in Extension activities since the turn of the century, when administration and Wisconsin citizen leaders introduced the Wisconsin idea that a university serves all of the communities in a state. The Regents have more recently charged the University of Wisconsin-Extension with providing jointly with four-year institutions and two-year centres a programme of outreach services that would bring the total resources of the university system to bear upon needs and problems confronting the people of the state.

The University of Wisconsin-Extension has a Chancellor and four Deans responsible for 12 programme areas that range from agriculture to business management, health and human services to youth and family living. Community-based faculty Extension Agents in every county employed co-operatively with the county's board of supervisors, work closely with the University specialists and other faculty to respond to specific educational needs of communities, groups and individuals.

Number of academic staff: 600
Number of students: Each year University of Wisconsin-Extension serves about a quarter of the state's adult population through its programmes and services in addition to more than 200,000 students.
Income: $US 18 million

II. The innovation/system being studied

Name: Instructional Communications Systems
Date founded: 1965
Nature: Interactive Distance Learning Systems throughout the state of Wisconsin.
Internal organizations: Director, Associate Director, 4 Department Chair People, Engineers, Production, Operations and Technical Design.
Number of academic staff: 10
Number of non-academic staff: 12
Number of students: About 45,000
Income: $US 385,000 is a total income reflected of $US 18 million for the institution.

NOTE
1. The Electrowriter, manufactured by Victor Comptometer Company, was an early pioneer in visual telephone devices. Recent developments in telewriting and televideo systems are reviewed above, on pp. 120-1.

REFERENCES AND BIBLIOGRAPHY

Axford, W R (1969) *Adult Education the Open Door*, International Text Book Co, Scranton, Pa

Baird, M A (1976) Designing teleconference programs: some clues from the Wisconsin experience, in Parker, L A and Riccomini, B (eds) *The Status of the Telephone in Education*, pp 41-50, University of Wisconsin-Extension, Madison

Blackwood, H and Trent, C (1968) *A Comparison of Face-to-Face and Remote Teaching in Communicating Educational Information to Adults*, Kansas State University, Cooperative Extension Service, Manhattan, Kansas

Braun, D, Gilbertson, D and Hansen, H C (1976) ETN: a technical system, in Parker, L A and Riccomini, B (eds) *The Status of the Telephone in Education*, pp 51-74, University of Wisconsin-Extension, Madison

Flinck, R (1975) *The Telephone as an Instructional Aid in Distance Education: A Survey of the Literature*, 49 pp, Pedagogical Report 1975-1, Department of Education, University of Lund

Holmberg, B (1981) *Status and Trends in Distance Education: A Survey and Bibliography*, 200 pp, Kogan Page, London and Nichols Publishing Co, New York

Hoyt, D P and Frey, D W (1972) *The Effectiveness of Telecommunications as an Educational Delivery System*, Kansas State University School of Education, Manhattan, Kansas

Jackson, Parker and Olgren (1978) Teleconferencing and telewriting = continuing education in Wisconsin, *American Society of Engineering Education Monograph*, July 1978, pp 63, 88

Johansen, R, McNulty, M and McNeal, B (1978) *Electronic Education: Using Teleconferencing in Postsecondary Organizations*, 176 pp, Report R-42, Institute for the Future, Menlo Park, Ca

Klus, J P et al (1974) *Continuing Education for Engineers: A Case Study of the University of Wisconsin-Extension Engineering Department*, Unesco International Working Group on Continuing Education of Engineers, University of Wisconsin-Extension, Madison

Machover, C, Neighbors, M and Stuart, C (1977) Graphics displays: factors in systems design, *Institute of Electrical and Electronic Engineers Spectrum*, 14(10), 23-7

Monson, M (1977) A report investigating teaching techniques used over the Educational Telephone Network at the University of Wisconsin-Extension, in Parker, L A (ed) *A Design for Interactive Audio*, University of Wisconsin-Extension, Madison.

Parker, L A (1976) Teleconferencing as an educational medium: a ten year perspective from the University of Wisconsin-Extension, in Parker, L A and Riccomini, B (eds) *The Status of the Telephone in Education*, pp 1-26, University of Wisconsin-Extension, Madison

Parker, L A (ed) (1977) *A Design for Interactive Audio*, University of Wisconsin-Extension, Madison

Parker, L A and Baird, M A (1977) Continuing education by telephone: a party line for professionals, hospitals, *Journal of the American Hospital Association*, November 16, 51, 105-9

Parker, L A, Baird, M A and Gilbertson, D A (1977) Introduction to teleconferencing, in *The Telephone in Education (Book II)*, University of Wisconsin-Extension, Madison

Pellet, V L (1970) *The Comparative Effectiveness of the Educational Telephone Network and Face-to-Face Lecturers for University Extension In-service Training*, Unpublished doctoral dissertation, University of Wisconsin, Madison

Rao, P V and Hicks, B L (1972) Telephone based instructional systems, *Audio-Visual Instruction*, 4, 18

Seaman, M (1976) Operational aspects for program planning, in Parker, L A and Riccomini, B (eds) *The Status of the Telephone in Education*, pp 27-40, University of Wisconsin-Extension, Madison

Short, J, Williams, E and Christie, B (1976) *The Social Psychology of Telecommunications*, 206 pp, Wiley, London

Telecommunication Systems Course Team (1976) *Telecommunication Systems: Unit 15, Teaching by Telephone*, 56 pp, Open University, Milton Keynes

7. Radio and television universities in New South Wales

Derek Broadbent

'I pass, like night, from land to land, I have strange power of speech'

The visitor to the Division of Postgraduate Extension Studies may hear these or some other lines from the Ancient Mariner in the full tones of Richard Burton, for the development of Radio University, the first university-owned and controlled broadcasting station in Australia, has been a major activity of the Division.

The purpose of Radio University is to transmit lectures to listeners in their homes, the broadcast lectures being supplemented by printed notes and diagrams. This type of teaching was quite new in Australia, although it had been successfully carried out by a number of universities in the United States. Its immediate advantages are: 'in a time of an acute shortage of teachers, a single lecturer can speak directly to each of many hundreds of students, and in a time of an acute shortage of accommodation there is no need to provide lecture rooms for these very large classes.' This was written by George Caiger, Editor, in the University of New South Wales journal, *Technology*, in 1963 about two-and-a-half years after the start of Radio University and reflected the thinking and conditions in Australia at that time. These conditions have since changed but Radio University and its electronic media offshoots still flourish 20 years later — why?

This chapter aims to give some information which will help the reader to assess, in his or her own situation, the chances of using modern technology successfully in education. It starts with the beginnings of an outline of a case study, the author's own institution, and then deals with the general area of communication media and distance education before returning to the case study of Radio University and Television University, where some of the technical considerations are mentioned. Later we deal with quaternary education, or the Postgraduate Open University concept, and finally return to the technology that will determine the directions we can go in the next two decades.

The institutional context

The University of New South Wales started as the New South Wales Institute of Technology in the late 1940s when the 'technological revolution' was perceived. It was closely associated with the New South Wales Public Service Board and its Chairman, Sir Wallace Wurth, and was initially based in the Sydney Technical College. Later it took over a race course near Randwick and it has been said that it has been racing hard ever since! Clearly it was science and technology oriented but it also instituted a General Studies department of arts disciplines to give undergraduate engineers and scientists a more catholic education than they got in any other Australian university. Like all new institutions it could afford to be innovative and there were departments or schools of traffic engineering, highway engineering, fuel and food technologies, textile technology, optometry and so on. It became the University of New South Wales in 1959 and when a Faculty of Medicine was instituted, Radio University produced and broadcast 'Medical School of the Air' in conjunction with Sydney University — so patching up to some extent the bitter feeling that Sydney University had in earlier times about this upstart institution, a feeling shared by the Prime Minister of the day, Sir Robert Menzies. But time makes everything respectable and now the University houses the Australian Graduate School of Management and the Tri-services Academy; it has certainly arrived as far as Canberra is concerned. In the early 1960s the atmosphere and finances were conducive to innovation; it is unlikely that the Division of Postgraduate Extension Studies would have been launched at that time, with its radio and television stations, in a traditional university such as Melbourne or Sydney. We had to wait until 1974 for Adelaide University to fund the second Australian educational station, 5UV, with substantial help from a private benefactor. Now there are quite a number of universities, colleges and institutions which operate radio stations to provide external courses.

Communicating media

Communicating media can affect markedly the education of persons at tertiary and quaternary level living at a distance from the teaching institution. 'Media' is not the peripheral aspect to the teaching process that some traditional educationists would have us believe, for we do not mean by 'media' just audiovisual teaching aids which may or may not improve the presentation of the material in a lecture. We mean by 'media' the technology which determines whether an educational programme can be mounted at all! Methods of personal transportation, printed material, postal services, language, radio, telephone, television, teletext, communication to video display terminals; these are the different media that will affect us. It is the technology, or the state of the art of media development which calls the tune, not the political requirements or the educational desirabilities of an educational programme. To quote the Duke of Edinburgh: 'The fact is that technology has a far greater and more direct social impact than any other -ology.' I am sure that he would agree that this is true of communication technology for extramural education. Australia, because of its great distances, was one of the first nations to use new communicating media this century, such as aeroplanes and radio, for education and information transportation. It has been said that, like all innovators, Australia is now suffering the reaction of a conservative educational administration in not developing broadcasting and other early ideas. However it is worth looking at these innovations as a guide to others. The country has a population of 13 million of which over 60 per cent lives in the six state capitals. The gross national product per head is one of the world's highest, but only 9 per cent of the 18- to 22-year-old age group is involved in full-time education and about the same percentage in part-time education of some formal kind. It is these small but growing groups of part-time and external students with which we are concerned, because they are the ones for which new communicating media hold most promise.

By the end of the century Australia, like many other developed nations, will be a 'post-industrial society'; in other words the majority of the working population will be engaged in tertiary (education, public services, transport and business) and quaternary (information, computers) industries. These industries are more information oriented and require fewer practical skills than do primary and secondary industries. This will have a marked effect on education, particularly quaternary education (ie education of a continuing or refresher nature).

The Australian Telecommunications Commission (1975) has forecast that by the year 2000, when the population will be about 19 million, the Australian information industry will have:

Telephone wire pairs	8.7 million
Computers, including domestic and office stand-alone or connected microcomputers	0.4 million
Data links	0.5 million
Facsimile terminals	0.6 million
Mobile radio transceivers	0.1 million
Cable television connections	0.3 million
Domestic and office recorders, audio/video	8.7 million

The telephone wire pair will be the basic communicating channel for the next 20 years, providing a low energy substitute for personal travel and for mail. These wire pairs can provide facsimile and two-way information terminals in the home or workplace which can include computer facilities and voice-accompanied alpha-numeric and graphic video displays using a domestic television set or equivalent. While these estimates are now six years old, the only way they can be dated is in their conservatism with respect to technical development; for example the mass produced silicon chip will drastically alter the cost and therefore the frequency of several of the above, particularly the second item.

Distance education

The good features of part-time and external studies programmes include the following: study is at home or at work in one's own time and hence the student saves travelling or accommodation expense and earns income; all part-time and external qualifications are equivalent to full-time qualifications in Australia; mature students can overcome an earlier low assessment of educational ability by taking later part-time or external study, and many do; transfer from part-time to full-time courses is possible without loss of credits; in spite of initial misgivings, postgraduate engineering and technology courses have been taught satisfactorily part-time and externally; radio, television, audio and videocassettes are used extensively and experience (and possibly software) can be interchanged between organizations and even between countries.

The unfortunate features of part-time and external studies programmes include the following: college staff tend to prefer full-time students because of research (and hence personal promotion) potential; drop-out rate is high compared with that of full-time students; the annual cost to the teaching institution is similar to that for the full-time students (but is less to the student, industry and possibly the community); technology subjects cannot be offered at undergraduate level through external studies without complicated practical work arrangements.

Let us look at what has been called 'distance education', as part-time students to some extent, and external students to a great extent, will be concerned with education remote from the teaching institution. Probably the first attempt at organized 'distance education', in the mid-nineteenth century, was that of the Sir Isaac Pitman Correspondence School of London which had a study programme using postcards giving messages from the Bible. These were to be coded by the student using Sir Isaac's new system of shorthand and returned for assessment. The Authorised Version must have had an effect, which the prim and proper Queen Victoria approved, on the style and vocabulary of the business correspondence of the period. What is of more interest however is that the start of this distance education programme coincided with the introduction of the British penny-post; in other words it was made possible only by the development of a new medium of communication made possible by, in its turn, the technology of transportation – the railways.

Certain media today can make economic the servicing of educational needs of people living remote from centres of population and training institutions. Alternatively, these media can provide a service to people who, though working in a city, are remote from an appropriate training institution in the sense that their needs are highly specialized and the educational material they need is not locally available.

Learning packages, for example audiocassettes and printed matter, sent to the student provide part of the answer, but remoteness will still exist unless feedback facilities are available. If this feedback can be immediate so much the better. What then are the media that can be used in distance learning? In developed countries people are familiar with the transistor radio, the telephone and the television set, and the capital and recurring costs of these items have largely been paid in most households. In developing countries perhaps only the radio is relevant. From economic considerations, these media should be exploited first if at all appropriate. Package learning through the mail and learning by personal transportation have much higher incremental costs. Radio and TV broadcast and the telephone media have the possibility also, at little extra cost, of making library facilities available through some form of terminal; for example, Teletext of the TV networks and Viewdata of the British Post Office's telephone service are basic forms of such a facility in that they can provide access to a library of pages at low cost on the domestic TV set.

Radio University

These were the sorts of arguments and forecasts that were put to the University's Professorial Board and Council in 1960 by the author in support of a proposal for distance learning by radio and television, although of course some of the information above was not available 20 years ago.

The reactions ranged from the enthusiasm of the then Vice-Chancellor, Sir Philip Baxter, who was frequently enthusiastic about new ideas (although it has been said that in those days he was only right 51 per cent of the time), to violent opposition from some professors who said quite openly that any change from the live lecture theatre presentation of teaching would put them out of a job.

However, in January 1961 a submission was put to the Australian Universities Commission by the Vice-Chancellor for a Special Commonwealth Grant of £A13,500 to equip an educational radio station at the University of New South Wales. Parts of the submission read:

> Educational broadcasting by its nature and applications falls between the correspondence course and the typical university lecture course to a large class; it could be argued that for teaching certain subject matter it is superior to both. A recent survey made by the University of Wisconsin showed that correspondence students do at least as well as classroom students as far as the assimilation of subject matter is concerned. The same factors that produce this application by correspondence students should apply to students in the type of extension radio broadcast course dealt with below. (In this type of course it is important that material, similar in nature to correspondence material, is supplied to the student to provide the visual link with the lecturer.)
>
> An added consideration that appears to support the establishment of extension radio in the University of New South Wales is the shortage of accommodation in the evening during term time, particularly for large classes, at Kensington. Extension radio is cheap and requires negligible accommodation irrespective of the size of class.

> *The Nature of Proposed Radio Courses:*
>
> Courses of this nature could with advantage be offered to:
> (a) adult students requiring special courses. The range here is from the fairly high level (subject matter) course to the course supplying entertainment plus;
> (b) adult students requiring professional refresher courses;
> (c) country students requiring certain undergraduate subjects, for credit if later found desirable;
> (d) adult graduates requiring graduate courses;
> (e) high school students who are required to make good certain university entrance deficiencies.

The students could participate as:
  (i) individual students in their home;
  (ii) a group sharing a receiver; this arrangement would enable helpful group discussion on the subject matter;
  (iii) a group under a tutor at an Extension Centre.

Estimated Cost of Radio Station:

		£A
1.	Transmitter + standby equipment	4000
2.	Audio equipment control console	1500
3.	Audio equipment editing console	1000
4.	Monitoring receivers and equipment (radio/television)	500
5.	Two soundproof studios (sprung rooms) 25' x 25' at £500/100 sq ft	3000
6.	Radio mast 100 ft structure (including erection)	3000
7.	Studio equipment	500
		£A13,500

The result was a grant of the money asked for and the installation of Radio University VL2UV broadcasting on 1750 kilohertz. The great majority of university staff supported the venture but a powerful minority had, and still has, reservations and this is why the words 'if later found desirable' were included in item (c) of the list above. The transmitter and studios bought with this grant were not actually in operation until early 1963; however, a temporary service was started in May 1961 with an ex Royal Australian Air Force transmitter of World War II. The licence for Radio University was authorized by the Postmaster General's Department in April 1961. It was for a frequency of 1750 kilocycles/second with a maximum aerial power of 300 watts under the call sign VL2UV, and this is still the case. The provision of this licence handicapped the university radio station in some ways, for it placed VL2UV outside the tuning range of an ordinary receiver; students therefore need to have a modification made to their sets to receive the University. Secondly it restricted VL2UV's transmitting power to 300 watts, compared with 50,000 watts used by the national stations and 5000 watts used by the commercial stations at the time. Thirdly, it prohibited the playing of music, hence the transmission of poetry as a 'bridge' between lectures.

In the initial stages, the University itself purchased a number of special radio receivers designed to pick up 1750kHz and hired these to students for five shillings per week. Later, several brand-name radio manufacturers produced radio receivers which covered the broadcast band and also VL2UV, while several 'converters' were placed on the market to extend the tuning range of any ordinary set to 1750kHz. These old valve units were quite expensive, in today's values over $A100 each. Radio University now sells transistors adjusted to include VL2UV, for seven dollars.

The second effect of the licence was that Radio University was very limited in transmitting power. Radio listeners have been conditioned by the fairly high-powered transmissions of broadcast stations to expect loud clear reception in any weather without needing to erect a radio receiving aerial. To receive Radio University, operating with 0.6 per cent of the power of 2FC, the local Australian Broadcasting Commission station, an aerial was, in those days, absolutely essential at a distance of more than a few miles from the transmitter. At the outset, many students undoubtedly were put off by the contrast between what they heard from 2FC or 2UE and what they heard (or half heard) from VL2UV.

The third handicap was the prohibition on the broadcasting of music. This meant that Radio University was restricted in that the usual musical bridges to which radio listeners are accustomed could not be used. The University's solution was to play recordings of poetry between lectures, read by such people as Richard Burton and the late Neil Burgess, Professor of English at the University. These, no doubt, had certain educational value, but none the less accentuated the general air of unfamiliarity to the listener. This restriction in the licence has now been removed and music is played between lectures and in 'comfort breaks' during lectures. Despite these handicaps, VL2UV began transmissions in May 1961 from the Electrical Engineering Project Laboratory at Kensington.

Field surveys and studies of reception reports from students showed that reception was loud and clear within a radius of about 15 kilometres of Kensington but that as one moved away from the University, and in the outlying suburbs, reception was poor. It was realized that better use would have to be made of the 300 watts authorized, and that moving the transmitter to a marshy location would be equivalent to doubling its power output. Late in 1961, the Concord Municipal Council kindly transferred to the University the lease of some Council land on which a steel radio mast, once used by 2UE, was still standing. Beneath the mast a building was erected to house another ex Air Force transmitter which had been modified by the staff to work on the University's frequency. This transmitter was remotely controlled over landlines from the University's campus some 22km away. When this transmitter was placed in service in October 1962, listeners in nearly all areas reported an immediate increase in signal strength. The point to be made is that perfectly viable broadcasting can be initiated without a large expenditure of money.

In the early years Radio University transmitted only tape-recorded material. There were three reasons for this. First, it was essential that a university radio station should have a high quality of presentation, and pre-recording reduced the possibility of mistakes on air. Secondly, most of the lecturers who would be called upon to present material found it more convenient to record their lectures in the daytime than to appear before a microphone in the evening. Thirdly, tape-recorded lectures could be made at any time, even months before their broadcast date; they could be stored and played again, or copied and sent out to extension groups who would play them on their own tape-recorders. It was not until 1972 that Radio University introduced 'open-line' sessions in which the lecturer or a panel received telephone calls from students in the now accepted talk-back mode. Nevertheless most sessions are still pre-recorded and the 'open-line' or a studio audience performs the function of a discussion period at the end of a lecture series.

Nor does pre-recording apply only to the lectures themselves. All announcements, including station identification, introductions and statements of copyright, are recorded on tape and edited into each evening's programme. Fortunately, in 1961 the University already possessed a small recording studio under the direction of Roy Caddy. In this soundproof room, many university lecturers learned for the first time the special techniques of lecturing to a phantom audience behind a microphone, without the reinforcement of facial expressions, gestures and blackboard demonstrations.

It quickly became evident that the new medium had its own special advantages and special limitations, and a new technique was required for successful transfer of ideas from lecturer to listeners. Many of the speakers were helped by the fact that they had taken part in radio and television broadcasts, but all had to adapt themselves, and their material, to the new medium. While most of the lectures consist of material presented by a single speaker, some take the form of a discussion between two speakers, with one interviewing the other, or both jointly developing a theme. A number of panel discussions have also been used, groups of from three to five experts in some field discussing a topic.

In some courses all the lectures have been given by the same speaker; in others a different speaker prepared each lecture, developing the subject in 'round robin' style, with perhaps a panel summing up at the end. Each lecture lasts for about 45 to 50 minutes, allowing time for opening and closing announcements, while remaining within one hour.

For radio lecturing, special attention had also to be paid to the preparation of notes to be supplied to students. One function of these notes is to replace the blackboard. All diagrams, graphs and formulae normally chalked up on the board are printed and mailed to the students in advance of the broadcast lecture. The notes, of course, varied greatly with the subject and lecturer; on some occasions the notes contained as many as 27 closely typed foolscap pages for one lecture; on others, five to six pages, consisting mainly of diagrams, formulae and tables.

During 1962, Radio University extended its services in several ways. It established suburban extension centres where groups of students could listen to broadcasts and hold discussion afterwards. It introduced tape-recorded correspondence courses for groups of students beyond the range of VL2UV. These extension groups were sent copies of the broadcast tapes and three sets of notes, and they listened to lectures on their own tape-recorders. Another new development in 1962 was the holding of live seminars at the University at or near the end of a radio course. This is in line with the system of having radio lectures supplemented by live tutorials. For example, seminars were held after biology courses, being supplemented by closed-circuit television demonstrations of films and microscope slides.

Early in 1963, the Division of Postgraduate Extension Studies moved into new headquarters on the top (sixth) floor of the Biological Sciences Building at Kensington, where Radio University had a transmitting room, control room, editing room and two studios. In 1973 with fee-paying student enrolment topping 4500 each year, the Division moved to larger premises on the top (sixteenth) floor of the Mathews Building where new studios, a seminar room and laboratory, workshops, tape correspondence and printing areas, offices and radio and television broadcast controls were housed. In a roof structure there is also the UHF television transmitter with antenna mast above.

Television University

The innovation of Television University VITU of the University of New South Wales in 1966 was much smoother from the point of view of the academic staff, but the technical difficulties of installing the first UHF-TV service in Australia made up for this. Closed circuit television had been used in the University for first-year lectures from September 1962 and this had helped to get videorecordings accepted as a useful educational tool by the Professorial Board.

Educationists will disagree on whether a teacher can present his material to students best in person, where he might have the use of visual aids such as filmstrip and overhead projection, or whether he can present it best on a pre-recorded videotape with the content drawn from a number of sources, including those above. There can be no doubt, however, that if neither a teacher nor the facilities required to accommodate students are available, then from an educational point of view a pre-recorded transmitted television presentation is attractive. Staff are often not available at times to suit students in courses involving groups of students who are professional working people, and it is mainly with such groups that this television education is concerned.

The procedure of recording lectures for later replay overcomes these difficulties. It has been stated elsewhere that these are not unlike difficulties that would be experienced in providing teaching facilities in underdeveloped countries (Broadbent and Brook, 1966). There are, however, a number of other educational advantages in using videorecordings. There is the possibility for the teacher to edit the recordings to compress or expand the length of an event he wishes to show or to compress or expand the field of view to be displayed to the student. A further advantage is that he can make up the recording in sections over quite a long period if necessary. An increase in the number of recipients of a television picture does not result in increasing difficulty of perception as is the case with attended lectures; one simply installs more monitors or receivers. Again, unusual situations which need to be shown to the student can only be captured in this way. Animated video presentations are essential in demonstrating certain things which are difficult to describe in words or with still pictures. Despite these obvious advantages, many university teachers, when confronted with the possibility of having to work with an instructional television system, have fears both about their own professional security and status and about any possible adverse effects which an inflexible television programme might have on

131

the students. This is a very real problem and emphasizes the fact that television is not a panacea for our educational difficulties.

Television broadcasts from the University started in 1966 with a low power UHF transmitter broadcasting on 10 watts to viewing centres located in the Sydney metropolitan area. In 1969 a 1000 watt transmitter was installed with an effective radiated power of 20kW. The majority of broadcast television lectures were and still are arranged to be taken in conjunction with the broadcast radio lectures from the University's radio station. These have been directed to professional workers and postgraduate students over the years. In contrast to the closed circuit television presentations previously referred to, which are for undergraduates, the broadcast lectures provide professional refresher courses and higher degree courses. Here, television is used as a complement to the radio lectures to show animated sequences essential to the development of the subject. There might be four radio lectures followed by a television demonstration, which in turn is followed by a live seminar for student/teacher discussion, thus making up a unit. A graduate course may have as many as five such units. The preparation of radio and television lectures involves considerable planning, as does the preparation of printed notes and study guides which provide the detailed visual link between lecturer and student. With a radio lecture a substitute for the blackboard is essential, while the resolution of a television screen leaves a lot to be desired when detailed material is to be shown.

The TV programme centres
The major closed circuit television studio is equipped with two colour cameras, a telecine chain incorporating a camera control unit, facilities for audio and vision mixing, two-inch transverse scan videotape recorders and several helical scan videotape and cassette recorders. The latter are used for recordings intended for the university departments and the College at Broken Hill, where identical machines are installed for replay purposes. Audiovisual aids used in closed-circuit television include graphics of various kinds, chalk-boards, magnetic boards, 8mm filmloops and photographic enlargements. The telecine equipment is used for the presentation of 35mm slides and 16mm film. Other aids include a caption roller, microscope projector, rear projection equipment, models, mock-ups, etc. Facilities are also available for the preparation of 16mm film animation.

When mass media techniques and equipment are to be directed to relatively small groups of postgraduate extension students the cost of production and presentation is the essence of the problem. For this and for educational reasons, depending on the type of material presented, a lecturer-controlled television studio was designed for the broadcast programmes. In the postgraduate area the best person to control what the student sees and hears is the lecturer himself, just as the lecturer does when he controls a slide projector in a lecture theatre. He does not try to conceal the fact that he is controlling the picture and sound, and in fact simply uses the radio and television channel as an audio and video aid to explain his points.

In this special studio there are no cameramen, and in the early days no producer either; from a console the lecturer himself punched up the picture he wanted to show and about which he was talking from one of the outputs of two cameras, a slide projector or a cine-projector (Figure 7.1). The layout of the console and associated equipment enable the instructor to select video and audio from five sources, and to record his selection on videotape. The console includes three miniature monitors, which show the video from each of the two cameras and from the telecine chain, a text generator or a computer. One camera is normally fixed focused on to a blackboard or perhaps the lecturer's face; the other camera, which is fitted with a motorized zoom lens controlled by the lecturer, focuses on to a part of the console top on which demonstrations may be shown or diagrams drawn. The lecturer makes up his programme as if he were before a normal class, using a wide selection of visual aids. With this arrangement it has been found that production costs are low, and flexibility of operation is considerable, when compared with normal television production methods.

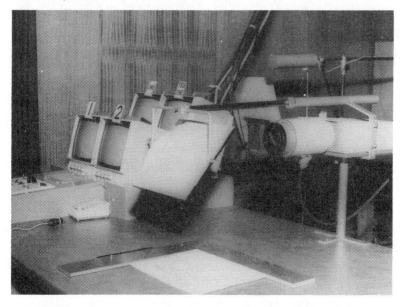

Figure 7.1. *The early 1971 version of the lecturer-operated TV Console. The graphics camera is now mounted vertically over the work area.*

The system works well but usually it is now organized so that a staff producer, who is familiar with the material of the lecture, assists in positioning the displays, in operating the zoom lens of the overhead camera, and in generally organizing the production.

A further development of the lecturer-controlled console was introduced in 1979 for the many computer programming courses offered. The display was restricted to the video output of a computer, with an audio accompaniment in the form of the lecturer's voice over. The advantage of such a system is that while the student never sees the 'talking head' of the lecturer, no studio or cameras are required. The TV signal is simply taken from the video display terminal connected to the computer. Animation in the form of keyed inputs and computer outputs of characters and graphics, stored or generated on the spot, are shown. The whole can even be transmitted to the students' centre over a telephone line at 300 baud if broadcast TV is not available, and the voice transmitted over radio or via another telephone line.

Quaternary education at a distance: the Postgraduate Open University

The distance education organization which the author knows best has now been operating for 20 years and has seen a number of changes which are worth noting, if only for the purpose of trying to forecast the future. This organization has always catered for the specialist recipient, in particular the college and university graduate who requires professional further education, and this fact influenced the choice of media through which the programmes were offered. The characteristics of such a group of students are:

- [ ] They are employed, sometimes at senior level, and any refresher education is done in addition to their normal work. Timing is therefore important.
- [ ] While cost of transportation is not necessarily important to these students personally, the time spent in travelling to an institution, even if a suitable one existed in the town of residence, would be inconvenient.
- [ ] The educational material required is often not included in traditional courses, and in consequence potential student numbers for a particular study programme are often low; for example, the number of engineers interested in a course on finite element analysis in the whole of Australia is limited.
- [ ] Professional journals are the main source of updating for professional people, so the material offered by a distance education system to such students must complement their journal articles. Properly designed video and audio displays are some of the ways this can be done.
- [ ] These students are associated with practical situations and problems; although often very sophisticated, the material presented must be related directly to the professional activity now or in the future. (This requirement again leads to the desirability for media having a greater potential than that solely of the written word.)

☐ Because of the seniority of these students the material presented to them should have a high 'multiplier effect'. In other words, courses which train people to train people have high priority, and the media used should have a high training or influencing impact. These features should be capable of being retained in recorded form.

The specialized nature of the material required by these students and the resulting limited enrolment relative to primary and secondary education precludes the use of expensive media such as printing by letter press and commercial film and television productions. On the other hand the traditional correspondence study media of duplicated notes used for small groups is inadequate for the reasons given above. A combination of telephone, TV, mail and cassette media, as appropriate for the best presentation of material, is required.

The media combination used by the Postgraduate Open University has consisted, over the years, of weekly radio broadcasts of lectures in the course of study, with monthly sessions using domestic telephone open-line broadcasted talk-back, and monthly seminars of television broadcasts to viewing centres followed by contact with the lecturer or tutor. Brief xerox printed notes are forwarded ahead of the radio lectures to take the place of the blackboard and the lecturer 'points' verbally to the tables, diagrams and equations contained therein. Such a combination of media shows up well on a cost/benefit index; indeed it can be shown to be economic for groups of students as small as 30, although course enrolment is usually much higher than this.

Such a system, it would appear, has the advantage of transportation of information at low cost in an attractive and effective form, according to educational research findings. It has, periodically, instantaneous feedback from student to teacher and presents an opportunity for student intercommunication and socializing. The television sessions display films, which may be difficult for the ordinary person to procure and show, together with low-cost videorecordings of such things as the working of apparatus in the university laboratories or elsewhere. The open-line discussion often comes from students with professional experience who contribute substantially to the session's educational content. The only disadvantages are that this Postgraduate Open University can have only two lectures in progress at any given time, one radio and one TV, and that student access to them is at fixed times. However, this formula for material presentation appears to be logical for the distance education of graduates and, as expected, a rapid increase in fee-paying enrolments (approximately $A2 per lecture is the fee) took place in the first six years of operation (see Figure 7.2). Over this period the transistor radio became reliable, cheap and of low battery drain. The television seminar broadcast to five Sydney metropolitan centres became a part of nearly every radio course in the late 1960s and from the early 1970s some courses were conducted solely by television.

The tape correspondence service started as an offshoot of the early

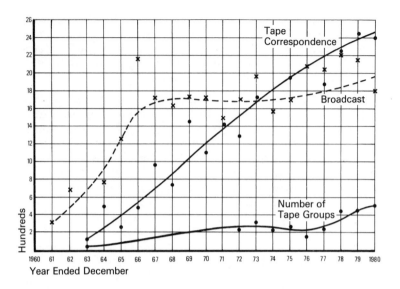

Figure 7.2. *Yearly enrolment for the postgraduate extension and school-university bridging courses by radio and television broadcast, and by audio and videocassette correspondence*

radio courses. As the lectures were recorded it became an obvious measure to hire out copies of the tapes with the associated student notes to people outside the range of the radio station. The tape correspondence student paid the same fee as the radio student, but because of postal charges the minimum group size was stipulated as three students. These tapes were first issued on seven-inch broadcast reels, later on twin-track five-inch reels as suitable recorders came on the market. More recently students have taken their audiorecordings almost entirely on C-60 twin-track cassettes, which they can now keep, as the technology improved and the cost of cassette players was greatly reduced over the ten years 1966-76. Over the period of advancing technology resulting in the introduction of the cheap reliable videorecorders of the last few years, there was a remarkable growth of videotape correspondence enrolments. It will be seen that audio and videotape correspondence enrolments now exceed the total broadcast radio and television enrolments, although this rise is mainly due to the number of students increasing from approximately three in each group to an average of just under six students per group. (The videotape correspondence groups tend to be larger in size than the audiotape correspondence groups.) The question that must be asked is that, with the trends shown for tape correspondence in Figure 7.2, do students, at least in the professional course area, prefer a programme which they can control themselves even if this control is at the expense of educational benefits such as feedback with the lecturer at formally arranged seminars and open talk-back sessions?

The answer is probably that they do. After all there are good grounds to believe that the serious music listener hears more music from a record or cassette system than from broadcast and attended concerts. Casual listening might be different but then an educational programme is not casual. It can be argued that broadcasting should give way to presentation via recorded media except where live material is involved, such as open-line connection to students, or where the delay inherent in a recorded presentation is intolerable. If so, the argument for retaining broadcasting for mass transportation of information is purely technical and economic, given the costs of the alternatives such as postal charges or land-line costs as well as the cost and reliability of audio and videocassette players. Some of these alternatives, such as postal communication, are labour intensive and therefore will become more costly in years to come, but eventually the cheap domestic information terminal will be with us when the postman as we know him will no longer exist.

Postgraduate Open University Programme
In the postgraduate professional area of continuing education where students are usually mature people with some seniority in their organizations, the old dictum can be rephrased: 'If the people won't come to our lectures, then our lectures must come to the people.' This forms the basis of operation of the Postgraduate Open University Programme of the Division of Postgraduate Extension Studies with the type of services it offers by radio, television and audio and videocassette.

The radio and TV venture has been successful in that enrolments are now running at about 2000 per year with a flow-on in the form of 2500 enrolments in groups using the tapes of the broadcast courses. The 40 or so courses offered this way each year range in length from full master's or graduate diploma subjects in engineering, science and human communication down to short series of five to ten lectures in such areas as computer programming, management, accounting, electronics and pharmacy.

About one-quarter of the courses are taken by qualified students towards graduate diplomas and master's degrees. Seminars and laboratory classes are held at Kensington. In an average year there would be over 100 subject enrolments by students taking advantage of these facilities to gain higher degree or diploma credit, but there are over 500 enrolled in these courses as non-credit postgraduate students. These subjects do not attract the large numbers of students that the non-credit short courses do both because of their length and because of the number of attended sessions required in addition to the radio and television lectures. Nevertheless, by using the media of radio and television, students who otherwise would not be accommodated in the normal graduate classes are able to take these courses.

When considering an external studies programme, it must be

remembered that, as in many spheres of activity, Australia is not a continent but rather an assembly of islands. The Postgraduate Open University radio and television stations provide for one such island, the Sydney metropolitan area, but for the others, the tape correspondence service provides the means for professional people to take refresher and updating courses. This fact has been realized by a number of industries, business houses and public service organizations wishing to provide senior staff training programmes. Enrolments for many of the groups are of this kind, each having between 20 and 70 students located in different places in Australia and overseas in the Pacific region.

Over the years the biggest enrolment in the Postgraduate Open University has been in data processing and computer programming — about 35 per cent of the total. Business and management courses come a close second at about 30 per cent. It is interesting to note that the enrolments in the human communication courses offered account for 17 per cent, indicating that this subject ranks quite highly in the minds of professional people when they review their educational inadequacies.

The courses leading to higher degrees, though open to the public, are naturally individually approved by the academic faculty responsible for examination and standards, but it was found desirable to arrange for all postgraduate open courses to be approved by the Professorial Board. This helps to ensure that the academic body identifies itself with the programme; consequently it is considered to be a normal and desirable thing for a staff member to give an extension course. It could be said that the scope for making courses 'open' is just as great for undergraduate courses and possibly greater in view of the number of people who can benefit by such sophisticated information. However one university is not quite ready for this yet.

Confrontation to broadcasting: alternative media

In terms of a media cost/benefit index analysis the best value in educational communication per dollar is given by the low power local radio broadcast and the low power local UHF television broadcast (Broadbent, 1966). However, unless a very large number of channels are available to service a relatively small receiving group of students per channel, the broadcast system will lack the capacity to serve as an information transportation medium to supply specialized educational material to the many diverse groups in the community. The audio telephone landline, another low cost medium, does not suffer from the fundamental limitation of broadcast space; but modern telephone exchanges are designed for a very low use factor per subscriber, and they would soon become jammed if the telephone system were to be used for bulk information transportation to and from the home. Let us look then at some of the media that have been used successfully in recent years and extrapolate the trends in time, bearing in mind the extraordinary developments that are going on in hardware design and manufacture.

First, there is the audiocassette. This is inexpensive to purchase, duplicate in quantity, and despatch to the receiving person and is easy to replay. An audio programme is relatively easy to produce and is suitable for intellectual concepts where animated video is not required. Visuals in the form of, say, pages of key-word vocabularies, data listings, equations, diagrams and photographs can be supplied and despatched by post at extra cost, but still reasonably cheaply, to provide the receiver with a more complete communication experience. Audiocassettes can be listened to in a motor car or in occupations which require only intermittent attention by the employee, for example some process workers and workers in loud noise environments (using radio-fed ear-protector phones). The main disadvantage has been the lack of general acceptance by the public of cassettes compared with, say, the transistor radio and the paperback book, which are its entertainment equivalents. However reductions in cost over time are resolving this.

The second medium that might be considered to present an alternative to local TV broadcasts or land-line CCTV programmes is the videocassette. This has almost taken over the role of the 8mm and 16mm film in the education area as the cost of video replay equipment reduces each year. It is equally suited to high cost sophisticated production and to low cost on-the-run recording of interesting events. Tape stock prices are relatively low (an off-air dubbing can result in a recording of less than one-twentieth of the cost of purchasing a 16mm film).

The third medium that presents an alternative to TV broadcast is the videodisc or equivalent. It is too early to say what the incursion into mass broadcast viewing will be, but an analogy can possibly be made between the hi-fi gramophone record and radio broadcasting. The videodisc has the attribute of 16mm film that the videocassette lacks, that is the capability for cheap high-speed multiple copying. It is also interesting to note that one such disc could comfortably contain a complete audio record library, enough for a year's listening, if indexing and access facilities were incorporated in the player.

There is, however, one serious and fundamental drawback with audio or videocassette and disc; it is the dependence on mechanical moving parts. This imposes a limitation in manufacture and reliability which is not experienced with purely electronic equipment. A record player with any moving parts is subject to abuse failure, failure due to wear, and failure due to lack of compatibility with other similar equipment because of mechanical tolerances — important features in the application to distance education. It is interesting to compare the development over the last few years of, say, the videocassette player and the pocket electronic calculator. Both have improved in performance, reliability, miniaturization and sophistication for the purchase price, but the solid-state integrated circuit calculator is far ahead of the videocassette player in terms of value per dollar, and is increasing its lead each year. The transistor radio and the TV receiver can also both be made to be very reliable at low cost, as they too have the benefit of being purely electronic and hence as reliable as solid-state large-scale integrated circuits.

The fourth medium, which like the videodisc has only limited availability at present but which has great future potential, is Teletext or Viewdata (Fedida and Dew, 1978; Goff, 1978). Both use a domestic television receiver as a home or workplace video terminal. Teletext uses the TV broadcast channels but is limited in its number of pages of information. With Viewdata one of 70,000 pages stored in a central computer can be dialled up through the telephone circuit. Both have access time of a few seconds. What is important from our point of view is the library search potential for education and the cheapness of producing the programme material compared with television production (Teletext requires only a key-punch, a TV set and a microcomputer with a disc store). It is technically possible to transmit both systems by a low cost radio transmission, a fact worth bearing in mind for developing countries.

The future: a 20-year forecast

In an attempt to make a forecast for the future, say for the next 20 years, and at the risk of proceeding too freely from the particular to the general, it can be said that society's education requirements, as has been the case in its leisure and work patterns, will become more complex and more individualized with the devolution of responsibility for education programmes to the local level. There will be a greater tendency for the student to pursue education in the home, or at work for the older student, and employment will be closely associated with education. This, after all, is only an extrapolation of present trends. Over the 1960s, in the developed nations, television saw to it that people stayed more and more at home for their entertainment. They still went out occasionally to the cinema or theatre, but not as much as in the 40s and the 50s. On the whole we have more and better entertainment and informative material than we used to (despite the deficiencies of present British, American and Australian television) and we receive it without the cost to the community of the travelling, extra building and seating facilities that would be required if all our present television viewing had to be undertaken at the equivalent of the local picture theatre.

These arguments must apply with equal weight to quaternary education and also to employment tasks, at least the non-hardware oriented tasks. Education is a much more complex communication process than that of passive entertainment, but the trend in the increased sophistication and cost reduction in technology shows that technology is, or soon will be, up to any task of information handling that is acceptable to educationists. It should be borne in mind that because of this increasing complexity and individualization of education programmes, macro-communication systems, such as satellite and conventional broadcast radio and television, will play a less important role as time goes on than will other forms of interactive media and bulk transportation media, if the latter are available. If these sophisticated media are used, the savings involved in avoiding duplication of workplace and travel for part of our present population could be great; but, of course, efficiency of communication must not be markedly affected. To achieve this, extensive provisions must be made for individual communication and group discussion. Provision will have to be made for student and worker to have access to full relevant library facilities via a terminal and for guidance in the use of sophisticated communication facilities.

This chapter has outlined some of the technical innovations used over the years, we think successfully, by Radio University and Television University. These innovations are not claimed to be substantial advances in the electronic art; components have been generally commercially available. What is of interest is the design of the system for the specific purpose of broadcasting integrated radio and television instruction to relatively small audiences — perhaps better called 'narrowcasting'. Costs, in terms of student and lecturer man hours expended, course materials and overheads also play a large part in the optimization process for this system design. An important feature, however, is the cost of technical facilities, capital and recurring, and one of the largest components in the recurring category is that of staff. The technical design of the radio and television installations was aimed at minimizing all these costs.

Narrowcasting to limited audiences requires a different philosophy of system design from that of conventional broadcasting. There is certainly a limitation in the type of material such a complex can handle. For example, drama and music programmes are excluded, but we have found over the years that the great majority of instructional material can be adequately catered for. Extensive use has been made of technology and modern methods of organization to provide this programme; however, the practice must not be allowed to rest there. In this context, technology and organizational methods, like books, are not ends in themselves; they are means to the end of education. Nevertheless, again like books, the newer technologies have opened up new avenues of teaching and, in particular, the teaching of external students. Developments must be watched and tested quickly if we are to keep abreast of this task, and at a reasonable financial expenditure. In this area, and with these pressures, it is advisable to live on the edge of the state of the art.

BASIC REFERENCE DATA (1980)

I. The host institution

Name: University of New South Wales
Date founded: 1949
Internal organization: 11 faculties with 57 schools and 14 independent departments; 7 residential colleges.
Number of academic staff: 1576
Number of students: 18,259 undergraduate and graduate enrolments + 8781 continuing education enrolments
Catchment area: New South Wales, Australia

Designated responsibility for off-campus activities: Responsible for courses by radio and television in Sydney metropolitan area and by cassette correspondence elsewhere.

Income: $A99.5 million

II. The innovation/system being studied

Name: Division of Postgraduate Extension Studies
Date founded: 1960
Nature: Responsible for offering postgraduate extension courses by various media and to offer a higher degree in human communication.
Internal organization: Departments of Radio Broadcasting, Television Broadcasting, CCTV, Cassette Correspondence and Human Communication.
Number of academic staff: 2
Number of non-academic staff: 22
Income: NA
Income as proportion of institution's total income: NA

REFERENCES AND BIBLIOGRAPHY

Australian Telecommunications Commission (1975) *Telecom 2000: An Exploration of the Long-term Development of Telecommunications in Australia*, 172 pp, National Telecommunications Planning Branch, Telecom Australia, Melbourne

Australian Telecommunications Commission (1978) *Outcomes from the Telecom 2000 Report*, 70 pp, National Telecommunications Planning Branch, Telecom Australia, Melbourne

Bethell, H (1972) *Education and BBC Local Radio — A Combined Operation*, British Broadcasting Corporation, London

Broadbent, D (1966) Programmed teaching and broadcasting for postgraduate courses, *The Chartered Mechanical Engineer*, 13(7), 330-3.

Broadbent, D (1974) An Australian Postgraduate Open University — Television University VITU, Radio University VL2UV, *Proceedings of the 1974 International Conference on Frontiers in Education*, pp 1-4, Institution of Electrical Engineers, London

Broadbent, D and Brook, D A (1966) *Report of the Commission of Enquiry into Television in the Territory of Papua and New Guinea*, Australian Government Department of Territories, Canberra

Broadbent, D and Mitchell, R C (1972) Television University and Radio University — a case study in teaching graduates, *Proceedings of the International Broadcasting Convention, London, Sept 1972*, pp 76-81

Fedida, S and Dew, B (1978) Viewdata in education, in Howe, A and Romiszowski, A J (eds) *International Yearbook of Educational and Instructional Technology 1978/79*, pp 76-86, Kogan Page, London and Nichols Publishing Co, New York

Goff, R (1978) A Review of Teletext, *Monitor — Proceedings of the Institution of Radio and Electronic Engineers, Australia*, 39(4), 18-26

IEC (1979) *About Distance Education, No 7*, International Extension College, Cambridge

Kanocz, S (1975) Part-time higher education using radio — an example from the Federal Republic of Germany, in MacKenzie, N, Postgate, R and Scupham, J (eds) *Open Learning: Systems and Problems in Post-secondary Education*, pp 163-81, Unesco Press, Paris

NAEB (1967) *The Long Range Financing of Educational Television Stations*, Report of Second National Conference, March 1967, National Association of Educational Broadcasters, Washington DC

Part 4:
Research and consultancy – new structures for the application of traditional strengths

8. Adult education and research: the case of Nottingham University

J E Thomas

The object of this chapter is to discuss some of the issues arising from the establishment of a Research Centre in the Department of Adult Education at Nottingham University. Not only should this be of interest as an example of innovation, but the creation of the Centre provides a useful case study of the potential, and the obstacles, which are present in university extramural provision in Britain. The British pattern of such provision has been a model for several English-speaking countries, even though healthy questions have been asked about its appropriateness as a model for other countries.

Education in Britain, in recent years, has been the subject of intense debate. Aspects of that debate, albeit indirectly, contributed to the establishment of the Centre, and a good deal can be learned about university adult education in Britain from this discussion of its functions.

The extramural tradition in Britain

Before describing these issues, it is necessary to explain something of the work of a British university extramural department. The traditional role of a department of extramural studies or adult education — the terms are interchangeable — is to provide liberal, non-vocational courses which do not, generally, culminate in examinations. Such courses are organized for the public of the region in which the university stands. Traditionally, these courses are mainly in arts subjects, although a modest number of social science and science classes can be found. The scale of the enterprise may be gauged by the fact that Nottingham, as one of the largest departments, employs some 40 academic and senior administrative staff, and that some 10,500 adult students attend classes each year throughout the East Midlands.

The spirit behind university extramural provision has its roots in that nineteenth-century liberal tradition of education, the most unrelenting advocate of which was J H Newman in *The Idea of a University*. This insisted upon the notion of education for its own sake, rejecting a profit and loss approach to educational provision. This rejection of utility took some odd directions, such as an embargo by the Ministry of Education on the teaching of 'practical' subjects such as music in extramural classes. Adult students in the traditional class may, therefore, listen to and discuss music, but may not play musical instruments or sing.

Such curiosities, deriving from the remarkable influence of nineteenth-century liberal educators, make university extramural provision an especially British phenomenon. Its singularity makes it difficult to transplant in its pristine form, but even so, there have been instances (which might inspire a Graham Greene or Evelyn Waugh) of English professors of adult education establishing model British departments in Africa and other areas which were reaching independence. Some of these attempts have been successful (New Zealand is a good example) but, generally, the milieu within which British adult education grew up is unintelligible to most university traditions in the world.

It is probably because of this faith in the value of liberal education that British university lecturers in extramural departments are, generally, committed to and convinced of the importance of their work to the community. As well as employing their own academic staff, extramural departments also arrange for colleagues from internal departments to teach adult groups. The result is that thousands of people who might be forgiven for viewing the university as an expensive, arcane institution for the young, now have an experience which may temper that view. The process of extramural education has built up a phalanx of people in the community who begin to understand what the university tries to do, and find that there are stocks of knowledge within it which are interesting and relevant to ordinary people.

One manifestation of the dynamism of this relationship between the extramural department and the local community occurred in 1979. The present Conservative Government's policy to cut expenditure on education has been heartily implemented by many local authorities, including those in the East Midlands. Since these authorities give the extramural department financial support, the latter was threatened. The Nottingham department asked its adult student population to consider writing a letter of protest to the local hierarchy. Several thousand did so, and the consequence was that the grant was substantially restored. This rather dramatic, but valid example of the relationship between university and community is a consequence of the mediation of the extramural department. The challenge to the local authority was of help to other adult education agencies, since they too were affected by the cuts. In short, extramural work has ensured that many people in the community understand and support much of what the local university tries to do. This is noticeably not the case in university towns (mainly new foundations) which do not have extramural departments.

It is clear from what has been said so far that a British extramural department is, above all, concerned about its relationship with the community — much more so than the average internal department with its relatively pliant, regimented student population. Because of this, extramural departments are more prone to self-examination, which sometimes becomes agonizing, about issues such as the fact that manual workers are under-represented in the extramural class. There are exceptions, such as the substantial provision of special 'day-release' classes for workers. Why is it — the question rings around every conference — that so few workers are found in our classes? I point out this phenomenon, and this example, of self-questioning because it is relevant to the establishment of the Research Centre. Much of this questioning has, in the past, been self-indulgent, and has culminated in some form of self-satisfied apologia, or the familiar bolt hole, a demand for more 'facts'. As a result of a number of new developments in adult education, several members of staff in the Nottingham department engaged in self-questioning which did not end in a convivial display of mutual congratulation for the maintenance of a 'Great Tradition', honourable though it is. Their mood was more abrasive and precocious, and their discussion took place within the context of several important debates and trends.

New developments in adult education

The debates of the 1960s

The future historian of British adult education will probably conclude that the intellectual turmoil generated by the university unrest of the late 1960s had a profound effect (a critic might say *should* have had a profound effect) on extramural provision. The central target for discussion in that unrest was education, and particularly its relationship with society, and its part in shaping that society. It was productive of anger, much polemical writing, a good deal of apprehension, and the disarray of academics who had survived hitherto as critics of stability and conservatism, only to be confronted with opportunities to be counted, which they declined to take.

Whenever discussions take place about education and the community, a reasonable expectation might be that these must have some effect on extramural activity. But, for the most part, in Britain these debates were kept at bay, and still are, by the weight of a tradition which was becoming fossilized and dogmatic. A severe critic might have used the word 'stagnancy' to describe the conviction that what had been developed as a pattern of provision early in the century was still appropriate, and was hallowed by experience which could not be gainsaid. This reluctance to be influenced by these fundamental debates about education was not, of course, universally true of extramural departments, or the individuals within them. Nor, or course, were extramural departments any more reluctant than internal departments to contemplate the basis of their operation. Universities are hardly noted for their propensity for change, or indeed taking a hard look at what is going on in the community. This aloofness, as one New Zealander wrote very succinctly, challenges the claim of universities to be taken seriously: 'Any argument which prefixes discussion with the assumption that university standards and, by implication, university roles, are the only fixed and immutable factors in an age of fluid institutional change, really invalidates the university's claim to have a larger role as a formative element in society' (Williams, 1970). Nevertheless, the enquiries generated by the debates of the 1960s still

147

affect education, and still leave extramural departments with questions, some old, some new, but all of an increasing urgency.

At about the same time there was a new interest in community development and community work. In part, this had as its source the debates about education and what it should be trying to do, and one of its effects was to renew the time-honoured discussion as to why manual workers and extramural provision seemed to be unknown to each other. This produced a number of interesting projects which attracted a good deal of attention. It also provoked a debate about the desirability of universities through their extramural departments becoming involved in such work: work which was variously described as too 'practical', too 'political' and 'non-academic'. The operation of such projects, and their critics, raised questions to which there were no answers. To those possessed of a questioning spirit, it was clear that there was a dearth of theory about adult education.

The establishment of award-bearing courses
This was confirmed by another development. This was the establishment of courses in adult education leading to the award of degrees and diplomas. Although such courses had been initiated at Nottingham under the direction of Professor Peers in the 1920s, it was not until the end of the 1960s that such courses were established in several universities elsewhere. The demand arose from an increasing awareness of the need for adult education (often for 'economic' reasons), and a consequent growth of professional structures for adult educators in the local authorities, which in Britain are responsible for almost all public education. This new interest in adult education led to the establishment of a major Committee, the Report of which (Russell, 1973) gave further impetus to the creation and expansion of these professional structures. Similar developments took place in many overseas countries, especially in the Commonwealth. The latter, as they always had, looked to Britain to provide courses to fill their professional needs, and there began a tradition of such groups coming to Britain to attend award-bearing courses. Such groups, together with the new indigenous adult education professionals, comprised a new 'audience' for the extramural departments. It was natural that those who wished to learn about adult education should turn to the agencies which had accumulated a considerable amount of experience in teaching adults, and who habitually proclaimed the importance of the task.

Not all British universities responded to this new interest, although several did and continue to deploy substantial resources to the development of appropriate programmes. The Nottingham department, for example, has seven full-time and a number of part-time academic staff exclusively employed in this work, although, as has been pointed out, this has its roots in the 1920s.

Research
Because of a failure by several university extramural departments to interest

themselves in this new field (for reasons which will be dealt with later) and because it was clear that there was a dearth of scholarly and well-researched writing about adult education, those university departments which were interested formed a conference to stimulate research work, and its application to teaching adults. This Conference was called the Standing Conference on University Teaching and Research in the Education of Adults (SCUTREA). Established in the late 1960s, the Conference is held annually and is attended by members of those university departments who are eligible to join by virtue of the fact that they have training and research programmes. This is a qualification, incidentally, which excludes a large number of extramural departments. There are other conferences of adult educators in Britain but these are mainly concerned with organization and 'in-house' matters with a modest amount of intellectual debate, and they are dominated by senior members of the staff of extramural departments. One of the interesting features of the SCUTREA Conference, in contrast, is that it gives a platform to younger members of staff who are engaged in an increasingly interesting and impressive array of research projects. SCUTREA, which publishes its papers annually[1], is attracting increasing attention outside Britain, as is evidenced by the foreign visitors who commonly attend as speakers and guests.

Not only has SCUTREA become very prominent in the attempt to develop a body of knowledge about adult education, but it has also made an important contribution to the new emphasis on research which led to a milieu in which the prospect of a research centre could even be contemplated. The contribution of SCUTREA is well illustrated by the fact that it was at the 1976 Conference that Dr Colin Fletcher and Mr Brian Harvey, both of the Nottingham staff, conceived the idea of a Research Centre, and proposed it to the Department's staff. A number of exploratory meetings were held, and a Steering Committee was established to try to define the possible direction of such a Centre. This was possible because a tradition and acceptance of research was by now well established in the Department. Another important advantage was the existence of a publications unit. This, it was expected, would be an outlet for research findings, as indeed it has been.

The reasons why Fletcher and Harvey were interested in this idea are important. Fletcher is a professional research worker, currently engaged on a major study of a community school complex in Nottinghamshire. The role of the contract researchers in the formulation of the idea of a Centre is crucial, and it is significant that part of the impetus for the idea came from this relatively new segment of an extramural staff. Harvey is a senior lecturer in economics in the Department, with a sound interest in research and its potential for extramural departments. At the back of their deliberations was the wish to transform research findings into materials for adult learning. There were, in addition, certain developments which were peculiar to the Nottingham department. These were identified by Fletcher and Harvey to support their initiative.

The first of these was a notable increase in research activity within the

Department. It is appropriate, at this point, to redress what may appear to be a misapprehension about research in extramural departments. In the light of what has been said so far, the impression may have been given that research in these departments is rare. That is not the case. A considerable volume of research is carried out by extramural staff, and as a consequence, individuals are acclaimed as international experts in their academic disciplines. Furthermore, adult students are often involved in research projects. Two notable examples are in local history and in sociology. In respect of the former — a subject which is especially noteworthy in extramural history — very many excellent publications have appeared as a consequence of the involvement of a local history class as a research team (see, for example, Meller, 1971). Similarly, extramural lecturers have produced scholarly work in sociology which is the outcome of a realization that an adult class is ideally situated to study its own social environment, to temper the hypotheses of abstract theorizing with live experience, and from the two to develop a synthesis which is both intellectual and coherent, not to say convincing (Coates and Silburn, 1968). Since these attempts to involve students in research into matters pertaining to their environment have been successful, an interesting question might be whether or not they could be involved in research which focused on the very process in which they are involved — that of adult education. This might be an especially productive area of development.

The aims of the Research Centre

The notion of a Research Centre was not advanced, therefore, because of an utter absence of research. On the contrary, it was advanced because there was an *increase* of individual research activity in the Department, because of the potential which had been identified and used in the form of involvement of adult classes in research, and because outside funding, some of it substantial, was increasing. This last factor was especially important because it involved the employment of contract research workers, who, while they were not dissatisfied with their position, as they were quick to point out, felt that they could make a more effective contribution if some structure could be devised to enable them to do so.

The contract researcher is still rare in extramural departments. At the time when the decision was taken to establish the Research Centre, there were several working at Nottingham. Indeed, there still are. They are, of course, engaged on a temporary basis to take part in team research. As a group, they are well qualified, intellectually forceful, and interested in what other research workers are doing. They present one demand which is especially alien to an extramural department. It is for the creation of an intelligible framework within which their individual research interests, and their collective interest in research, can meet and find expression. Because of the structured diversity of extramural departments, such a framework did not exist, and a resultant effect was a feeling that their overall contribution to the work of the Department was not as great as it might otherwise have been.

This same feeling could be found amongst the members of another new group — the higher degree and diploma students. Their need, like that of the contract researchers, was recognized by the originators of the Centre, and one positive outcome has been the establishment of regular postgraduate seminars which act as a focus for the discussion of research projects. In essence, what was sought was the establishment of a coherent action research policy. This, it was hoped, would be achieved by pursuing a number of aims, which were eventually formulated by the Steering Committee. To understand exactly what the Centre was intended to do, it is necessary to set these out. They were:

1. To provide a framework of support for all research activity in the Department.
2. To produce and circulate an annual register of research interests in the Department and include, where possible and relevant, the interests of our part-time teaching staff.
3. To compile a register of relevant expertise within the University and elsewhere.
4. To promote the winning of external funds.
5. To assist the efforts of staff members to attract funds and facilities by advising them on the writing of research proposals and, if necessary, by supporting them in the process of negotiation.
6. To promote strong contacts with the community with a view to the identification of research ideas and funding.
7. To secure and encourage a pool of equipment, accommodation and services.
8. To support the development of the postgraduate research programme with particular reference to attracting students, vetting MPhil and PhD proposals and to encouraging staff in the Department to undertake supervisory duties and support them in so doing. Additionally, where appropriate, it would ensure the provision of a minimum of training in methodology for both students and supervisors.
9. To encourage the publication of research findings.
10. To encourage strongly links between research and the Department's teaching.

These objectives, boldly stated, are clear enough. The compilation of registers of research is relatively easy, and was indeed long overdue. Such registers are of great interest to other institutions working in the field, but they attain an equally important objective, which is to let people in different parts of the Department know what colleagues are engaged upon. The acquisition of material and visible signs of an existence, such as accommodation, is not easy nowadays, but this has been done. In the same way the encouragement of the publication of research findings is facilitated by the existence of our own publications unit.

151

A second level of desiderata is rather more difficult. An example would be the encouragement of links between research and the Department's teaching. This goal is a useful reminder of the fact that the whole of this innovation is designed, ultimately, to improve the quality of our educational service to the community. One example of our 'encouragement' in this area has been the financial and professional support given to a group of part-time lecturers who teach a 'communications' course to trade unionists. These lecturers are anxious to discover the effect of their teaching, and how it might best be improved. To that end they are carrying out a survey of their students with a view to culling their experience and with the eventual aim of improving their contribution to the industrial programme. This would appear to be a concrete example of the fulfilment of one of the Steering Committee's aims.

Obstacles to change

The most difficult problem is in the implementation of those several aims which seek to involve 'the staff' of the Department. At the root of the problem is the historic diversity, academic and often geographical, of extramural staffs with a concomitant deeply ingrained tradition of autonomy. This is a matter which has been touched upon several times in this account, and if one had to identify a major problem in the attempt to develop an intelligible research strategy of the 'collective' or 'team' kind which the proposers of the Research Centre advocated, this might well be it. Put briefly, it concerns the traditional role of the extramural lecturer.

The lecturer in a British extramural department is, in every sense, a university teacher. For example, he is paid the same salary as his internal colleagues, and their respective claims for promotion are judged on equal terms. The extramural lecturer, like his counterpart, is recruited to teach a special subject, and he may, in addition, have some responsibility for organizing an area. This is what is meant by academic and geographical diversity, a structured and integral part, perhaps the corner stone, of the fabric of the extramural department. It follows that the extramural lecturer has a remarkable degree of autonomy, and is nurtured in a tradition of individual preference which is, for the most part, unlikely to conflict with the needs of the Department. The central organization of the latter may be thought of as a federal government in its dealings with states which are barely dependent, except, of course, in financial terms.

It is vital to understand this because included in the aims of the Centre are several which threaten this historic arrangement. These include the 'encouraging' of staff to undertake supervisory duties in respect of higher degree students, and less threatening, the proposal that the Centre should 'provide a framework for all research activity in the Department'.

The classical organizational structure, at present at least, makes the achievement of these aims difficult. Probably all members of staff in a university extramural department joined that kind of department as against, say, an internal department, because of certain distinctive characteristics of extramural work, such as working with adults, and the extraordinary, and quite luxurious, autonomy which may be enjoyed. Faced therefore with an exhortation to become involved in some kind of a team approach, some are likely to resist because of the implicit danger of an erosion of their autonomy.

Another form of resistance, if it is sufficiently conscious to have such an active noun bestowed upon it, springs from another well established feature of the organization. This, too, has been mentioned several times: it is subject specialism. This is, of course, perfectly respectable, but there is little correlation between teaching an academic subject at a high level to adults, and an interest in the theory of adult education. Extramural staff are, naturally, aware that teaching adults is a specialized task, and are proud of their particular skills in doing so. But it is only exceptionally that an extramural lecturer might be discovered reading a new book on the effects of aging on learning skills, or a progress report of an experiment in community development. To do so betokens a broad view of the discipline of adult education which is unusual amongst British extramural lecturers. But, it should be emphasized, this is not to suspect their commitment to their work.

The 'team' approach to research in adult education which the Nottingham Research Centre regards as cardinal, threatens to erode the autonomy of staff, insists that they develop a scholarly interest in adult education, and, arguably, puts them in some danger of losing control of the direction of research to which they would like to apply their energies.

This is exacerbated when another aspect of the Steering Committee's purpose is considered — 'the winning of external funds'. The interest in adult education which has grown up in Britain has been accompanied by an interest in research by bodies which are able to provide funds. The Department of Education and Science, and the Advisory Council on Adult and Continuing Education (ACACE), are two examples of bodies which can dispense research largesse. Their custom is to define which topics justify research, and, sometimes, contracts are put out to tender. Various groups compete, and the contract is duly awarded. This is done on the terms of the awarding body, naturally enough, and all the necessary paraphernalia of Steering Committees and so on are brought into being. The lecturer now finds himself on a research project, the thrust of which is decided by someone else, where he is called upon to collaborate with other people, and where he is made accountable to a steering committee which is going to take a close and insistent interest in his progress. Furthermore, he is likely to be constrained by something which is especially anathematical to university staff — a time limit. Add to this the fact that his real academic interest may be in medieval history, and the exhortation of the Research Centre Steering Committee to become involved in research might appear somewhat unattractive.

This area of tension — between the 'individual' and the 'collective' has been a subject of prolonged discussion amongst the seven members of the Steering Committee, both in respect of the policy or 'house style' of the

Centre, and its management. With regard to the latter, the force of tradition was evident in the expression of the opinion that a 'formal' structure might be inappropriate. What was needed instead was, in the words of one member, Dr Graham Mee, 'a learning system'. This would, he went on to note, 'be able to adapt in response to new pressures and opportunities'. It was for this reason that the Committee was chosen to represent a broad range of the Department's work. Perhaps one of the problems with this structure is that the apparent validity of representatives from the several distinct areas of the Department's work can be invalidated by a lack of interest on the part of those representatives who are not keen on educational research. It may be that the Committee will eventually comprise a group which is not 'representative' but consists instead of a cadre of committed people prepared to subordinate some degree of autonomy to the collectivity which the Centre seeks.

This same problem arises in respect of the administration of the Centre. The organizational overtones of the term 'Director' have caused a good deal of discussion, motivated by the same apprehension about the consequences of 'direction' which is so much in conflict with the traditional *modus operandi* of an extramural department. There is a certain feeling that the way to make the Centre operate effectively is by a loosely structured dialogue of members who are marshalled by an elected convenor.

Evaluation

This diversity and the problems it creates have been dealt with at length because diversity is the key to understanding the obstacles which the traditional extramural department faces when a change is contemplated. What has been said about the problems of developing a research organization is equally true about the creation of a segment of the organization to teach adult education to higher degree students. In several British universities it was decided that the existing department did not have the appropriate skills, and so a second department was established. There then arises a situation where there is a department of adult education, the members of which teach qualifying courses but do not engage in dealing with the classical audience, and a department of extramural studies which continues to provide the traditional programme but whose experience is not readily available to degree and diploma students. This solution has a certain amount to commend it — notably that the campus-based department attracts young staff with a highly developed interest in research and teaching in adult education. The major defect is that such staff may have limited practical experience, and that the body of experience which does exist in the extramural department is not exploited. It would be tempting, since the Research Centre is faced with just this problem of trying to 'collectivize' a group of individuals, to acknowledge research as a special discrete area which need not impinge on other parts of the Department. To do so would negate the very reasons for its existence, in order to make a difference, ultimately, to the quality of our provision.

The University generally may be said to be supportive of the Centre. For example, accommodation and furnishings have been procured from a helpful Works Department. One would not really expect hostility for a number of reasons. First, each department is heavily preoccupied with its own business, and, increasingly, its problems. Next, because of the complex nature of funding, adult education is not a constant financial competitor. But a much more positive reason lies in the fact that each British extramural department has built up over the years a body of academic staff, in various departments, who are sympathetic to the tasks which adult education tries to achieve. These are people, often very senior, who support adult education enterprises, including this research initiative.

It is too early to make claims about the success of the Research Centre. This year has been especially difficult for adult education because of the massive assault upon expenditure by the Government. A good deal of the energy of many members of staff has been deflected into attempts to resist this onslaught. We have only recently been able to establish ourselves in accommodation, before which we had to say, with the Hollywood wit, we have a home, but no house to put it in. And we are still discussing styles of management and research.

Even in the years ahead it will be difficult to evaluate just how effective we may be. Some measure of effectiveness may be the amount of fund-raising which is achieved, but a major difficulty here would be distinguishing whether the Centre or the eminence of an individual had attracted a grant. In the immediate future we can try to create an atmosphere which will encourage research, where help can be given when staff or students wish to engage upon it, and where we can provide facilities for and try to forge links between higher degree students, contract research workers, and the staff at large. This is, of necessity, vague, because one is talking of influences which shape the choices people make. An example of the problem of determining influence may be seen in the interesting effort of Mr Derek Cox, a member of the Steering Committee, to collect valuable documents to build an East Midlands Miners' Archive which will, eventually, be an excellent research source. Of course, initiatives such as this arise from, and are fuelled by, the academic interests of members of staff in the first place. However, a department with commitment to research, of which a Research Centre stands as the most visible manifestation, is of considerable importance in establishing the appropriate atmosphere in which this type of proposal can be nurtured and encouraged.

This account is an attempt to set out, accurately, some of the difficulties and problems associated with the establishment of a research centre in a highly traditional academic context which, apart from historical study, has little tradition of rigorous research. The deflection of resources to the Centre and the initiative and interest of the staff who created it, are signs that adult education is taking on new interests and new directions. It is also evidence that the debates about the whole complex subject of adult education are becoming more sophisticated as well as more urgent.

It is remarkable that Britain, which has such a famous tradition of university adult education, should lag behind some other countries in its research work. There is at the present time only one other British university research organization with a primary interest in adult education. This is the Institute for Research and Development in Post-Compulsory Education at the University of Lancaster. The shortage of such centres should not be seen as proof of a lack of interest or concern in what many think will be the most important area of education in the next 20 years. It is more a reflection of the weight of traditional structure, and the considerable resolve which is needed to vary it. Given determination, any extramural department should be able to set up a structure to carry out research. What should be recognized is that if such departments, which should be eminently qualified to do so, fail to take this initiative, other agencies might well do so, thus failing to draw upon a mass of useful experience.

This account began by emphasizing that the extramural tradition in Britain consists of trying to make university values intelligible to the community. It also seeks to make the knowledge of the university available to the public who pay for its operation. Adult education is, as Asa Briggs once remarked, the university's off-licence. It is worth concluding with a reminder that the purpose of encouraging research through the Nottingham Centre for Research is to ensure that the best that a university can offer is made available to the community, and that the method of doing this is the best that can be devised. Adult educators have problems in reaching as much of the community as they would like. The Centre may help us to look at community needs, and appropriate adult education to meet them. Most important, it may help us towards an evaluation of our effectiveness.

BASIC REFERENCE DATA (1980)

IA. The host institution

Name: University of Nottingham
Date founded: 1881
Internal organization: British provincial university structure. Seven faculties: Arts, Law and Social Sciences, Education, Pure Science, Agricultural Science, Applied Sciences, Medicine; subdivided into 50 departments.
Number of academic staff: 750
Number of students: 7000
Catchment area: National
Designated responsibility for off-campus activities: Responsible for university adult education in the East Midlands; also the work of the Industrial and Business Liaison Unit
Income: £Stg 25 million

1B. The host department

Name: Department of Adult Education

Date founded: 1920
Internal organization: Directorate and divisional organization
Number of academic staff: 40 full-time plus 260 part-time
Number of students: 10,500
Catchment area: East Midlands (national for higher degrees)
Income: £Stg 1 million

H. *The innovation/system being studied*

Name: Centre for Research in the Education of Adults
Date founded: 1978
Nature: Focus of national/internal research
Internal organization: Director and Steering Committee
Number of academic staff: Variable
Number of non-academic staff: 1
Income: £Stg 0.25 million

NOTE

1. The papers reflect the particular theme of the Conference, and therefore range over a very wide area of adult education. Copies can be obtained from the Secretary, SCUTREA, c/o The National Institute of Adult Education, 19B De Montford Street, Leicester, UK.

REFERENCES AND BIBLIOGRAPHY

Coates, K and Silburn, R (1968) *St Ann's: Poverty, Deprivation and Morale*, Department of Adult Education, University of Nottingham
Meller, H E (ed) (1971) *Nottingham in the Eighteen Eighties: A Study in Social Change*, Department of Adult Education, University of Nottingham
Russell Report (1973) *Adult Education: A Plan for Development: Report of the Committee appointed by the Secretary of State for Education and Science, chaired by Sir Lionel Russell*, 334 pp, HMSO, London
Williams, A (1970) Continuing education, in Bates, R (ed) *Prospects in New Zealand Education*, pp 170-8, Hodder and Stoughton, Auckland, in association with University of London Press
For a discussion of broader issues see:
Fletcher, C (1980) The theory of community education and its relation to adult education, in Thompson, J L (ed) *Adult Education for a Change*, pp 65-82, Hutchinson, London

9. Interfacing with industry: Loughborough Consultants Ltd

Universities and industry: the universities' response

Although most British universities had had substantial contact with
industry in the past, from about 1965 to 1970 three-quarters of the
university institutions in the United Kingdom established some formal
activity to co-ordinate and increase the amount of work for industry
undertaken in universities and to encourage industry to use alternative
mechanisms for sponsoring work in the universities. As well as long-term
research work, wholly or partly funded by industry, opportunities were
advertised for consultancy work, contract research, product development,
technical problem solving, access to equipment and specialist in-house
short courses. Each university established an organization which was
thought to be appropriate to its needs and the emphasis placed by each
of these university liaison organizations depended on the strengths of the
university, the inclination of the staff and the previous experience of the
person appointed to manage the liaison activity.

A number of British universities have not established formal
organizations and amongst those which have not are found some of the
most active in the field of collaboration with industry. These universities
have taken the view that collaboration with industry is an integral part
of a university department's life, particularly in engineering and science.
Therefore, far from requiring a formal organization, collaboration should
be developed as part of the normal responsibilities of academic heads of
department. Even those universities which have formal organizations
undertake a substantial amount of work in which the industrial liaison
office is not concerned. In these cases the office is there to advise and to
increase the opportunities over and above those which would have arisen
naturally. Again, in some universities the brief of the industrial liaison
centre has been defined to include only certain aspects of collaboration
with industry and in some cases the liaison centre is only concerned with
part of the academic expertise of the university, leaving other areas of the
university to operate independently, and possibly to establish a second
and perhaps different type of liaison centre.

During the past ten years industrial liaison centres of various sorts have
been becoming a significant activity in many universities and the people
engaged in this work have banded together in an informal group of
University Directors of Industrial Liaison in order to discuss problems
that are common to all universities, to build up the expertise of the

members of the group and when appropriate to represent the industrial liaison activity in universities to external bodies. These have included a select Committee of the House of Commons, the enquiry into the operation of financial institutions under the chairmanship of Sir Harold Wilson and the Advisory Council for Applied Research and Development working under the Civil Service Department. It has also been found advantageous to represent the spectrum of university views to such bodies as the Science Research Council and the National Research Development Corporation.

Each university in the United Kingdom has created its own different type of liaison activity. They may be grouped into three or four types. An Office of Industrial Liaison under a Director is a form favoured by the majority of universities. In other universities one or more units offering particular technologies based upon university departments have been set up. In one case this has resulted in the creation of seven different laboratories offering specialist services to industry. Limited liability companies have been established by some universities in order to market the expertise of the university and provide some protection for the academics engaged in such research work. A few universities have appointed, within their own administration, commercial managers whose task is to ensure that the contracts between the university and outside industry are drawn up in an appropriate form.

Loughborough University of Technology

Loughborough University of Technology decided in 1968 to establish a limited liability company which began operating in the summer of 1969. The company emerged as a result of the deliberations of a working party established under the chairmanship of the then Vice-Chancellor to review research, consultancy, industrial collaboration and a whole range of other external activities undertaken by the University, sometimes formally, but frequently on an informal basis.

Loughborough University of Technology was granted its Charter in 1965. Loughborough College had existed since the end of the first world war as a college funded by Leicestershire County Council. The institution included departments of engineering, science, physical education (for which Loughborough became very famous) and a department of art and design. The integrated institution existed until after the second world war when Loughborough College was divided into a number of separate units. A College of Technology with a grant from the Department of Education and Science was the institution which eventually became the University of Technology, having in the interim been one of the ten Colleges of Advanced Technology established to offer degree level courses in engineering and science. Recently the College of Education, another of the units, has amalgamated with the University, thus by a curious turn reforming the institution that had existed more than 50 years previously.

Loughborough University of Technology now consists of four schools:

Education and Humanities, Human and Environmental Studies, Pure and Applied Science, and Engineering. There are 25 departments and these departments are the operating units of the University itself. The University is governed by a Senate which is responsible for all academic matters and by a Council which is charged with the general oversight of the University. Council includes a number of academic staff and lay members appointed by various external bodies. Much of the detailed work of managing the University is carried out by Joint Committees of Senate and Council and to a very large extent these committees control, through finance, the activities of the University. The chief executive of the University is the Vice-Chancellor, with the University administration being headed by the Registrar.

The creation of the Company

There is no doubt that one reason for the establishment of the Company in the University was that it was a novel concept as far as universities in the United Kingdom were concerned at that time. There was also an increasing desire by heads of department and senior administrators in the University to have consultancy work managed and administered rather more formally than it had been in the past and also to increase the amount of such work undertaken for industry by University staff acting alone or as members of small teams. The company structure was chosen because it would give industrial clients an organization with the same structure as themselves to whom they could address their enquiries. By maintaining a legal separation between the University and the Company, the University could protect itself against claims made in respect of consultancy work undertaken by staff members. At that time there was a fear that universities might be exposed to substantial claims in respect of negligent work undertaken by staff members. Those claims would have had to be satisfied using public funds and clearly no university would have willingly undertaken the risks which are associated with the undertaking of commercial project work.

At the time of its formation a number of universities were creating organizations intended to make the university more responsive to industry and there was considerable pressure from industry and government for universities to organize themselves so that more work for industry, not necessarily of a long-term nature, could be undertaken by academics using the substantial resources that had been built up during the 1960s.

The Company was conceived by the Vice-Chancellor. A small group of people including the Registrar, the Managing Director designate of the Company, the University Solicitor and one or two heads of department converted the embryo idea into a working concept. Formal proposals were put to the University Council and accepted by it in order that the Company could exist on the University campus. Arrangements were made for the University to underwrite the activity for a period, not exceeding two years, and to provide the new Company with the modest resources in terms of space and equipment that it was likely to need.

The Company was seen by the academic staff as a means of increasing their private consultancy income; it was seen by administrators as a means of controlling the work of academics; it was seen by heads of department as an organization that could provide project management and help academics to remain in close touch with industry. It was seen by a small minority as just another bureaucratic organization that was going to restrict their freedom of action. In general the University welcomed the idea of a company and a considerable amount of support was offered by heads of department who, realizing that the University's own funds were at stake, became determined that the Company should succeed.

The University Council sought the approval of the University Grants Committee, which controls the finances of all universities in the UK, for the use of its own funds to underwrite the activity. Loughborough was therefore unique in that it commenced its operation of a liaison centre without any external funding. Most other universities received funds from the University Grants Committee; from the Ministry of Technology, the Government Department which together with the Board of Trade represented the industrial activity of central government; from the Wolfson Foundation or from the Science Research Council. Since the activity was to be funded by the University itself, of necessity it began life in a very modest fashion. The initial staff comprised a managing director and a secretary, occupying a single office rented from the University, with a separate telephone line and a small budget for publicity and travel. The venture was experimental and the Company had to break even over the first two years in order to survive.

The Company came into existence by resolution of a small group of individuals who thus became the first members of the Company, which was limited by guarantee of its members rather than by share capital. A Board of Directors was formed with the Chairman of the University Council as Chairman of the Company, the Vice-Chancellor as Deputy Chairman, the Registrar as Secretary. A number of members of the University Council who were in industry were appointed to reinforce the academic staff members who were mainly heads of department. The Board of Directors then proceeded to establish the authority of the Managing Director to enter into contracts on behalf of the Company and to determine the initial policy that the Company was to pursue. Some simple publicity material was prepared. This comprised a ten-page brochure and the first of what eventually became a series of ten leaflets. A press notice was circulated widely.

The early days

Much of the early work, for which the Company became the contractor, was brought to it by members of the academic staff who felt that the Company could provide them with a project management service, some insurance protection and a simple accounting system. The early publicity brought in a few enquiries to the Company itself, and contact was made with many organizations who were thought to have the potential for generating business for Loughborough Consultants Limited. The Company was offered the chance to manage a major project on behalf of the University and as a consequence of all this activity the company broke even in its first year with a turnover of some £Stg 50,000.

In the early days virtually all the projects were small and typically only occupied two or three days of academic staff time each. The Genesys Centre, the major project referred to above, was on the other hand a much more serious undertaking, since it meant that the Company had to employ technical staff who were to be supervised by a seconded member of the staff of the Department of Civil Engineering. The scale of this venture was such that it was the first and, to date, only contract undertaken by the Company on a cost plus basis.

At the time the Company was formed the University had an active interest in consultancy work in the environmental noise area. The Vice-Chancellor was an established consultant in the field and was offered the opportunity to carry out the predictive work on behalf of the British Airports Authority in connection with the selection of a site for a third London airport. He was also consultant to a number of local authorities and felt the need for technical staff to support him. Similarly the Engineering Design Centre of the University found itself unable to respond to a number of enquiries for assistance since it lacked draughtsmen and junior designers to support the professional staff within the Centre. These two initial groups of staff became the nucleus for two substantial activities for the Company, one of which has grown and developed into a major Design Group employing 20 people with substantial resources at its disposal.

The Genesys Centre, the Noise Group and the embryo Design Group gave the Company an identity but put more demands on the University for the provision of space. These were met by renting offices in academic buildings and by the provision of a number of temporary buildings. At about this time the instrumentation and electronics laboratory in the Department of Transport Technology found itself being asked increasingly for instrumentation systems for use by industrial research laboratories and the Head of that laboratory became involved with a number of projects which were undertaken in his laboratory by technical staff of the Department. From this grew the Company's Electronics and Instrumentation Group which now has a turnover ten times greater than the entire Company did in its first year.

The Company was initially seen by its originators and by the University as a mechanism for making available the expertise of the University and its staff to industry. It was intended to provide a professional management service for project work and to acquire expertise in one or two areas such as patents and licensing, project cost estimating and the establishment of clearly worded contracts between the consultants and their clients. The realization that the University lacked certain resources led the Company to employ its own staff in supporting roles, but these were initially seen to be individuals acting in a manner which would be co-ordinated by a member of the academic staff in every case.

The potential clients for the Company's services began to regard the Company as a different entity from the University and therefore began to expect the Company to behave more like a commercial research and development company than an offshoot of an academic institution. Fortunately the Company was able to respond to this demand, albeit in the early years in a somewhat fragmented manner.

The principal initial constraint was money. The Company was established without a share capital and existed on a modest overdraft from the University intended to provide working capital to cover the salaries of its administration and its tiny staff. After five years the Genesys contract came to an end and the amount of work in electronics, in the design field and in noise control was sufficient to justify a plan to increase the number of staff and to regard those staff members as the permanent staff of the Company rather than of the University. It should be emphasized that no short-term contract staff have ever been employed; the continuity of employment has depended on successive contracts being available.

Expansion

At this point the Company's demand for finance was modest, but in the three years following 1973 the staff numbers began to increase, people were employed at several levels and the character of the Company began to change rapidly. By 1976 the present senior managers were all in post working for the Company. Of the four, three had previously worked for the University, including the Manager of the Electronics and Instrumentation Group and the Manager of the Design Group. The Accountant who had been seconded from the University had become a full-time employee, and a Manager to assist the Managing Director with University project work in particular had been recruited from a major electronics company where he had been a production manager. All this time the staff were occupying rented or borrowed accommodation in University departments and the rate of growth was such that the use of other people's accommodation was no longer feasible. The capital employed by the Company which was available in the form of a loan from the University had reached some £Stg100,000 which was more than ten times the total overhead cost of the Company in its first year.

Clearly the time had come for a careful review of the operation of the Company. It was necessary to determine the Company's future policy and make a number of decisions which, at the time they were taken, appeared to be very bold. The University needed to consider whether the Company was fulfilling its original objectives or not; how successful it was; whether it should be encouraged to develop further in the direction it had taken in the previous few years, and finally what commitment of resources the University could afford or justify making in the future.

It was apparent that the Company was still fulfilling its original objectives in that it provided project management to staff who wished to bring projects in; it was finding a substantial amount of project work for individual members of staff to carry out and it was acting as the managing and marketing agent for a number of department-based activities. Some of these were long lasting and some, such as the work connected with high alumina cements were of short duration. The Company had also successfully exploited a small number of patents granted to university inventors, but this activity had not grown quite as rapidly as some university staff hoped that it might.

On the other hand the work undertaken by the staff of the Company itself was developing. The Electronics and Instrumentation Group undertook a substantial amount of its work without involving the University and the Company was also contemplating in that field acquiring manufacturing rights so that sub-contractors could be used for products which would be effectively sold by the Company. Clearly some of the decisions were concerned with matters of principle and the others with matters of expediency, particularly in terms of cash requirements.

After a great deal of thought and discussion within the University it was decided that the Company should be allowed to develop its business in the way that the Board of Directors thought appropriate, that the financial arrangements between the Company and the University should be put on to a more formal basis, and whilst the University was happy that products should be manufactured by contractors for the Company, the University had no wish to see a manufacturing operation, no matter how modest, established on its own campus. The University agreed to lend to the Company up to £Stg 200,000 at a rate of interest 1 per cent below the minimum lending rate and to guarantee loans from the Midland Bank Limited to the Company up to £Stg 100,000 in the first instance. Both of these limits were increased by £Stg 50,000 at the beginning of 1979.

These arrangements enabled the Company to borrow external funds for the provision of its own building which was occupied in March 1977. This building was a conventional single storey brick structure giving 4000 sq ft of usable space to the Company for its administration, design and electronics activities. The increase in borrowing limits approved in 1979 enabled the Company to double the space available and at present the Company has 8000 sq ft of usable space. A further consequence of the decision to set a borrowing limit was that the Board of Directors could look ahead and plan the way it wished the Company to develop. So far most of the decisions have really been that the Company should continue to expand its present areas of business since these were felt to be the areas where the Company was likely to be successful both technically and commercially. Since the borrowing limits were set the Company has maintained cash flow control and carries out monthly predictions of the cash situation for the ensuing six months. Apart from one or two occasions during the past five years the Company has always had at least £Stg 100,000 of spare cash available and the likelihood is that the Company will attempt to repay the money provided by the University on loan in the same way as it is repaying its medium-term bank loans. It is possible that this repayment will take ten years and at the end of that time the University will have to decide once again on its mechanism for controlling the Company activity. At the end of 1980 the Company employed more than 50 staff. Most were members of either the Design or Electronics Group but a further activity which has developed during the last three years provides employment for about six scientists. This activity is concerned with surface analysis and the Surface Analysis Centre will be discussed a little later.

The decisions taken by the University some five years ago mean that in effect the Company has changed from being an exploiter of University expertise only into a business which is established on the University campus with access to the University expertise and facilities. This means that many industrial clients are now able to obtain a service from the Company which is virtually unique in the United Kingdom in that it combines the benefits of a permanent professional staff with ready access to substantial expertise at a high level. It also means that major projects in a very wide range of industrial areas can be undertaken. The proposals that the Company makes are credible because of the resources that are available.

The Company's range of activities

The projects undertaken by each of the three operating groups — Design, Electronics and Instrumentation, University Projects — vary widely. The Design Group has, at the present time, a project to design and build to prototype stage an agricultural rough terrain fork lift truck intended to meet the present and likely future European Economic Community regulations for such equipment. That Group has also, during the same period, designed and supplied equipment for the handling of pharmaceutical materials and for the manufacture of chefs' paper toque hats. At the other end of the product size spectrum, industrial design work has been carried out on two internal telephone systems for electronics companies and, with the Electronics Group of Loughborough Consultants Limited, a very competitive burglar alarm system has been developed. In the past, design staff working with academics from a number of departments have designed a first attendance fire appliance which has been sold extensively abroad, three other construction vehicles and a transportation system for Whipsnade Zoo, the extensive Zoo Park operated by the Zoological Society of London. Also included in current products are three items of medical instrumentation, a hand held bearing compass for small boats and a toilet seat adaptor for use by disabled people. This range of activities is probably only possible in the environment in which the Company operates.

The Electronics Development and Instrumentation Group covers an almost equally wide range of industries, although the techniques used are probably more limited. The skill in the Group lies in the identification of the problem and the conversion of that problem into electronic terms and also, at the practical level, in making electronic systems work in unfavourable environments.

The Electronics Group has designed and built equipment to operate on coal mining machinery, on the underside of diesel locomotives and experimental railway vehicles, on construction plant, military equipment and ships. Some of this equipment is permanently installed and includes a torque measuring system installed on the cutter of a harbour dredger such that the system operates on the sea bed 40 metres below the surface. Torque measuring systems are designed and built for a wide range of customers and the Group offers a problem-solving capability which is one of the best in Europe at the present time in this field. Other equipment of the same type has been built for Vickers Limited, who subsequently exported it to the Soviet Union and the People's Republic of China as elements in tyre and brake dynamometer systems. The systems are also installed on power station boiler water feed pumps in New Zealand and on a number of large ocean going ships.

The Group has experience of product development incorporating digital logic and microprocessors and this has resulted in a number of systems being designed for clients to manufacture, including equipment used in the medical field, the alarm and protection industry and for the control of fire service turntable ladders. A considerable number of experimental projects are undertaken which require complex equipment to be built and this in recent times has included a substantial amount of work in connection with the British Rail Advanced Passenger Train, with mine winding equipment and with underground coal conveyors. The Group is recognized by its many clients as being one of the most competent in its field with a long track record of successful design, development and construction.

Many of the University projects are not concerned with the design of products but with solving problems for manufacturers. In many cases these projects are smaller in size, but they require a substantial amount of management effort. In 1980 the Company completed more than 600 separate projects, 400 of which were carried out by academic staff of the University with an average contract size of only £Stg 500. Inevitably this means that the consultants acting for the Company have to manage many of their projects themselves and the Company provides an administrative framework within which those projects can be satisfactorily undertaken. Some no doubt could be managed successfully without the Company being involved, but over the years an understanding has been developed with so many members of the University that the use of the Company system is in many cases automatic.

A brief reference was made above to the Surface Analysis Centre. This is in many ways the most intriguing of the developments with which

Loughborough Consultants Ltd has been involved. Three years ago the University purchased an Auger Electron Spectrometer and asked the Company to be responsible for the commercial exploitation of a fraction of the time available on the instrument. In order to do this the Company employed a graduate experienced in the operation of an Auger Spectrometer and aided by a member of staff of the Physics Department actively sought business for the instrument. This was so successful that within nine months a second operator was required and the Company became established as one of the leading providers of surface analysis facilities in the United Kingdom. There were several instruments on which commercial projects were undertaken in the University but the surface analysis activity has easily been the most successful. The principal reasons for this success have been the active co-operation of the University Physics Department over a long period of time and the quality of the service which it has been possible to provide because the operator is responsible to the University Projects Manager of the Company. At the beginning of 1980 a second, larger instrument was installed in order to carry out X-ray Photo Electron Spectroscopy (ESCA or XPS). This instrument was leased by Loughborough Consultants Ltd, leasing being feasible for the Company but not for the University owing to the charitable status of universities in the UK. The University would have been unable to recover value added tax paid and has no income against which it can set the leasing charges, which is essential if the cost of leasing is to be justified. During 1980 the instrument became profitable with two operators providing a service to industry which is complementary to Auger Electron Spectroscopy. The acquisition of a further large instrument is now being considered with the decision depending entirely on the likely use by industry of the facilities to be provided. This is an excellent example of collaboration between the Company and a University department which has resulted in substantial income for the University enabling the University to acquire advanced instrumentation at a time when money is strictly limited and enabling the Company to make significant profits on its own equipment.

A substantial amount of the time on the instrument is used by research workers at Loughborough and at other universities. The Company staff and University staff have combined to publish a number of papers and are now highly regarded in the surface analysis field. The important factor was the initial decision by the University to make the considerable capital expenditure needed for the first instrument. The Company was then able to develop its marketing expertise in a low risk venture which eventually enabled it to take the very considerable risk of acquiring an instrument whose current price is well in excess of £Stg 100,000. The third instrument which is even more expensive will be purchased to provide a service in which the Company has increased its marketing capability and its understanding of the nature of the problems that industry needs to solve in this advanced analytical area.

Future developments

So much for the type of activity currently undertaken by the Company staff and the academic staff who operate under the aegis of the Company structure. It becomes interesting to speculate on the way the Company will develop over the next five and ten years, particularly when one compares the Company as it is at present with the original concept and the way in which the Company operated in its first few years. It would be easy to say that there will be simply more of the same type of activity. It is, however, likely that other new initiatives could be taken and it might be of interest to consider some of these at the present time.

The Design Group is likely to develop further along its present lines. The areas of expertise in vehicles, manipulative machinery, medical equipment and consumer products, provide it with a base from which it can develop both at home and overseas. The Group almost certainly will undertake an increasing fraction of its business overseas and active steps are being taken to seek contracts in Holland, Belgium and India where the Company is beginning to be known. Overseas marketing is expensive and proposals for project work are most likely to be accepted in overseas markets where the Company has at least a modest track record.

The Electronics Group presents a number of interesting problems. It is apparent that in many cases our clients would like to see us both designing and manufacturing for them. Some products such as safe load indicators for construction equipment and cranes are already supplied by the Company having been manufactured by sub-contractors. If this activity develops the Company will require more production management expertise than it has at present, but the rewards for such activities in financial terms are considerable. The balance has to be maintained in order that the Company is not seen to be a manufacturing company either by clients for design work or by the University itself. The tendency for the instrumentation and electronics work to be carried out for significant engineering companies will inevitably increase. The type of problem that the Company staff are best able to solve and the level of documentation that it has become our habit to supply, puts many potential clients out of reach on cost grounds. At the same time the most interesting technical problems inevitably turn up from the larger organizations, a number of which have been referred to earlier. The trend here is inevitable. The Company has recently diversified into microprocessor-based instrumentation systems and products, but at the same time it has been restricting its activities to ensure that the quality of engineering work is maintained. It is possible that telemetry systems of an advanced nature will feature in the Company's range of expertise in the near future, this being a natural development from the type of work undertaken at the present time. There is the possibility that joint manufacturing ventures might be considered with outside bodies providing production management expertise and Loughborough Consultants providing product development skills in particular areas on an exclusive basis for those manufacturers. This type of stability is attractive in many ways but might conceivably reduce the options available to the Company. This may be more of an imaginary fear than a real one because the Company is already limited in one way in that having undertaken a substantial development programme for a manufacturer it cannot then undertake similar work for the original client's competitors.

Within the University area more effort will be put into the exploitation of patents and inventions, but in this part of the Company's business one could conceivably develop a number of original or near original initiatives. One that is currently being considered is an industrial nursery. This would involve the provision by the University of a piece of land on which very small industrial units could be established. As they grew in the helpful environment that the University can create they would eventually come to a size where they could be transplanted to a conventional industrial estate, having had the benefit of contact with the University in the early years where both the management skills and the product development skills of the entrepreneur are most tested. A venture like this in partnership with a financial institution and local government agencies is one way in which the University through its Company can contribute to the local community a supply of new jobs for the next generation and for those who are being made redundant because their skills are no longer required in traditional industries. The generation of new job opportunities is an area in which universities in the UK can play a significant role both to their own benefit and to the benefit of the community at large. In order for this to be rewarding for the University and its staff a mechanism has to be created which will ensure that the contribution of the University is recognized.

An interesting paradox is developing in that the University wishes the Company to remain within borrowing limits established some years ago despite continuing inflation and even wishes the Company to repay the loan and become eventually self-financing. This has to be set against the desire of the University to regulate the type of activity in which the Company will become involved. Therefore the choice of venture cannot be made purely on the basis of financial return. The Company has no funds to invest of any size and therefore the task of achieving self-sufficiency is difficult. Joint ventures with the University such as the industrial nursery, referred to above, the exploitation of major instrumentation facilities and the extension of the Company's business away from its traditional technological base into management and other areas would find favour with the University. It remains to be seen whether there is sufficient commercial advantage to enable the other objectives to be met. At the present time it seems to be possible.

Conclusion

In conclusion one must evaluate the establishment of a Company such as Loughborough Consultants Ltd in a university environment by considering the reactions of various groups of people, some of whom may have somewhat conflicting criteria for success.

There is no doubt that the industrial clients of the Company by and large consider the Company to be successful. The project proposals that we make appear to be widely accepted both on technical and cost grounds, with the Company able to make a profit, providing expertise to companies that have either excessive demands on their own resources or lack the expertise to carry out the work. At the same time, in most engineering disciplines, major companies make judgements on the costs put to them on the basis of what it would cost them to carry out the work themselves and therefore a considerable skill is needed to make a profit in such circumstances. The University appears to be satisfied with the Company in that the University Council sanctions annually the continuation of the loan made to the Company for working capital. Close contact is maintained with senior officers and particularly the Vice-Chancellor to ensure that developments contemplated by the Company are likely to meet with the approval of the University if the Board of Directors decides to implement them. In a University community there are many different points of view and there are still people who do not think that the University should be involved with a Company of the type that Loughborough Consultants has become. At the same time a majority seems to find the Company at least acceptable and frequently helpful. Being able to please most of the people most of the time would appear to be the best that one can expect to achieve in an organization where views which are very diverse are likely to be expressed.

Other universities in the UK and overseas have followed the development of this Company with interest and whilst the structure that has been created does not always satisfy their requirements there is considerable evidence that there has been extensive borrowing from the concept which has been created in Loughborough. This is common amongst academic institutions and Loughborough University is itself very pleased that other institutions have found something that is worth imitating at least in part. The Company receives frequent visitors from other institutions and members of the staff have always taken a great deal of trouble in the response to their visitors' questions. We, of course, learn from colleagues in other institutions, although being something of a front runner and committed to a particular structure, we cannot always take up the good ideas that we see.

Government agencies including the British Council and a number of government departments visit Loughborough to learn about the way the Company operates. The mechanism for industrial collaboration that has been established is widely recognized as one of the potentially most successful forms of collaboration that can be contemplated. It is always made plain to such visitors that the formal mechanism that is chosen is only a small part of whatever success has been achieved in any academic institution. The principal ingredients for success are clearly a desire by the institution to carry out substantial industrial project work and the establishment of a mechanism with sufficient resources to enable work to be attracted which might not otherwise have found its way on to the University campus. Sufficient management resources are important but possibly even more important is the creation of teams of skilled whole-time staff who can carry out such work. Even those universities without a formal mechanism for this type of activity have found it necessary to maintain considerable numbers of research workers and professional engineers in order to be successful.

Locally there is increasing recognition that Loughborough Consultants Ltd, like all the successful small companies in the area, is a provider of jobs for qualified staff. During the periods of recession experienced by British industry the University Company has grown without any check until at the present time it provides over 50 jobs, the majority of which are held by locally recruited qualified staff. If further growth needs to be justified it can be justified on that basis alone in the present and likely future economic climate in the United Kingdom.

BASIC REFERENCE DATA (1979-80)

I. The host institution

Name: Loughborough University of Technology
Date founded: As Loughborough College, 1916; university charter, 1965
Internal organization: The University was formerly a College of Advanced Technology, ten of which were created in 1957 from large technical colleges in the UK. Organized in four Schools: Engineering, Pure and Applied Science, Human and Environmental Studies, Education and Humanities; and 25 Departments.
Number of academic staff: 513
Number of students: 4754 undergraduates; 1197 postgraduates
Catchment area: Students are drawn mainly from the UK with about 10 per cent from Commonwealth countries and 4 per cent from other overseas countries.
Income: £Stg 14 million: 62 per cent UGC grant, 25 per cent tuition and other fees, 9 per cent Research Council and Industrial Research grants

II. The innovation/system being studied

Name: Loughborough Consultants Ltd
Date founded: 1969
Nature: Company limited by guarantee, without share capital
Internal organization: Organized in three groups: University Projects, Electronics and Instrumentation, and Design
Total staff: 50, including 40 graduates
Income: £Stg 850,000; all contract work for industry and government
Income as proportion of institution's total income: 6 per cent

REFERENCES AND BIBLIOGRAPHY

Advisory Council for Applied Research and Development (1978) *Industrial Innovation*, 43 pp, HMSO, London
Lees, F A (1981) *Industrial Liaison and the Academics*, 91 pp, Swinburne Applied Research and Development Division, Melbourne
OECD (1980) *University Consulting Services: Issues and Experiences*, Proceedings of Eighth Special Topic Workshop, April 1980, Organisation for Economic Co-operation and Development, Paris

10. Business development: a consultancy service at the University of Otago

Richard Higham

The Business Development Centre has existed for eight years as an exciting innovation, bringing the resources of a major university into the commercial sector of the South Island of New Zealand. Two basic challenges led to the creation of the Centre: these were, first, the slow growth rate of a largely rural area when compared with the faster growing urban centres in the North Island and, secondly, the challenge of creating a business education in the University which would be of real relevance to undergraduate and postgraduate students.

The idea

A proposal for 'a small business centre' was presented in May 1972 by Philip Rossell, the newly appointed Professor of Management at the University. Surveys had previously been carried out into local business skills, and weaknesses were identified in the individual firms: these were as might be expected to be apparent to a professional who had worked for some time in a large international corporation – for instance, poor business planning, inadequate administration, lack of production planning and control, poor feasibility studies, and a lack of professional marketing skills. However, the proposal also contained a section on the need for better planning at the regional level – leading to rationalization of industry, greater skills in Otago businesses in exploiting direct shipping links between their port of Dunedin and the Australian market, and the undertaking of feasibility studies as a basis for new ventures and the attraction of venture capital.

Formal proposal
Philip Rossell's paper proposed that the University establish the Small Business Centre as a pilot project. Three objectives were drawn up and discussed by the University's Commerce Faculty; these were:

☐ to promote regional development, through general research studies into regional industrial problems
☐ to provide small businesses in the region with assistance in specific management areas
☐ to improve the education and training of managers.

The proposal sold the Centre as a logical extension of the University in society: in drawing up terms of reference, a structure was created which involved both the University and local industry. For instance it was envisaged that the unit would establish its programme of work in consultation with companies and through discussion with regional and local development groups. This consultation would be formalized through a Management Advisory Committee composed of invited representatives of industry, government departments and the University. A Director of the unit would be the Executive Officer of the Committee; he and his staff would undertake some teaching in the University's embryonic business school and reciprocally involve members of the school in the work of the unit.

Local debate

The proposal was widely debated in the University and generally accepted as a good move, particularly in the opportunity it created for developing New Zealand case study material and for deploying Commerce Faculty and other faculty skills in the business community. However, the view was taken by the local accounting profession that a subsidized consulting service could have dangers, and reservations were expressed about the wisdom of the Centre as a long-term institution. During this debate, the name Business Development Centre was coined in preference to the Small Business Centre, to indicate that work would not be confined simply to owner-managers.

Whatever the merits of the case for a Business Development Centre, it has been maintained in retrospect that without the 1972 General Election and its emphasis on regional development programmes by the two main political parties, the Business Development Centre would not have emerged as it did.

The South Island context

Two thirds of New Zealand's population lives in the country's North Island, with major cities in Auckland, Hamilton, and the capital, Wellington. In the South Island a million people inhabit an area half the size of the United Kingdom, with developed sheep farming on flat and upland country producing wool and meat for export via two main ports (Christchurch and Dunedin) and three smaller ports (Picton, Bluff, and Timaru). The rapid growth of farm output during the 1960s had been accompanied in the South Island by diversification into timber products, fishing, processed foods, and engineered goods. However, with the main European market remote and under the Common Market regulations subject to increasing restrictions, the economy slowed in the early 1970s, productivity remained stagnant and living standards gradually declined.

The election in 1972 saw regional development as the main issue in the South Island and programmes were created to foster economic development. Regional Development Councils were proposed to encourage local commercial initiatives and to co-ordinate a government backed programme of loans at low interest rates. The Development Finance

Corporation was to expand its activities, with a well publicized portfolio of loans for manufacturing and processing of agricultural output aimed particularly at the smaller enterprise.

The creation of the Business Development Centre has thus to be seen against its background. Three factors may be identified as crucial: the interest of the Commerce Faculty in teaching both theory and practice in Management, the interest of the Government in fostering local initiative in the South Island, and the interest of the local business community who saw some of their problems in marketing and management terms, and wanted an advisory service in their locality.

In the event, a chance meeting between Philip Rossell and the then Minister of Trade and Industry, Mr Brian Talboys, at one of the west coast towns in the South Island, brought about agreement that the Centre should be funded with a small establishment grant and an annual grant to cover salaries, of $NZ 35,000. This was to be paid to the Centre for administration by the University, with the proposed Advisory Committee deciding priorities for action. The University asked Philip Rossell to be the first Director of the Centre, in addition to his professorial duties in Management. He quickly set about recruiting four consultants and used his influence in the local business community to create suitable assignments for his new staff to investigate.

The BDC as part of the University

The University of Otago was New Zealand's first university, founded in 1869. It has faculties of Arts and Music, Science, Law, Medicine, Commerce, Dentistry, Home Science, and Theology, and a School of Physical Education. It offers the only university courses available in the country in dentistry, theology, home science, physical education, pharmacy and land surveying. The Otago Medical School, established in 1875, was the only training centre for doctors in New Zealand for the first 90 years of its existence. The University has a strong scientific tradition and a considerable medical research team is attached to the Medical School, which has an international reputation in some research areas.

There are approximately 7000 students enrolled at Otago, including a number from overseas. More than 70 per cent of them come from beyond the city, and about 1400 live in colleges and halls of residence.

Because the University was founded only 21 years after the first shiploads of Scottish pioneers reached Otago, it has literally grown up with the city of Dunedin. This has resulted in a strong rapport between town and gown and made Dunedin the nearest thing to a university town to be found in New Zealand. In economic terms, the city sees the University as a major industry which annually puts millions of dollars into local circulation. There is also pride in the tradition of learning which is part of Dunedin's heritage. In turn, while continually engaged in the true functions of teaching and research, the University of Otago has always been ready to respond to community needs and it reaches out into the city and province in a variety of ways.

The Business Development Centre is one of three organizations which work from the University in society. The first of these was founded as an offshoot of the Home Science School: it became the Department of University Extension which expanded its activities quickly into formal education courses in the more remote areas of the South Island, and into vocational or general interest studies mainly in the arts and more recently in the political and social sciences. However, it has never been envisaged that the Department of University Extension would undertake a wide-ranging consulting or advisory role.

This has fallen to the Business Development Centre and to the University's Technical Advisory and Consulting Service. The latter, known by its initials as TACS, was started at the same time as the BDC and specializes in bringing technical skills to bear on development problems in industry — water quality, chemical analysis, pollution control and a host of other matters which university staff are qualified to investigate.

Some of the first assignments for the Business Development Centre were undertaken in conjunction with TACS and a harmonious relationship was established quickly. The Department of University Extension, by contrast, concentrated mainly on its teaching skills based on the arts and the social sciences: thus, except for an overlap in identifying opportunities for the improvement of life in the South Island in the broadest sense, there was less opportunity for co-operation between the BDC and the University Extension staff.

The early years of the Business Development Centre

At the start, it was expected that fees would not be charged to the predominantly small business clients the Centre was intended to attract. However, following critical evaluation by the Society of Accountants (who saw Government sponsored competition as unethical and undesirable) and from members of the faculty and local businessmen, it was decided to charge fees at professional rates and to use the grant on a discretionary basis to help small businesses as yet unable to afford full consultancy rates, and regional development organizations or associations whose efforts were considered to be in the best interests of local development.

The Centre recruited overseas staff during its first years, hoping thereby to acquire a measure of marketing and production expertise learnt in larger companies. The first recruit was a production consultant whose university degree had been taken in New Zealand, but whose industrial experience was in the motor industry in the UK. His particular interest had been the rational supply of components to the car industry and he had seen at first hand the problems of the owner-managed business in this trade. He therefore fitted easily into the South Island scene and made an immediate impact on the smaller engineering and timber componentry companies, particularly in the improvement of their production methods. A second consultant was also recruited from the UK: he had a commercial background in the chemical industry and had undertaken research at the London Business School into small company marketing and financial problems. Further recruits, also from overseas, had marketing skills in the textile industry, and production engineering in the ceramic industry.

While consultants brought a wide range of large and small company skills to bear on local problems, they had quickly to adapt their approach to a land of small companies (by overseas comparison miniature companies). While the problems faced by such companies may be typical of the owner-manager in business, there is the added difficulty that expansion invariably leads to trading at a huge distance from markets. A South Island businessman wanting to export to the main New Zealand market, which is located at the other end of the North Island, faces freight costs which are the equivalent of a trip from London to Milan — and he does so via a single railway line and a union-dominated inter-island ferry.

Early assignments of the Business Development Centre
The wide range of consulting assignments undertaken during the early years of the Business Development Centre indicates a further aspect of the Centre's work – the need for people who had specialized in one or another aspect of management to generalize and bring in other skills where necessary. Thus one of the larger clients was a City Council considering the manufacture of metallurgical coke in its town gas plant. The production process was one from the previous century — indeed one of the main problems was the very antiquity of the machinery being used and the inefficiency of the operation even to produce town gas. In the event, a feasibility study (Higham, 1974) indicated that metallurgical coke was well beyond the capability of the plant and the management, and a phased run-down of the equipment was recommended.

In another assignment, a multi-branch national company asked staff at the Centre to investigate its organizational problems and recommend a strategy for expansion of its activities. As a first phase in this exercise, the local branch was assessed and preliminary recommendations made concerning improvement in management. The subsequent investigation of the whole company indicated two fundamental difficulties — the highly decentralized operation had but two executives at the Head Office and decisions were being made in any one of 25 locations which could affect the viability of the whole unit. In addition, only one of the accountant staff in the company kept figures to indicate the return on capital being made by the enterprise and his figures applied to one main branch out of seven. Recommendations for change were made leading to a substantial improvement in financial ratios, and a more viable company emerged. The benefits of this exercise for the South Island were that some of the production processes were concentrated where labour was skilled and freight differentials lowest.

A third example will illustrate the range of activities required of the Centre. A group of enthusiasts, foreseeing the development of one of the South Island's major rivers (the Waitaki) as a threat to the introduced salmon run, proposed a salmon hatchery near the river mouth as a means of preserving the run and creating a saleable product for export. An investigation was undertaken (Higham and Rossell, 1974) into the commercial viability of this proposal which, though it was not subsequently taken up by a local company, brought two of the country's major food producers into competition to establish the best river for development of such a hatchery. A long term proposal of this kind has, in the New Zealand climate of fierce local independence, provoked competition for resources between the 'acclimatization societies' (who oversee the introduction and control of animals and fish for recreational purposes) and the state Ministry of Works and Development (which has created massive hydro lakes and canals out of a large number of the country's previously wild rivers). A feasibility study has to tread a careful path between environmental, commercial, recreational and state development interests. In the event the salmon hatchery was eight years away from the feasibility study but the early work of analysis and measurement may yet pay off.

Other assignments included a construction company attempting to expand its activities and a university hall of residence experiencing financial difficulties. There were of course also a large number of smaller owner-managers, particularly in the furniture and cabinet-making industries.

Many of the clients of the Business Development Centre in this early phase were skilled businessmen wanting to improve their activities rather than the unskilled business managers identified in the proposal which led to the creation of the Centre.

Progress by 1976

Staff of the Centre taught postgraduate and third year undergraduate courses, and thereby were able to select the more able students as junior recruits. By 1976 the Centre employed six staff members and had been commissioned to undertake a cycle of resource surveys for Regional Development Councils in the South Island (Duffy and Higham, 1975). The five Regional Development Councils in the South Island had been operating since 1973, with Government appointed local businessmen and officials promoting industrial growth. Two of these Councils initiated resource surveys to identify what was available and to ascribe priorities for development particularly where constraints of water or soil availability became apparent. The 1975-77 cycle of South Island resource surveys, pioneered by the Centre's staff, went one better than those drawn up in the previous generation by the Department of Industries and Commerce, which catalogued the resources but ascribed no development programmes.

By 1976, therefore, the Centre was engaged in four South Island provinces and was building an active stance in advising managers, undertaking feasibility studies, and discovering which best routes to follow in developing new business activity.

Reduction of grant

In 1976 it was announced that the Government grant would be reduced the following year from $NZ 35,000 to $NZ 10,000. The reliance of the Centre on a measure of Government support, to enable its consultants to travel widely in the South Island and help wherever the need was expressed, was not taken into account in a Government budget which aimed simply at reducing expenditure.

The Centre's programme of activities was continued at the previous level for a further year, using the reserves of grant and fees which had been used as working capital previously. By the end of the year these resources were depleted and despite urgent requests to the Government for a restored grant, no promises were forthcoming and decisions had to be made about the continued existence of the Business Development Centre.

A lesson was learnt in this process: despite any benefits which derived to the University from its accommodation of the Business Development Centre, no financial support was forthcoming to replace the Government grant. The University did not see itself as responsible for the provision of an advisory service, nor did it direct resources towards the Centre to maintain the admittedly small teaching component of its work.

Early in 1977, four of the six consultant staff found alternative employment, and thereby enriched local industry. Two staff members joined companies to undertake marketing work; another joined a city council on the financial side, and another transferred to the University's Management Department where he undertook teaching work in production systems.

There remained two staff members whose skills could be turned to more commercial assignments, thereby eking out the small Government grant expected for 1977. In the event, the decision to restore the Government grant to the previous level was taken three weeks after the fourth staff member had left — and there remained the arduous task of rebuilding a team from scratch. Four important questions were faced in this process and the solutions to these questions gave the Business Development Centre a second opportunity to establish its style and work programme.

The BDC's 'second wind'

The first problem was faced by the then Director of the Centre, who besides the duties of running the Management Department of the University and undertaking consultancy work in his own specialization of manpower planning, was heavily engaged in designing and administering the country's first Master's Degree in Business Administration. The pace set in this dynamic process was always perhaps a little faster than could be easily tolerated by a university and, in the ultimate struggle, Professor Philip Rossell resigned as Director of the Business Development Centre

179

and as Director of the MBA programme. The directorship then devolved on one of the Centre's staff, who had been serving as Deputy Director for the previous three years. The appointment was thus not of a full-time University employee although the individual concerned had been previously offered tenure of his post in the University as though he were a full-time University member.

The second situation which faced the Centre was one of recruitment and terms of employment. Where previously the Centre had gone overseas for its staff, there was an increasing drive to employ local people and advertisements were placed accordingly. In the event, the BDC staff numbers increased with two executives from local industry, one skilled in marketing, the other skilled in quality control and product evaluation. There then followed, during a period of close harmony with the Faculty of Commerce, recruitment of students from the MBA class and a routine was built up whereby the Business Development Centre would attract a junior consultant and then release him for studies on the MBA, subsequently to supervise his project work and re-employ him at the end of his study period. This has had a profound effect on the relationship between the BDC and the University.

The third problem facing the Centre was the deployment of expertise. Where previously assignments had been undertaken by individuals with advice or constructive criticism from colleagues, one assignment was requested of the Centre which tested not the individual skills so much as the team work skills of the staff. It involved a study on behalf of a timber industry guild of the impact of a reduced supply of indigenous timber to five mills in western Southland (Rush *et al*, 1977). In the event, a formula was discovered of penetrating higher value markets with more sophisticated products, and thereby using less of the scarce indigenous resource but at maintained levels of employment. This report was undertaken under pressure and its results have been used in other parts of the country where a similar problem has emerged. Beyond that, however, the report gave the Centre a good reputation for innovative impact work and created a team work ethic in the Centre which has subsequently stood the test of time.

Fourthly and finally, where previously the Centre had been located in offices adjacent to the Management Department, a relocation of the Commerce Faculty found the BDC accommodated in an attractive Victorian house in the middle of the concrete high-rise buildings which now constitute the University — a small focal point for all sorts of activities beyond those involving management or purely commercial skills.

Six service programmes

By the middle of 1980, the Business Development Centre had established six programmes of work, in direct response to requests made by organizations for help in solving problems:

The first, and main programme is described as the Centre's Corporate Advisory Unit. Four staff members help businesses to improve their management efficiency, along the lines developed by the Centre over the last eight years.

A shift may be detected in the creation of this unit, away from the very small companies and the growing owner-managed companies to the large local and large national companies. Whereas before the Centre concentrated on broadening the owner-manager's approach as he developed a new product or penetrated a new market, the corporate advisory staff undertake a 'corporate audit' of the organization, discover areas of weakness, and concentrate on improving these as a means of improving business performance overall.

The main management weaknesses of these organizations are as set out in the preliminary documents to the creation of the Business Development Centre. It is, however, only after working extensively with a wide range of small companies, that the Centre has built a reputation which allows it to move into the marketing and organization problems faced by the well established firms.

The second programme is that deploying a similar corporate advisory service in Christchurch. This is currently staffed by two consultants, both ex-MBAs of Otago.

Christchurch is the largest city in the South Island, twice the size of Dunedin. Besides its University it also has in the nearby Lincoln College an institution offering courses mainly in the agricultural sciences. There is also a large and active Polytechnic, and this has been chosen as the base from which the Christchurch branch of the Business Development Centre operates.

During the first year of its existence, the Centre worked closely with the local branch of the Small Business Agency and concentrated its efforts mainly in the small company. During the second year of its activities the range of assignments has been broadened to include a social impact assessment (Lindop *et al*, 1980) and two assignments for larger companies, one in the retail and one in the clothing manufacturing sector.

The classic problem of New Zealand parochialism has been to a certain extent overcome by creating a Christchurch Business Development Centre and playing down the fact that the Christchurch service is administered from Dunedin. This balances the need for a team approach, which is now basic to the BDC service, with a unit which has to be seen as a Christchurch based operation so as to serve the local market.

The third programme in the Centre's service is based on experience in the north east of England where Alan Gibbs has pioneered the Enterprise Board system (Gibbs, 1977 and 1980). Following consultation with Alan at the Durham University Business School, a similar effort has been made in Ashburton in the South Island of New Zealand, with a three-man Enterprise Board encouraging new entrepreneurs to bring their ideas for analysis, subsequent sponsorship and general help.

Ashburton is a city of some 5000 people servicing the commercial requirements of the mid-Canterbury Plain. The town is vital and self-sufficient but, as in all similar places in New Zealand, local companies

181

find it difficult to expand their activities beyond the immediate market, for they then enter into competition with those who are placed near the main markets of Auckland and Wellington. The Enterprise Board has discovered, however, that many of the new ideas which have been turned to business propositions in Ashburton (and these include a solar water heater valve, and a tree seed export business) can be introduced to overseas markets at a profit to their organizers. The Enterprise Board members are in this instance a local engineer, a local accountant, and a local agricultural produce entrepreneur. All have run successful businesses and are able to turn their contacts in trade to advantage for others with different products and services.

It is hoped that, following the Ashburton experiment, a series of Enterprise Boards may be created in the South Island to help other rural and urban communities to develop new products. The Business Development Centre's role in the Enterprise Board system would continue to be the provision of a secretariat and the formulation of brief 'desk-top feasibility studies' for new ideas.

The fourth programme is in its embryonic phase, with one consultant identifying applied research worthy of commercial development (Rush, 1979); the model has been the development of a new heat pump in the University of Otago's Physics Department (Heat Pump Group, 1981). This is currently being given commercial tests by one of New Zealand's leading engineering companies and it is expected that marketing and production will follow.

Applied research, or technology transfer, is a well known graveyard for many reputations both in the banking and the commercial sectors. The formula appears always to rely on a spectacular success underpinning other less commercial ideas. The BDC has been lucky in that its first attempt has been the spectacular success based on two skilled members of the Physics Department, who have made a genuine breakthrough with commercial potential.

The role of the Centre has been to cement relationships with the companies who wish to develop the commercial potential of the heat pump, so as to allow the University to continue with basic research and the company to undertake practical research. Further developments may follow from the Medical School and from the Chemistry Department of the University.

The fifth programme has been developed from the skills of one of Otago's MBA class members, in Forestry. With a growing resource of timber available in the South Island over the 1980s and 1990s, the large number of owner-managed timber processing companies offer an excellent opportunity of co-ordinated overseas marketing of furniture, componentry, and semi-processed timber (Nicolson, 1979). This is, however, a competitive area requiring judgement and skill — and these are being fostered by a three-man team in the Business Development Centre. The prospect is of an export consortium being created, with in the earliest phases Government or Development Finance Corporation investment, to create designs appropriate to the American market for manufacture in New Zealand.

The sixth programme is named 'Impacts and Models'. Its origin lies in work undertaken in the Centre over the last two years which has led to the recruitment of two social scientists skilled in identifying the consequences of the economic rationalization and/or restructuring currently undertaken in the regional and national interest as Government economic policy (Houghton *et al*, 1981). Clearly the undesirable consequences of too rapid restructuring should be avoided, so work is commissioned of the impact and model staff to predict what may happen in particular industries or areas.

Problems and opportunities in the 1980s

The Business Development Centre rarely undertakes repeat performances of assignments, preferring to see the professions actively engaged along lines pioneered by the Centre. Indeed, feeding back solutions to often difficult development problems, to the students and to others interested in development issues, allows the lessons learnt in one instance to be applied quickly and effectively in others. However, this tends to reduce the repeat work which brings in regular fees and the Centre is thus often working at fever pitch for several months only to find work relatively short during the subsequent period. This has not proved a constraint on development — new projects always seem to materialize at the appropriate time.

But, as in many other institutions of a similar kind, the Business Development Centre staff, working long hours and often away from home, are treated with amused indifference by some members of the academic staff of the University. It takes time for the Centre's work to be understood by some; yet others are active in their promotion of the Centre's work and help in a wide variety of ways, in offering their consulting services or bringing good students to the Centre for project work, thereby benefiting local society with innovative solutions to problems.

Thus the close liaison between the Business Development Centre and the staff of the Master's Degree in Business Administration is advantageous to the University in providing practical case work for teaching, and to society in offering enthusiastic and innovative solutions to problems.

BASIC REFERENCE DATA (1980)

I. The host institution

Name: The University of Otago
Date founded: 1869
Internal organization: Typical of older redbrick English and Scottish universities.
 Eight faculties: Arts and Music, Science, Law, Medicine, Dentistry, Home Science,
 Commerce, Theology; subdivided into 57 departments
Number of academic staff: 662 full-time equivalent

Number of students: 7004 undergraduates and postgraduates on campus,
358 extramural

Catchment area: Students in general faculties come mainly from Otago and
Southland; students in professional training programmes come from anywhere
in NZ.

Designated responsibility for off-campus activities: Responsible for university
extension activities throughout Otago and Southland. .

Income: Approx $NZ 27 million per year over the period 1980-84, subject to
annual adjustments for inflation.

II. The innovation/system being studied

Name: Otago University Business Development Centre

Date founded: 1973

Nature: A business advisory service in an area of slow economic growth.
Complementary activities include research and management training. Special
attention has also been directed at resource development.

Internal organization: A multi-disciplinary group, working in *ad hoc* teams, under
a University-appointed Director. A branch in Christchurch operating in a similar
fashion, under local day-to-day control.

Number of academic staff: 8 full-time staff appointed by the University Staffing
Committee. Part-time associate staff taken on as required.

Number of non-academic staff: 1 full-time and 1 part-time secretary

Income: $NZ 285,000: 38 per cent from Government grant subject to annual
revision, 62 per cent from fees charged to clients

Income as proportion of institution's total income: 1 per cent

REFERENCES AND BIBLIOGRAPHY

Duffy, P and Higham, J R S (1975) *South Canterbury — A Regional Resources
Survey*, Business Development Centre, University of Otago [Other resource
surveys have been undertaken by the Business Development Centre in Mid-
Canterbury (1976) Marlborough (1976) and Otago (1977)]

Gibbs, A (1977 and 1980) *Enterprise North*, Durham University Business School,
Durham

Heat Pump Group (1981) *Interim Report on the Development and Demonstration
of a Hot Water Heat Pump* (Prepared for the NZ Energy Research and
Development Committee), Heat Pump Group, Physics Department, University
of Otago

Higham, J R S (1974) *Report on the Financial Feasibility of Providing an Economic
Supply of Gas to Oamaru Private and Commercial Consumers by Producing Gas
by both Normal and Metallurgical Coke Processes, either with the current or
with unexpanit capacity*, Business Development Centre, University of Otago

Higham, J R S and Rossell, P E (1974) *Commercial Feasibility Study of the
Establishment of a Salmon Hatchery on the Waitaki River*, Business Development
Centre, University of Otago

Houghton, R, Gold, U and Woodhead, M (1981) *The Social Impact of a Major
Business Collapse: Mosgiel Limited*, Business Development Centre, University
of Otago

Lindop, T W, Sanders, G and Woodhead, M (1980) *Ashburton Borough Council
Business and Employment Study, 1979-1980 Survey*, Business Development
Centre, University of Otago

Nicolson, D (1979) *Markets for Radiata Pine in the 1980s*, Business Development
Centre, University of Otago

Rush, B (1979) *Technology Transfer — Problems and Opportunities*, Business
Development Centre, University of Otago

Rush, B, Menzies, P and Higham, J R S (1977) *Indigenous Forestry in Western
Southland*, Business Development Centre, University of Otago

11. The community role of university teaching clinics

Daniel W McKerracher

Universities which have encouraged professional training schools to become incorporated into the university establishment have been engaged for many years in offering services to the public as a by-product of the practical elements of training involved. Trainee dentists and doctors, for example, work under supervision in a variety of clinics and teaching hospital environments.

Many kinds of clinics are operated as part of medical and allied health personnel training. However, existing hospitals and social or educational agencies are mainly used as temporary placements for university students, who are not therefore the main providers of the service. The agencies — not the university — retain direct responsibility for client welfare, though this distinction is blurred where staff are partly employed by university and partly by the service agency.

There are some arrangements in the USA, Canada and Australia where a non-medical university department is itself a major source of community service. The professional skills of staff members and their supervised students are made available to the public through course practicums and subjects such as counselling, remedial reading, behavioural analysis, individual assessment and so forth. The difficulties with this kind of service are the establishing of a flow of clients, the superficial skill levels and inexperience of the students, difficulties of timetabling coherent and regular services, and interruptions of services for long periods of time during university vacations. Is it, then, feasible for a university department with professional training interests to mount a viable programme which is based primarily upon university resources and premises, combines an adequate service to the public with satisfactory quality of academic preparation, and is operational for most of the year? The training scheme for educational psychologists described in this chapter sets out to meet these criteria.

The local setting

New Zealand universities are more closely integrated into the life of the community than is the case in many other countries. This is especially true of those situated in relatively small cities or towns of no more than 100,000 inhabitants where there is considerable communication between 'town and gown'. Otago University, in the city of Dunedin, plays a prominent part in local affairs and the daily newspaper frequently features the contributions made by departments and individual staff members.

A good example of direct service to the community is the leadership role which Otago and other NZ universities have fulfilled during the last 40 or 50 years in piloting guidance and counselling services in the major centres and laying the foundations for the official introduction of government-employed vocational guidance counsellors, school counsellors and psychological service personnel (Winterbourn, 1974).

At Otago University a lecturer in psychology, appointed jointly to the areas of philosophy and education, pioneered a part-time child guidance service in 1931 (Rosenberg, 1945). In 1936, an Education Department was formed in the University and gradually assumed total responsibility for providing clinical and educational services to the community in the absence of a state service. This work was continued and expanded during the term of office of Professor F W Mitchell (1945-70). The clinic catered mainly for school referrals but a substantial number also came from parents, doctors, the child welfare division, the vocational guidance centre, speech clinics and other social agencies. The major services provided were intellectual assessment and educational guidance for backward children and children with behaviour problems. They were aimed principally at the primary school level but included secondary school children too (Mitchell, 1954).

Interestingly, the Otago clinic did not go into demise after the introduction of a state psychological service in 1953, as did the clinics associated with the Victoria University of Wellington (which functioned from 1926 to 1942) and with the University of Canterbury (1923-46). The Otago clinic continued to function as an adjunct to the new state psychological service, providing, for a modest and waivable fee, an alternative source of guidance for schools, parents and agencies. Staff members interested and qualified to do so undertook much of this work themselves but some practicum classes of graduate and undergraduate students, particularly those studying educational assessment, also participated under supervision. There was a tendency for the emphasis to change from public service to teaching and research, so that the service became a by-product of student and staff academic objectives. With varying fortunes the clinic continued to function until the late 1960s, dealing on average with 40 to 50 cases per academic year.

The three major drawbacks with a clinic operated on this basis are:

☐ Inexperienced students studying one or two papers on behaviour modification or cognitive assessment amongst their options in a general degree are very limited in the kinds of service they can provide for the public. Without a thorough preparation in psychological theories or methods of research, and lacking the structure of a training programme with closely supervised practice, there are many dangers for the public in being assessed and advised by enthusiastic would-be psychometricians; or in being behaviourally influenced, during the course of class projects in applied

behavioural analysis, by inexpert practitioners acquiring skills
through trial and error.

☐ Academic supervisors who have not themselves trained or practised
as applied psychologists are not always well equipped to carry out
any more than a dilettante kind of public service. They are certainly
not capable of satisfactorily supervising students to do so where
the ratio of staff to students exceeds 1 : 10 and there is no extensive
support from experienced professionals in the field.

☐ Unless the host university of the clinic is prepared to recognize that
practical training of students through actual case work is a legitimate
form of university teaching whose time-consuming nature often
erodes the personal research time of participating staff members,
making it difficult for them to compete in volume of publications
with less engaged members of staff, then it is unrealistic to expect
them to become heavily involved in the manning of a continuous,
year-long, coherent range of clinical services without financial
inducements of some kind. The operation of a clinic implies an
organization that is designed to bring together skilled personnel
with those in need of their skills. This assumes availability of some
premises with reception facilities and certain back-up clerical staff
to ensure standardization of data collection and also synchronization
of appointments with use of equipment. The more numerous the
therapists and the more complex the treatment methods being used
(eg videocassette recording or biofeedback training), the more
essential does such organization become.

Following Mitchell's retirement, the education clinic was only partially
used and the feasibility of continuing to operate a clinic as an adjunct to
teaching without an associated training programme and a professional
qualification to accompany it, was being seriously questioned. At the same
time, the Psychology Department of the University had established a
postgraduate clinical training programme with a Diploma of Clinical
Psychology qualification, but had no clinical premises and insufficient
clinical staff. This resulted in the temporary suspension of its trainee
intake. Discussions between clinical representatives of both departments
explored the possibility of merging clinical resources and introducing a
joint training programme for a Diploma of Applied Psychology similar to
the development at Rutgers University, New Jersey. Unfortunately, a
mutually satisfactory formula could not be negotiated, largely due to the
fears of non-clinical staff members in both departments that such a
rationalization might lead to a reduction in the establishment of each
department through the more efficient use of existing staff complements.
Difficulties were also encountered in reaching agreement about
prerequisite education and psychology qualifications for eligibility to
enter the applied psychology programme. There was some opposition in
both departments to the basic concept of an applied psychology
programme and a preference for retaining separate identities for
educational and clinical psychologists. The merger failed to materialize,

although joint teaching in one paper, common to both departments, still survives as does a joint staff-student clinical seminar.

The Otago University Education Department was invited in 1976 by the NZ Department of Education to participate in the training of up to nine psychologists per year for the state education service, giving a much needed boost to the clinical psychology area in education. At the same time the clinical unit in the Psychology Department was granted an extra post making its continuation as a separate entity quite feasible. The mounting of the joint paper and seminar serves the interests of both departments and allows at least some minimal interaction between students of both programmes. But each programme maintains a separate clinic using different premises.

The question of the differing roles of clinical and educational psychologists (and, by implication, of justice, industrial and vocational guidance psychologists) was obviously a major stumbling block to the development of a joint clinic at Otago and to the co-ordination of both programmes. Ironically, the original clinic had been a joint one, more than 40 years before; whilst the idea of running education and psychology clinics that were able to collaborate closely had flourished 50 years earlier at Victoria. The issue is whether the training of applied psychologists can be organized around a nucleus of knowledge and skills common to all established branches and divisions of the profession; or whether each application of psychological techniques to specific environmental and social institutions necessitates a training that is unique for that purpose.

General aims: role definition and general training objectives of applied psychology programmes

There is a history of tension between educational and clinical psychology training programmes (Begin *et al*, 1967) which spans continents. In North America, school psychologists, trained in university education faculties and benefiting from the support of the education power structure, have a strong service orientation. Conversely, clinical psychologists trained in psychology departments have a vested interest in promoting an experimental approach rather than a service approach to the needs of clients. Indeed, in the applied sense, psychology is a relatively new professional discipline which developed rapidly in education, health and justice only after the second world war and there is evidence of conflicting ideas about the role it should play (Montgomery and Sunberg, 1977; Zangwill, 1966).

In a stimulating article entitled 'What should we do with applied psychology?' Pond (1977) drew an analogy between psychology and medicine. He pointed out that university training in general medicine provided a structure for uniting several disparate specialities into a common training experience. This led to a common degree, followed by registration and entry into a powerful profession, that maintained its *esprit de corps* despite numerous subdivisions of skills and interests. Pond argued that educational, clinical, occupational, forensic psychology and some elements of social work could be combined into the single concept of applied psychology. This would be akin to the concept of general medicine. The psycho-social skills for dealing with many problems of the deviant, the handicapped, and the disabled now exist. They could be taught within the framework of a similar professional degree.

There are two impediments to such a development: there is as yet no generic course comparable with the long medical programme; and there is an absence of properly organized psychological facilities that could combine training and service with academic education in a manner analogous to a teaching hospital. Pond suggested that the university would need to have, under the direct control of senior academic teachers, various organizations and services such as special prisons, schools for the maladjusted, rehabilitation units, family therapy centres and so on, before an applied psychology course could hope to compare with a medical course. Pond admitted that there never could be one building that was the equivalent of a teaching hospital. The nearest facsimile he could suggest was the cross-appointment of university staff with a number of agencies or organizations scattered throughout the community. Thus a professor of education might also be the headmaster of a school for maladjusted children; a professor of clinical psychology might also be director of a psychology department in a general hospital; or a professor of guidance and counselling might also be head of a marriage guidance bureau. Academics embroiled in the psycho-social sphere in this fashion would, of course, be subjected to social and professional restraints, but it was Pond's hope they could foster new ideas in service organizations through their influence as leaders.

The power of Pond's suggestions about applied psychology as the common denominator for psychology, education, counselling and social work, lies in its capacity to encompass the divergent views of academic psychologists. At one extreme are those who wish to remain experimental scientists; others are clinicians interested in social applications of experimental findings; and others still are more concerned with client welfare than with scientific rigour. He points out that if experimental biochemists, keener on molecules than on humans, can have a part to play in the training of general medical practitioners, then similar roles must await specialist interest groups in psychology, if they contribute to the general preparation and training of a new breed of applied psychologists.

The weakness in this proposition is that there is as yet no satisfactory university administrative establishment in which such a concept can flourish. To be accurate, the analogy would require a faculty of applied psychology to be compared with a faculty of medicine. However, faculties of behavioural sciences and social sciences do exist in some universities and they probably possess the best opportunity of developing Pond's model. Pond is concerned with the broad canvas of administrative arrangements for departmental co-operation and not the detail of the content of the curriculum, nor the emphasis given to different aspects of psychology. Quite rightly, he points out that wrangles over the content of medical curricula still occur, without the unity of training in that discipline being destroyed. Differences of opinion will probably always exist in psychology too, but provided that the training is founded on working with people in their real life situation, then academic curriculum differences are not so important.

Some published opinions about ideal directions for development in Australia and New Zealand are very similar to those described above. Keats (1976) contends that educational psychology is not a discipline distinct from other branches of psychology, but merely provides a different setting in which the same psychological principles may be applied. It is also essential that educational psychologists are able to co-operate and work with many other kinds of professional people when striving to resolve children's problems. Sheehan (1978) agrees with the tenor of Pond's suggestions that an autonomous profession must have an agreed area of basic abstract knowledge and theory, plus adequate field training and commitment to services in which can be practised the skills that society regards as being within the profession's exclusive competence.

Views in the recent literature (eg Raeburn, 1978) resemble some of the major guidelines for the future expressed earlier by Himmelweit (1963), Rawlings (1964) and Wright (1963). In the 15 intervening years there has not been much progress. The probable reasons for this, proposed by Montgomery and Sunberg (1977), are the inadequacies of pre- or in-service training, the lack of co-ordination over minimal qualification levels demanded for employment, and the lack of properly integrated programmes where academic knowledge and practical fieldwork are adequately combined.

The present functioning and suggestions for future development of educational psychology in New Zealand were outlined by Brown *et al* (1977). It never has been a service that was limited to schools as in North America, nor shackled to psychiatry as it was in Britain for many years. New Zealand educational psychologists have always operated from autonomous psychological centres with a great deal of independence. By contrast, clinical psychologists have been largely confined to hospitals and rehabilitation institutions until quite recently. Now there is a general trend towards developing community-based services (Bradshaw, 1975) with emphasis upon multi-disciplinary co-operation, following the recommendations of the Trethowan Committee (1977).

Reflecting upon the opinions reviewed above, a pattern of recommendations about training requirements can be discerned which is very similar from country to country, though the terminology sometimes differs. Ten of these priorities are presented here because they are the ones most relevant to the training programme to be described:

1. The ideal administrative structure to house psychology training programmes is a faculty of behavioural and social sciences,

allowing all facets of psychology, education and social work to be represented.

2. The training schemes should provide multi-disciplinary experiences and team approaches to social problems, to prevent professional rivalry and jockeying for power being encouraged.

3. Granted that there is adequate general education of a more academic type in the first years of applied psychology training, there should be concentration in the clinical years (4 and 5) upon practical work designed to prepare trainees with particular knowledge and skills that will be useful to them in dealing therapeutically with the public.

4. Trainee applied psychologists need to be provided with a wide spectrum of social and personal problems to deal with.

5. University academic appointees in psychology training programmes should be experienced in the clinical sense, in addition to their academic credentials. They must also be prepared to spend longer hours than their colleagues in personal contact with students for field supervision as well as academic purposes. (This extra demand is not always recognized by university administrators and can sometimes jeopardize promotion prospects.)

6. De-institutionalization of training preparation and a community-based service orientation are the major needs for future training programmes.

7. Training programmes have to be lengthened so that satisfactory periods of time are made available in which trainees can learn to apply the various skills necessary for competent professional practice through increased fieldwork.

8. Appropriate support funding for postgraduate training should be available on a competitive basis so that private means do not become a factor and selection of the most academically suitable candidates can be made.

9. Whilst there can never be uniform agreement about what constitutes the ideal model for applied psychology training, it is important that there be some unifying principles underlying each training programme.

10. Social and political pressures upon universities to become generally more accountable for the nature and standard of their teaching programmes are specifically applicable to professional training programmes.

Formative steps in establishing the Otago programme

In 1975, although clinical psychology training programmes existed in most of the New Zealand universities, only one educational psychology training programme was available — at Auckland. This had been initiated in the mid-1950s at the instigation of the NZ Department of Education in order to supply trained personnel for the state psychological service.

Joint consultations between university and state department representatives and joint interviewing of applicants, led to the selection of up to 11 teachers per year who were appointed for one year to probationary public service posts at salary levels commensurate with their teaching experience. At the end of this period they were viewed as holding public service posts for the next one or two years. The length of programme decided upon by the selection committee depended upon what was considered to be required to bring each of the trainees to the same uniform level of qualification. At the end of their training, graduates sought employment in the state psychological service on a competitive basis, by applying for vacant positions around the country. The two- or three-year training therefore included one or two postgraduate years at university and one internship year. Practicums of various kinds in connection with courses were offered during the university-based second year, but no regular clinical services from a university centre were offered to the public and the bulk of practical experience in the field occurred during internship placement. Field supervisors rather than university personnel therefore exerted the greatest influence upon trainees during this important aspect of their programme. A postgraduate Diploma of Educational Psychology was awarded at the end of the practical training year. This depended upon satisfactory completion of university examinations and presentation of written evidence of acceptable casework. The major drawbacks in this system were:

☐ University representatives were sometimes urged by state representatives to accept candidates who lacked sufficient academic qualifications in psychology or education, because of their strong teaching records or potential as desirable employees. Special arrangements were sometimes necessary to provide extra make-up courses in such cases. Funding of successful candidates was ultimately a state decision and considerable pressure upon selection could be exerted by simple refusal to fund candidates desired on academic grounds by university representatives, if they failed to meet state department criteria in terms of teaching experience. Clearly this arrangement militated against the concept of integrated applied psychology training, as it effectively cut out promising applicants with a strong psychology background but no teaching experience.

☐ As 11 places per year was the calculated number necessary to supply the state psychological service with replacements and allow for some growth, the onus was upon the university to accept a full quota each time. If the number was not reached by the end of the usual procedures of advertisement and selection, then late applicants were supplied by the state department until the quota was filled. The university trainers found it difficult to establish control over the internship training year, as the state department reserved the right to post trainees to whatever psychological service offices they wished for administrative, as distinct from training reasons. This sometimes resulted in trainees being exposed, during their crucial practical training year, to psychological models of functioning that were not always ideal and might even have been antithetical to what the university wished to be taught. In other cases, the office might be so distant from the university as to reduce to a minimum the contact between a trainee and his university supervisor.[1]

☐ A crucial problem existed over the fact that, after satisfactory completion of one year as a probationary public service appointee, the candidate automatically qualified as a permanent public servant even if he failed in succeeding years of the training programme. Because of the nature of the programme a successful pass at the end of the first year was wholly or largely based upon academic achievement, and not upon applied skills in the field. If a candidate did not show his personal ineptitude for psychological work until he undertook substantial clinical work with people, then it was too late to stop his being granted a permanent public service post even when the university judged him to be a failure. This meant that the state might have invested at least two years' salary to train an individual who then failed and for whom a post elsewhere had to be found. No definite provision was made for repeating a year of the training with funding, so considerable assurances were sought by the state department that every effort be made to ensure there were no failures. Clinical trainers were placed in the awkward situation of trying to satisfy two masters: the state, whose direct funding of trainees made the programme possible at the cost of some loss of academic autonomy for the university to make independent decisions; and the university, which still expected academic standards to be upheld.

In 1976, the NZ Department of Education decided upon a policy of expansion of the psychological service in response to the Educational Development Conference recommendations (Lawrence, 1974). Two further universities were invited to participate in the funded training schemes, Otago being one of them. The proposal was that each university should cater for up to nine trainees in each year of a three-year programme. It was requested that the first year could be waived, if proof were provided by the applicants that parallel courses to those prescribed for this pre-clinical year had already been successfully studied elsewhere at an equivalent level. The same conditions of selection and funding prevailed at Otago as have already been described for the Auckland course. The same advantages and disadvantages therefore still applied. One additional problem, common to all three training programmes, was that they were situated in liberal arts faculties. At Otago this meant that there was no precedent for housing a professional training programme with direct occupational objectives. Clearly the formulation of the administrative regulations necessary for the introduction of a new qualification was the foremost problem to be dealt with in that setting. Naturally this involved specifying the objectives of the programme before framing regulations that would allow them to become operable.

Objectives

A series of meetings was held involving all the staff of the Otago Education Department and agreement was reached that the Otago course would attempt to put into practice some of the ten suggestions for improving psychological training programmes outlined on pp. 190-91. It was also agreed that the programme should be based around the long-established education clinic which provided direct access to the public. The aims of the programme as it has now developed are to produce educational psychologists competent to work in a variety of areas and settings in co-operation with other disciplines and based upon an integrated educational and clinical training. There is an emphasis upon broad community orientation to strengthen the trend, already occurring within the NZ Psychological Service, of extending a psychologist's function beyond the limitations of a consultative role in connection with schools and school-related problems, to those of a community-based specialist able to assist in the introduction of innovative health and educational services to the community. The maintenance and improvement of existing case work methods are also aimed at through scientific practice and interdisciplinary collaboration.

Qualifications

No suitable qualification was available to supply a structure for the new three-year, practically oriented, professional psychology training programme at postgraduate level. At that time the Education Department contributed academic papers towards a general BA and a new BEd for primary teachers; a Postgraduate Diploma of Arts, which was regarded as the equivalent of master's papers, and an MA gained by papers and a thesis. On the grounds that the BEd was a professional degree, it was considered logical that a higher level professional degree (MEd) should be introduced to allow advanced professional studies to be offered to those with the basic qualifications. The Otago course is offered principally for applicants with a first degree which includes the study of both education and psychology to the second-year undergraduate level and a major in one of them. Previous professional experience, either in teaching or in some related discipline, is normally regarded as essential. A special series of papers, principally aimed at funded psychologists in training, is built into the Otago course. But some leeway is allowed for non-funded students to have limited entry, if the ceiling number of nine students is not reached. It was decided by the Department that a compulsory two-year MEd degree, oriented towards practical studies and applied professional activities, is a better basic qualification for an applied psychologist than a professional diploma with only an option to complete a master's thesis before or after finishing the diploma. In point of fact, it has been found recently (McKerracher and Walker, 1980) that 40 per cent of New Zealand educational psychologists in the psychological service do not have a master's degree and so obviously have not always exercised that option in the past.

The new two-year MEd is designed to allow an academic orientation towards baseline courses in the first year (*pre-clinical year*) albeit with considerable practical experience. It is followed by a second year (*professional year I*) which is mainly practical in emphasis, and in which students assume case work responsibilities under the direct supervision of university clinical staff. The equivalent of a full-time psychologist seconded from the local office of the state psychological service is made available by the NZ Department of Education to assist with the teaching and training.

The third year (*professional year II*) is regarded as the internship year and a Postgraduate Diploma of Educational Psychology has been introduced, necessitating the attendance of trainees at university for the equivalent of one day per week during their attachment to the state psychological service as assistant psychologists. This circumvented the problem of the university having difficulty in establishing appropriate supervision of internship training during this period. Additionally, an arrangement was agreed whereby half of the internship students are seconded full-time to the university for six months, to work in the department clinic and its associated community programmes. The other half are placed full-time in the state psychological service, with the exception of one day per week for joint seminars at university, attended by university and psychological service clinicians. At the end of six months, the latter trainees rotate from placement with the state psychological service to university clinic placement whilst those in the clinic move into psychological service.

Candidates who are not accepted into the diploma programme may graduate with an MEd on completion of research report requirements, but will not, by virtue of this degree alone, have achieved the qualifications necessary for employment or practice as psychologists in the view of Otago University: both qualifications are compulsory for this purpose.

Outline of course contents

Pre-clinical MEd papers: Four part 3 honours papers or their equivalents are regarded as compulsory from the five core elements which students must all possess before embarking upon professional years I and II. These papers are: advanced learning theory and behavioural analysis, advanced child development, research and evaluation methodology, individual assessment in education, exceptionality and psychopathology. In addition to the 12 hours of seminar time per week, a total of at least 200 field hours is expected during term time in connection with the core papers (ie about eight hours per week). The remainder of the time is for private study and project preparation.

Professional I papers: There are no options in this year; trainees take a paper on educational guidance and counselling, one on applied assessment and therapy, and one on remedial education. These papers are heavily practical and involve supervised case work in schools, hospitals, community agencies and in the clinical and special education unit of the University Education Department. Reading projects and other assignments are based around cases for which trainees share responsibility with staff supervisors.

The equivalent of one full day per week is devoted to academic work at university. Seminars are held in the morning, afternoon, and evening. The morning session involves the presentation of academic discussion material connected with the practice of psychology. The afternoon session concentrates upon case-oriented topics and specified case work issues. The evening session deals with the theory and practice of guidance and counselling.

The equivalent of two days per week is spent in field work placements. Students are allocated in groups of two or three to several agencies, in order to gain experience of working in co-operation with staff from other disciplines. The three major areas for practical applications involve:

☐ *Clinic-based activities:* trainees are attached for a period to the main clinic in the University Education Department. A variety of services are provided to parents and children who seek assistance directly, as well as to cases referred by other professional workers and agencies (eg the probation service, the Society for the Intellectually Handicapped).

☐ *School-based activities:* trainees are attached to the Dunedin school system to gain experience of working with children with special learning and behavioural difficulties who present primarily as referrals from schools.

☐ *Health and community-based activities:* trainees are attached for a period to a health-oriented system (adolescent adjustment unit at the local psychiatric teaching hospital) and to a multi-disciplinary community-oriented system (Mosgiel Health Centre).

Each group of trainees rotates through each of the three placement areas during a ten-month period.

Professional II papers: The third year of the course is an internship period which demands the equivalent of four full-time working days in the field, where supervised psychological practice is engaged in by trainees as they rotate through a variety of settings. Each trainee spends six months with the state psychological service and six months in the clinical and special education unit of the University Education Department.

Whilst working in the latter placement, services are extended by trainees to the three areas outlined in professional year I. Part of the responsibility undertaken during this period is to assist the course lecturers with supervision of professional I trainees as they carry out their practical case work duties. In some respects their function is analogous to that of a junior houseman in medicine.

Trainees are also required to take a psychological practice paper based upon the presentation of a folio of the best ten cases dealt with during the year and accompanied by appropriate evidence of literature consultation in connection with each case; plus a further paper which is in part designed by the trainees themselves in order to ensure that social, philosophical, ethical and practical issues which had not been covered satisfactorily or to sufficient depth in the other parts of the programme are given some coverage during the last year. An oral examination is held at the end of the year for the practical paper and this involves an external examiner from another university joining the internal examiners to cross-examine candidates on their work. A written examination is arranged for the other paper.

The Otago programme is primarily designed as a three-year programme because of the inter-linked nature of academic teaching and practice. It is difficult to cross-credit academic courses from other universities in the first year of the MEd because of the specific behavioural, counselling and assessment methodologies employed at Otago to prepare students for their practical application in the two professional training years that follow.

The teaching clinic

The administrative arrangements outlined above are a reflection of the consultant liaison developed over time between the education clinic and other clinics or agencies or university departments involved in provision of health and education services to the public. This includes cross-referral of cases, joint participation in therapeutic interventions, assistance in setting up individualized programmes for clients, and staff training exercises. Placement of trainees in the Psychiatric Department's children's unit facilitates observation of methodologies employed by the disciplines of psychiatry, social work and nursing in dealing with deeply disturbed children and adolescents.

The clinic also continues to provide direct autonomous services to the public by accepting requests from parents or schools or from university students for guidance and counselling. A nominal registration fee is charged on a sliding scale for this aspect of the work, to help support replenishment of clinic supplies, but is often waived entirely, depending on the social circumstances of the clients. The intention here is to provide an alternative source of support for those who, for one reason or another, are unable to obtain satisfaction from services provided by the state. A child advocacy approach is adopted, but this means that some situations are politically delicate to deal with, particularly where aggrieved parents feel dissatisfied with the handling of their child's problem by a school or by the state psychological service. The need to maintain harmonious relations with the school system and the psychological service is very important in co-operative training. Equally important, however, is the maintaining of a non-aligned viewpoint, with the child's welfare as the main focus. This is particularly helpful where parents feel intimidated by teachers or headmasters and unable to make a direct approach to the school. An outline of the clinic's function appears each year in the published directory of Otago social services. General guidelines dealing with situations of conflict between parents and schools, agreed to by the school inspectorate and by the local association of headmasters after a meeting with clinic representatives, have clarified the role to be played by university clinicians in these matters.

Development of special community services

University clinical teachers from the Education Department contributed heavily to the formation of two special innovative community service schemes. They helped to evolve the ideas and also to put them into practice. In the second year of the programme, a Family Health Counselling Service with a multi-disciplinary child and parent unit was introduced at a community health centre, staffed partly by Education Department staff and students. In the third year, an activity centre classroom was introduced into the University Education Department, for children threatened with expulsion from the school system whilst still under school-leaving age. A teacher and teaching aide were supplied by the NZ Department of Education and consultant support was made available from the clinical staff and trainees in the educational psychology training programme.

Community health centre project

A certain amount of opportunism is necessary in developing a training programme with community service links. It involves being able to locate appropriate openings for student placement, or to grasp the possibilities for relating existing services together in new patterns by taking advantage of local developments. The arrangements to provide students with specified experiences are therefore liable to be regional in flavour. But in spite of this, the principles, goals and objectives can be similar amongst programmes. The two major ingredients for success are: the ability to relate well to other disciplines, and placing the needs of the community being served on an equal footing with those of the trainees being trained.

A practical orientation makes it more difficult to plan a tidy academic coverage of material to be learned in a logically consistent series of topics. What is lost in terms of cognitive precision is, however, more than compensated for by increased motivation in the students. They are able to improve their professional skills through actual practice and arrange their reading and seminars around the series of nuclei provided by the different cases with which they have to cope as they occur. It has been found most useful to have the trainees build up a clinic library of articles and books on various intervention strategies for problems with which they have to cope. This ensures an expanding and continually updated reference resource for teachers and learners alike.

The Otago programme is fortunate in that a full array of health and education services is available within a relatively confined area in the city of Dunedin. However, none of the existing agencies have organizational structures that encourage multi-disciplinary interaction where each professional discipline can be on an equal footing. As in most traditional professional settings, the team members tend to work alongside each other rather than with each other and a certain amount of interdisciplinary rivalry seems inevitable. However, in 1976 the state health department floated a national family health counselling scheme and allocated funds to the main centres throughout the country with the request that each region find its own means of evolving a new community service for families (Hospitals Amendment Act, 1976, clause 6). At Mosgiel, a dormitory town to Dunedin, situated some ten miles south of it and with a population of approximately 9000, a family health counsellor was appointed to the local health centre by the Otago hospital board with a mandate to develop a co-ordinated service for that community. The health centre had been created some years previously by all of the local doctors banding together to centralize their practices in one building. A full range of medical support services was added over the years. Adjacent to this health centre is a rural general hospital with a maternity unit, a pharmacy and a two-storied nurses' residence that was not much used. The Department of Psychological Medicine (ie psychiatry) had supplied adult and child consultants on a weekly basis for some time and offered extended outpatient or institutional care from its Dunedin base. It was found that Mosgiel residents were reluctant to make the journey into Dunedin for such help because of lack of adequate public transport facilities. The way was clear to develop a more readily accessible counselling service in Mosgiel itself.

Good relations had been established between the University Departments of Psychological Medicine and Education. This made it easy to discuss the possibilities of establishing a broad-based counselling unit with the family health counsellor at Mosgiel and link her needs for skilled personnel to the training needs of both departments.

One of the difficulties to be overcome was associated with the absence of a full-time school psychologist in the district. Only 20 per cent of one staff member's time was available for the Mosgiel area by Dunedin office. The result of this appeared to be that many parents consulted their general medical practitioner (GP) about their children's school difficulties. This is often the pattern in New Zealand even when psychological help is available. Some parents seem to feel threatened by schools and headmasters when there is no demonstrable reason for this. They apparently find it easier to consult their GP. The drawback of this latter arrangement is that when health professionals, such as medical social workers, school health nurses or even family counsellors attempt to intervene in schools about education-related topics at the request of the GP, there is some reservation on the part of teachers about this course of action being appropriate. It had been found at Mosgiel that the school medical officer was the most acceptable general figure to represent the welfare of the child, both in health and in education matters, but there was a lack of sufficiently available psychological expertise to back up this liaison function of the medical officer.

What was needed was a family counselling service, mutually acceptable to both schools and families, that could be accessed through education or health initiated referral routes and which fulfilled a child advocacy role. A school and family care unit, conceptually a part of the family health counselling service, seemed to be the most obvious means of meeting this need. Accordingly, discussions were held with the GPs and paramedical staff at the health centre; then with the state psychological service seniors in Dunedin, the school medical officer for the district and the headmasters of all the schools in the town. Eventually, a joint proposal was prepared by the family health counsellor and the consultants representing the University Departments of Eduction and Psychological Medicine. It was submitted to the hospital board and approved on a trial basis. It included gaining access to the bottom floor of the nurses' residence so that sufficient office and clerical space was obtained.

The growth of this aspect of the programme has been very satisfying. Approximately 150 cases are seen each year in the Education Department clinic and 50 per year at the Mosgiel family unit. A comparison of the sources of referral of education teaching clinic cases with those of family health counselling cases in the new service centre shows that while the latter encourages direct parental approaches (70 per cent) more frequently than agency referrals (30 per cent), the reverse is true of the clinical and special education unit (32 per cent versus 68 per cent). The age range in both cases is very similar, with no mean differences between the samples (general mean = 9 years; standard deviation = 4.5 years). In both instances, the ratio of boys to girls was between three and four to one, supporting the well documented fact that boys show more adjustment difficulties requiring intervention than girls.

Activity centre classroom

In 1979, the entire Education Department at Otago University moved into a newly completed building. A specially planned clinical section provided ample space for the programme. A reception area, more interview rooms with observation facilities, a playroom, an audiometric soundproofed room, an electrically shielded room for biofeedback apparatus and a classroom designed for emotionally disturbed children were all incorporated. The classroom had been planned some years previously with the prospect that a special class might be operated there in co-operation with the school system, as a demonstration teaching unit. However, the remedial emphasis in the intervening years swung away from the segregation of children with special needs into special classrooms. The more recent trend is a concentration upon the mainstreaming of such children, with the object of helping them to cope with the regular school system rather than extracting them from it. For a time it seemed as if the departmental classroom complete with time out room, curriculum room and learning carrels would not be used as planned. However, in response to an upsurge in unruly behaviour in the public school system, the NZ Department of Education had recently instituted several activity centres throughout the country. These were housed in special buildings, often older houses converted, or prefabricated structures, to which children under the threat of expulsion from the normal school system but still under school-leaving age were assigned, together with specialist teachers, in an effort to salvage something from their history of educational failure. Dunedin had not been included in this scheme at the time, although similar problems existed there as elsewhere.

After consultation amongst clinical representatives, the district senior psychologist and the senior inspectorate, a scheme was proposed to the NZ Department of Education to use some of the space in the university clinic area as an activity centre classroom. A specialist teacher and teaching aide dealing with up to ten children were to be appointed and paid for by the NZ Department of Education. Support was to be given to this class by a clinic consultant supervising senior trainees in the last year of their training. Further help was to be made available by involving other students in the production of programmed curriculum materials for use with departmental teaching machines and an APPLE microcomputer. The programme came into being in 1980 and has just completed its first year of operation (Dolby, 1981). Part of the project involves evaluation of the classroom's effectiveness and annual reviews will be conducted both by clinical university personnel and by the school inspectorate. Eight children have been admitted to the activity centre in the first year. They were added gradually so that the teacher had the opportunity to organize his programme and his curriculum resources. In a series of meetings with headmasters, it was repeatedly stressed that all existing channels of attempting to cope with the disruptive behaviour of the children in question should be exhausted before the possibility of their being candidates for the activity centre was considered. When principals decide that this point has been reached, they refer prospective candidates to a small admissions committee comprising the unit's teacher, a secondary school inspector, a senior educational psychologist and a senior university educational psychologist. This committee considers the pupil's needs and decides whether they can be met within the unit taking into account the composition of the group at that time. To facilitate prompt admissions, principals are issued with referral forms indicating the kinds of information the committee requires. A psychological assessment is usually undertaken by the state psychological service and the unit teacher interviews the pupil and the parents. No child can be admitted without parental permission. Since places are very limited, priority is given to pupils under the age of 15 years (school-leaving age in New Zealand) but any pupil may be considered and may be accepted if circumstances warrant it.

No doubt some pupils will complete their secondary education within the unit and enter the workforce either directly or through the Rehabilitation League. But it is hoped that others will be able to return to secondary school. With this in mind, liaison is maintained with the referring school to keep open this possibility. The orientation of the classroom is towards individualization of learning and considerable use is made of university resources such as the gymnasium in the School of Physical Education, visits to medical lectures in physiology and anatomy, use of university museums and of films from the Audiovisual Learning Centre and access to the Education Department's own library of special educational materials.

On admission to the unit the problems presented by the pupil are documented and realistic goals are established in consultation with the pupil himself. Initially these are short-term goals which are reviewed in the light of progress achieved or of difficulties encountered. It is essential that the pupil be encouraged to take a growing responsibility for his own programme. These programmes are related to the ability, attainments and social skill levels of the pupils. In cases of limited ability and attainment a very practical course with an employment orientation and with work experience is arranged. Basic reading and number skills are incorporated, capitalizing on areas of concern for young people, such as budgeting, hire purchase, the road code, survival skills, diet and meal preparation etc. Social skills training is included in the programme, stressing appropriate behaviours in a variety of social situations such as job interviews, taking meals in restaurants, requesting information, purchase of goods in shops, etc. For other pupils an emphasis on effective work habits is more important. Here individual tutoring to encourage mastery of material and the filling in of gaps in basic knowledge is considered essential.

Before a return to the school system is considered, regular reports and programmes have to be made available to the teachers concerned. If the next step is into the community, then the support of the Rehabilitation League is requested. In many cases work experience will have been provided by the League during the period the individual has spent in the unit. Liaison with the Departments of Social Welfare, Labour and the After Care Committee are important in ensuring continuity of help for young people when they leave the unit. It is too soon to say how successful this enterprise will be, but it is an interesting development within a university department and says much for the forbearance of members of staff in other departments that they have tolerated within their midst young individuals with such anti-social capabilities.

Evaluation procedures

In a wide ranging community undertaking of the kind described in this chapter, it is obvious that a complex evaluation problem exists because there are so many parameters to take into account. As the first group of trainees has just completed its final year, it is difficult as yet to say what the long term effects of the programme will be upon each of them, in terms of influencing their job attitudes. However, as a first step, a national survey of psychologists has been carried out (McKerracher and Walker, 1980) in which data was collected about how currently employed psychologists in health, education and justice are spending their time and ordering their employment priorities. It is planned to contact trainees emerging from the Otago programme and other programmes at yearly intervals for their first two years in employment and thereafter at three-yearly intervals. This will enable a close look to be taken at the patterns of professional style which are shown by each wave of new graduates, together with an examination of what happens to professional style with the passage of time and the influence of colleagues. Five-yearly random samples of pyschologists in service prior to the commencement date of this study will also be taken, in order to study differences between those emerging from the new training programme and those in the field before the programme started.

Shorter term aspects of evaluation involve judgement of specific elements within the programme rather than its total impact. For example, course evaluations of the usual kind relating to knowledge standards, relevance, interest, organizational structure and administration, teaching style, clinical competence of teachers and efficiency of communication of information, have all been gathered for each of the three years that the programme has been in operation. All the reports have been placed in sealed envelopes at the end of each year. This is to ensure that there is no possibility of frank replies by students having any deleterious influence upon teachers' grading of their practical performance. Only after final graduation of each cohort will the course evaluations be analysed. All that can be said at this point is that the students seem very satisfied: there are relatively few complaints; *esprit de corps* seems high and spontaneous feedback from other quarters (eg secretaries, teachers with whom students have spoken, students outside the programme etc) suggests that the trainees are proud of being an integral part of the programme and aware of the social responsibilities placed on them by the nature of their training.

Another specific form of assessment involves the collection of information from field supervisors and university supervisors about the professional competence of each student displayed throughout the year. This information is collated and made available to trainees at three-monthly intervals throughout the year so that relatively swift reinforcement of strengths and more immediate corrective measures for weaknesses can be applied. One major drawback of this approach appears to be that the consistent emphasis on evaluation and the perceived threat that they may not be considered of sufficient quality to merit gaining entry to the professional diploma programme creates considerable tension in the MEd students and saps their feelings of security and self-confidence. Coping with this problem will be a challenge. Some means of retaining the rigour of the assessment system but rendering it more humane, has to be found.

Distinct from the evaluation of trainees and the practical teaching programme itself, is the evaluation of projects within the programme, such as the family health counselling unit or the activity centre classroom. In both cases, social and personal identification data are being systematically collected. These allow a yearly statement to be issued about numbers, age range, sex distribution, nature of referral, outline of intervention strategies, outcome using academic data, behavioural observation data, client reports, teacher reports, and ratings and reports by parents or significant others. So far, the results for the family counselling unit indicate a clinical success rate over a one-year follow-up period of around 68 per cent. The remainder either showed little change or broke contact. For those who showed improvement, the success was not uniform in all aspects of the problem, but sufficient progress had been made to allow classification as a success. Where the profile of improvements was extremely inconsistent (eg marked improvement in school but deterioration at home) the case was not considered eligible for inclusion as a success. For the activity centre classroom, using similar criteria, the success rate during the first year of operation was 45 per cent. Although at face value this may seem a modest figure, nearly at the chance level of probability, it must be remembered in Bayesian terms that the base rate prediction of outcome for this highly disturbed group of children was 100 per cent failure, since all of them would have been expelled from the school system if they had not been referred to the activity centre classroom. Nevertheless, it is hoped that a higher success rate will be achieved once the curricula and personal conduct programmes are fully operational. Recently two microcomputers have been installed in the Education Department at Otago University. As part of their function, it is planned to use them as computer-assisted learning devices for drill and practice in arithmetic, remedial spelling and reading exercises and also as reinforcers through the medium of games such as 'space invaders' when playing time can be purchased with tokens earned in the classroom for good behaviour. Furthermore, by harnessing the practicum course work of an undergraduate class studying instructional strategies to the work of the special class, it is anticipated that a library of educational, remedial and games materials will eventually be assembled by lecturers and students in liaison with the class teacher.

Reviewing what has been accomplished in the first three years of the programme against the ten general objectives listed on pp. 190-91, the following tentative conclusions about the general objectives of the programme can be reached.

1. The programme is situated in a liberal arts faculty, which has posed some difficulties in having professional course requirements tailored to an academic system that is not designed to accommodate them. Fortunately, the flexibility of the Otago Arts Faculty in relaxing academic restrictions (eg the percentage of a final mark that can be supplied by practical assignments) made it possible to mount the programme without too many problems.
2. The programme is wholly committed to the concept of multi-disciplinary co-operation and provides ample opportunity for

trainees to learn to work amicably with professionals from other disciplines as proposed.

3. The structure of the qualification system allows for a three- or four-year bachelor's degree comprising specified minimal amounts of general psychology. This is followed by a two-year MEd which includes one mainly practical year. A third postgraduate year leading to a Postgraduate Diploma in Educational Psychology is wholly committed to supervised practical work. The propositions concerning increased proportions of practical work in the training of psychologists are therefore satisfied.

4. A multiplicity of training outlets has certainly been established, thus enabling a variety of contacts to be made with different individual, social and emotional problems. Whether this is as wholly satisfactory as the teaching hospital is in medicine, is difficult to say. There has been no opportunity to attempt to put into practice Pond's (1977) scheme for appointments being split between university and institutions or agencies. The nearest approach to this is the arrangement where an educational consultant from the university clinic works voluntarily in the family health counselling clinic at Mosgiel, discharging hospital board responsibilities in addition to his university duties. This occurs at times of the year when trainees are on vacation but a service has to be maintained. Such continuity is essential in maintaining good relations with agency staff and with members of the public. Regularization of this interim arrangement will have to occur after the honeymoon period of establishing the community link is over. One possibility is that a consultation fee could be paid to the university by the hospital board as a means of purchasing staff time and releasing the teacher from his other university responsibilities without disturbing the security or the privileges of his university appointment.

5. The clinical teachers in the programme are enthusiastically committed to an approach that involves supervision of trainees in their work with clients and other agencies. All of the university teachers are trained clinical or educational psychologists. Practical competence in case work is not therefore an issue. However, the long hours of teaching, supervising and giving advice on research theses, leave little time to the teachers for professional reading and personal research. There is no special consideration given within an arts faculty to the demands that clinical teachers have to meet. Consequently promotion is still heavily influenced by publication record and could make it difficult for younger members of staff seeking advancement. A choice may eventually have to be made between dedication to the programme and furthering one's personal career.

6. Orientation towards developing community-based services, contribution to innovative service schemes and the building of a

new psychological-clinical service area in the University Education Department all ensure that the de-institutionalization of objectives in this category has been vigorously attempted.

7. The length of the programme is six or seven years (three plus three or four plus three) depending on whether the bachelor's degree was at ordinary or honours level. Two clinical practice years are included. It therefore satisfies suggestions about duration in the literature.

8. The generous funding of trainees by the NZ Department of Education, the careful selection procedures, the emphasis on practical skill development and competent professional practice during the programme, and not on academic attainment alone, all follow the guidelines of the eighth objective.

9. The need for a model of professional conduct based on congruent theoretical principles is met to some extent by the focus upon behavioural analysis and learning theory in the core papers within the MEd. A scientific practitioner approach is applied to the major part of the casework, but in the practicum for the counselling paper and in the family health counselling unit there are too many uncontrollable variables for this model always to be applicable. A directive general counselling model is therefore also used. In view of the fact that over 90 per cent of all practising New Zealand psychologists report using general counselling as their most commonly used clinical method (McKerracher and Walker, 1980) this departure from the central model was not considered inappropriate, particularly as seminars are regularly held to discuss the strengths and weaknesses of the scientific model compared with those of other methodological models in the diploma year.

10. The last suggestion selected from the literature review pertains to the need to evaluate the impact of the training programme upon the community as well as upon the trainees. The efforts made in this direction have been fully described in the preceding section.

Overall, two major failures have to be admitted:

☐ Inability to mount a joint training programme in collaboration with the Psychology Department or to have a Diploma of Applied Psychology introduced as the qualification of choice.

☐ Inability to maintain control over trainee intake numbers. Because of recent national economic restraints, austerity measures of various kinds have had to be introduced by Treasury. One of those measures involved the number of funded psychologists in training being reduced from a national level of 27 per year to 11 per year. For Otago University this has meant a drop in numbers from nine to four per year. No doubt the programme will survive, but its ability to continue to serve a broad array of social agencies, institutions and members of the public is jeopardized now by lack of manpower and may lead to a constriction of functions in some areas in order to support continuation in others.

Generalization

No rigid translation of any programme from one context to another is possible. Adaptation to the limitations and advantages of each local region has to occur before a programme can develop its own identity. Attention to the ten general directives and to some of the innovative concepts discussed in this chapter should, however, increase the likelihood that highly motivated applied psychologists with a practical, inventive problem-solving approach to their work will emerge from programmes of similar type.

BASIC REFERENCE DATA (1980)

IA. The host institution

Name: The University of Otago
Date founded: 1869
Internal organization: Typical of older red-brick English and Scottish universities.
   Eight faculties: Arts and Music, Science, Law, Medicine, Dentistry, Home Science,
   Commerce, Theology; subdivided into 57 departments.
Number of academic staff: 662 full-time equivalent
Number of students: 7004 undergraduates and postgraduates on campus;
   358 extramural
Catchment area: Students in general faculties come mainly from Otago and
   Southland; students in professional training programmes come from anywhere
   in NZ.
Designated responsibility for off-campus activities: Responsible for university
   extension activities throughout Otago and Southland
Income: Approx $NZ 27 million per year over the period 1980-84, subject to annual
   adjustments for inflation

1B. The host department

Name: Department of Education
Date founded: 1936
Internal organization: Three interest areas: psychology, sociology, and
   history/philosophy of education; but no formal divisions.
Number of academic staff: 16
Number of students: Approx 1000 undergraduates study for degree and diploma
   papers offered by the Department. Approx 30 full-time equivalent students
   are enrolled for postgraduate qualifications of various kinds; about a third of
   these are in the psychology training programme.

II. The innovation/system being studied

Name: Education Department Clinical and Special Services Unit
Date founded: Original clinic founded 1932; new unit formed 1976.
Nature: Focus for professional training programmes in educational psychology and
   special education and for pioneering alternative methods of child and family
   therapy delivery.
Internal organization: Three sections: central education department clinic, satellite
   family health counselling unit, activity centre classroom.
Number of academic staff: Five full-time equivalent staff, plus 0.6 equivalent for
   field supervisors paid by state.

Number of non-academic staff: 1 full-time equivalent
Income: No independent allocation but approximately 1/6 of the Education
Department's recurring grant and 1/3 of the non-recurring grant is expended
on the clinic (approximately $NZ 2000) plus $NZ 200 in annual registrations,
in addition to staff salaries.
Income as proportion of institution's total income: 0.5 per cent

NOTE

1. The recent appointment of a liaison officer by the NZ Department of Education
for the purpose of integrating university and psychological service requirements
during internship has vastly improved this arrangement. Auckland is now in an
enviable position in this respect, compared with the unofficial liaison situation
persisting at Otago.

REFERENCES AND BIBLIOGRAPHY

Begin, A E, Garfield, S L and Thompson, A S (1967) The Chicago Conference on
Clinical Training and Clinical Psychology at Teacher College, *American
Psychologist*, 22(1), 307-16

Bradshaw, P W (1975) Lessening the marital bonds of clinical psychology:
psychologists in the general hospital, *New Zealand Psychologist*, 4(1), 4-8

Brown, D F, Standring, D E and Jones, B F (1977) *The Psychological Service:
A Critical Appraisal of its Present Functioning and Future Development*, 22 pp,
Position paper presented to Conference on Future Development of the
Psychological Service, Wellington

Dolby, D (1981) *The Dunedin Activity Centre: An Experiment in Dealing with
Difficult and Maladjusted Teenagers*, 16 pp, New Zealand College of Education,
Dunedin

Himmelweit, H (1963) A social psychologist's view of the school psychological
service of the future, *Bulletin British Psychological Society*, 16(52), 16-24

Keats, D M (1976) Psychologists in education, *Australian Psychologist*, 11(1), 83-93

Lawrence, P J (Chairman) (1974) *Improving Learning and Teaching*, 277 pp, Report
of the Working Party on Improving Learning and Teaching, Department of
Education, Wellington

McKerracher, D W and Walker, F A (1980) *Applied Psychologists in New Zealand:
Employment Characteristics, Qualifications and Training*, 233 pp, Research
Survey Report for Department of Education, Wellington

Mitchell, F W (1954) A note on the University of Otago Child Guidance Clinic,
Australian Journal of Psychology, 6(1), 15-17

Montgomery, R B and Sunberg, N D (1977) Current and alternative training models
in clinical psychology, *Australian Psychologist*, 12(1), 95-102

Pond, D A (1977) What should we do with Applied Psychology? *Bulletin British
Psychological Society*, 30(13), 13-14

Raeburn, J (1978) Clinical psychology versus the people: a community psychology
perspective, *New Zealand Psychologist*, 7(2), 41-5

Rawlings, G (1964) The school psychological service – final comments, *Bulletin
British Psychological Society*, 17(54), 1-5

Rosenberg, A (1945) *Some Aspects of Psychological Work in Vocational Guidance
in Relation to Child Guidance with Specific Reference to New Zealand*, 125 pp,
MA thesis, Victoria University, Wellington

Sheehan, P W (1978) Psychology as a profession and the Australian Psychological
Society, *Australian Psychologist*, 13(3), 323-30

Trethowan, W H (1977) *The Role of Psychologists in the Health Service*, 33 pp,
HMSO, London

Winterbourn, R (1974) *Guidance Services in New Zealand Education*, 163 pp,
New Zealand Council for Educational Research, Wellington

Wright, H J (1963) The School Psychological Service, *Bulletin British Psychological Society*, 16(50), 2-8

Zangwill, O L (1966) In defence of clinical psychology, *Bulletin British Psychological Society*, 19(64), 13-21

Part 5:
The performing arts – a synthesis of university/community expertise

12. Town with gown: the York Cycle of Mystery Plays at Leeds

Jane Oakshott and Richard Rastall[1]

It is clearly important that universities mix with the community at large, and the subject of this chapter, the University of Leeds, has a tradition of such involvement. From the time of its foundation in 1874 as the Yorkshire College of Science it has had close links particularly with the textile industry; and in the 1950s the University chose to consolidate its community links physically, by developing the existing site near the city centre rather than moving to a new campus in the open countryside to the north of the city.

At the same time as turning to the community, however, the universities must preserve their intellectual integrity, for they would otherwise be of use neither to their members nor to the community as a whole. The universities must lead, not follow, the community that they serve. This leadership largely stems from the research that the universities undertake and which, in its broadest sense, is one of the chief contributions made by universities to society.

It was with these two principles in mind that the production of the York Cycle of Mystery Plays, now known as the Leeds Experiment, came into being at the University of Leeds in 1975.

The performing arts are by their very nature an obvious area of communication between 'town and gown'. Drama and music in particular are good public relations subjects in that most performances are open to the public, whose presence is thus welcome in the university on a regular basis: indeed, university productions and concerts are often a major part of a town's facilities in the performing arts. Moreover, in drama especially, university facilities are frequently used to present works that would not be viable as a commercial enterprise: this may be for instance because they cater for a minority interest, or require too large a cast or complicated scenery. (Student casts do not demand payment and reasonable costs of scenery can be covered in a teaching budget.) Occasionally, instead of the public being invited into the university, productions may be toured to extra-university sites. The Bristol University Drama Department's performance in Cornwall of the Cornish *Ordinalia* (1969) is a rather special example of this, and the frequent tours in Yorkshire and elsewhere by the Leeds University Workshop Theatre are another instance.

In such cases as these, however, members of the public attend in a purely passive role, and the object is entertainment in its widest sense. While entertainment may include some educational purpose, it is seldom connected with the distinguishing concern of a university — research.

And rare indeed are occasions when the public is invited into the university on equal terms to participate actively in a research project.

What has become known as the Leeds Experiment was just such an occasion. In the performance of the York Cycle of Mystery Plays at Leeds University, 17-18 May 1975, members of the community were involved as participants as well as audience, and moreover the event was a research project of a most unusual kind. For the first time in 400 years the plays were produced processionally on pageant wagons — that is, in the performing mode for which they were originally intended. The production was an important innovation in terms of theatre history: but our present interest in it is as an occasion on which the public was invited to take part in a research project not as guinea pigs but as contributors.

The English mystery plays and the genesis of the Leeds Experiment

The mystery plays were a type of large-scale religious drama that flourished in England for over two centuries, from the middle of the fourteenth century to the second half of the sixteenth. Produced by the trade guilds and acted mainly by the townspeople, the mystery plays were civic drama which was 'the most truly popular drama England has ever known' (Kolve, 1966).

Only four English mystery cycles survive — the York, Chester, Wakefield[2] and N-Town plays.[3] The subject treated is on a large scale — the biblical story from the Creation of Man to the Last Judgement — and the original productions were on a scale to match: the York Cycle, which is the best documented, is made up of 48 separate plays, varying in length from five to 30 minutes and taking, in all, 17 hours to perform. Each of the 48 playlets was produced by a separate trade guild. Many guilds took an appropriate part of the Bible story: for instance, the Shipwrights performed the *Building of Noah's Ark*, the Nailmakers played the *Crucifixion*, and the Bakers took the *Last Supper* (as they did also in Chester).

As far as we can tell from the York records (Johnston and Rogerson, 1979) each guild played on its own special pageant wagon drawn through the streets to as many as 12 playing places or 'stations' set along a procession route. The audience in the streets would be entirely a standing one; the only seats were at the windows of nearby houses rented out for the occasion. The streets would be packed with spectators, food sellers, pickpockets and the processing actors and guildsmen. The atmosphere was one of festivity, a civic and religious celebration in one magnificent spectacle of which there is no single equivalent in twentieth-century England.

Modern performances of the plays have made them into a very different sort of event, the pattern for the next 30 years being set in 1951 by E Martin Browne's revival of the York Cycle.[4] Dr Browne did not aim to recreate the original setting nor to present an 'authentic' performance. Indeed he deliberately turned his back on what was known of the methods used at York in the fifteenth and sixteenth centuries. By placing the drama on one large fixed stage, in a statuesque mode of performance with a single cast and seated audience, he completely changed the relationships between text, actors and audience; and by reducing a full day's drama to a mere three hours he lost the enormous vitality and dramatic scope of the cycle as originally conceived. It would, of course, be quite unjust to Dr Browne to criticize him for his 1951 production on these grounds. At that time an 'authentic' performance would have been impossible for a variety of reasons, and his revival of a cycle play in any form was a visionary's act of faith from which all later productions took their inspiration. The pity is that at York (and at Chester where a similar condensed version is performed) no attempt has been made to follow that vision further by substituting the real thing for the second best.

The problems of large-scale authentic production are not confined to the cycle plays, however, but apply to other medieval dramas. Historically, an important turning-point came in 1969 with the performance of the Cornish *Ordinalia*.[5] Different as it was from a cycle play, this performance showed that an expert production that attempted to recreate medieval drama on its own terms could be a useful and proper tool for research as well as a dramatic success.

The next step was clearly to mount a production of a cycle play on wagons in such a way as to stand a good chance of answering some of the questions that were still merely (though rightly) points of academic argument. My production of the York Cycle at Leeds in the summer of 1975 was this next step. It aimed to present the plays using as far as possible the organization and staging techniques of medieval York — pageant wagons, 'stations', a separate acting group for each play and so on.[6] The actors would thus have to adapt their methods and acting style to the conditions of outdoor performance, using a very restricted stage and only such properties and scenery as could be carried (on or off the wagons) in procession. More important, perhaps, they would be faced with standing audiences[7] who could choose their distance from the actor and could come and go freely throughout the performance.

One of the important points of the experiment was to provide centrally the medieval setting and other external features, thus giving the individual producers a unified basis on which to work. The results of their practical approach to the plays, especially that of the experienced producers, was certainly enlightening on matters that could not be learned by armchair assessment of references in records and guild accounts.

The initiative for such a production would hardly come from the civic community itself: indeed, the examples of York and Chester show a quite understandable but total failure in this respect. The initial impetus was inevitably an academic one, for it was only among a few medieval specialists that the true nature of medieval cycle plays was recognized and appreciated. Since a university is also one of the few types of institution with the resources to organize and mount such an event, it is no surprise that Leeds University should provide both the intellectual impetus and the practical resources necessary. In the event, I first proposed the idea at the informal weekly meeting of the six drama specialists in the Graduate Centre for Medieval Studies[8] in which I was then a postgraduate student. The proposal met with much active enthusiasm and the Centre, having approached the University officially on my behalf, then remained the 'home base' for the production throughout. As it happened, the University was about to celebrate its centenary: and although the date proposed for the plays was rather later than the main celebrations, the University decided to accept the plays as the final item in the centenary programme and to support the venture accordingly.

It must be clear, however, that there are certain vital resources that the University could not provide. A sufficient number of competent, experienced actors was one; a body of producers capable of undertaking a cycle was another and much more important one. The first touchstone for success in the Leeds Experiment was therefore bound to be the matter of collaboration with non-university people. Would they join in? Would they remain? And would they, in the end, find it a worthwhile experience?

In such a project it is vital to approach the plays with humility. If one adopts a patronizing attitude to the medieval playwrights, the actors, or their methods, the project will fail, and rightly so. Any theatre historian will understand this, but it is not an easy matter to persuade the man in the street that a completely unfamiliar art-form is worth presenting in its own terms as a way to further understanding. Nevertheless it was necessary for me, a medieval specialist, to introduce medieval drama of this type to non-academics, and to do it successfully, before the project could feel the benefit of the non-academics' expertise. It is difficult to meet as equals when the areas of competence overlap so little: yet that is what had to be done.

The context of the Leeds Experiment

The University of Leeds has a government much like that of other universities, with the Senate as the main decision-making body of academics, chaired by the Vice-Chancellor and answerable to the Council and Court above it. In effect, Senate debates the recommendations of a number of bodies below it, principally the larger pemanent sub-committees of Senate, in which the bulk of the decision-making is done. At the time that the plays were proposed, however, the relevant decision-maker and provider of money responsible to the Senate was an *ad hoc* body, a Centenary Celebrations Committee chaired by the Vice-Chancellor, and it was to this committee that the proposal was taken. After a good deal of thought and enquiry, and discussion with the interested members of the Medieval Centre, I decided that we should ask the University for a cash grant of £Stg 300 plus 'full support by the University's facilities'.

A request at the same time so very low in specific terms but with such a wide margin of unspecified spending is I think unusual: but the reasoning behind it might be applied to any project of so experimental a nature. The £Stg 300 of course was straightforward — a budget very precisely estimated on the lines of any ordinary theatre production: principal items on it included costume hire and materials for set construction (in this case the basic superstructure and hangings for the wagons), which eventually came to £Stg 99 and £Stg 101 respectively.

The further non-specific request for support by the University's facilities was best thus formulated because of the experimental nature of the event. No such production had been attempted for 400 years, and we could not dare limit ourselves to a precise estimate of the unforeseen expenses which might occur. Analogy with a similar and familiar medium, such as carnival, was of limited use: it would not take into account, for example, the cost of communication with producers requiring constant information, reassurance, and encouragement in their dealings with the unknown. Furthermore, the University's contribution of the use of already existing facilities was far more valuable to us and far less expensive for the University than any direct financial aid. Indeed, the experiment was possible precisely because a university does have wide resources available: and one of the long-lasting effects of the production was to prove to University members just how much could be achieved by a pooling of these resources.

In the face of this request, the Centenary Celebrations Committee was not unnaturally a little cautious: but after consultation with the director of the Workshop Theatre the full request was granted.

In practice a wide range of University resources was tapped. At the most obviously financial level, the University bore the cost of telephone calls and postage. Local calls are not in any case charged to individual departments at Leeds, and the Medieval Centre, under whose auspices the post was despatched, did not have financial status as a department with its own budget. Under the heading of hidden costs was the very important support of the service departments:[9] the Fabric Office, for example, was invaluable in providing transport and labour for the erection of fair-stalls, help with clearing the site before and after the event, and lending of equipment; the Security Guards dealt with traffic and crowd control, among other things, kept roads clear and guarded the wagons overnight; and secretarial help was provided by the University's Secretarial Services.

Two services found themselves unable to help: the head of the Television Unit — although personally enthusiastic about the experiment (to the extent of playing God in Play 4, *Adam and Eve in the Garden of Eden*) — felt unable to commit staff and camera time to a weekend outdoor performance, the effect of which was so much a matter of conjecture. Videotapes of the production would have been invaluable for example for conference use, although their place has to a certain extent been filled by illustrated lectures and written papers.[10]

Much more serious was the non-participation of the Information Office, the University's public relations and publicity service. The importance of professional publicity in any large-scale artistic venture cannot be too highly stressed. It is not just a matter of attracting an audience. Especially in a production such as this, where the participants are asked to stick their artistic necks out and trust an unfamiliar medium, publicity from the beginning is an invaluable aid in maintaining interest and boosting cast morale. As it turned out, the event itself was an enormous popular and artistic success: but the time and energy spent on publicity could have been much better used on monitoring the experiment for further research; and without the support of the Information Office we did not have the resources to stake clearly the University's claim to the first authentic performance of a Cycle play. So Leeds University to a large extent lost the kudos of this first performance to the University of Toronto, which mounted a similar production two years later. (Of course, it must be remembered that in their widespread publicity Toronto had the advantage of following the Leeds production and so knowing exactly what they were publicizing. An innovation is difficult to advertise: yet pre-advertisement may be precisely what secures its success.)

Support from individual academic departments was considerable. The fact of the University's formal approval was an essential starting point, although in practice support depended upon the commitment of individuals in the departments. In some cases the resources of a department were placed unstintingly at the service of the plays. The most striking example was perhaps the Department of Civil Engineering. This department was offered the *Crucifixion* play, since they had the best chance of solving the immense problem of crucifying an actor on a pageant wagon three times in succession and doing it efficiently and safely. They not only worked from clues in the medieval script to design a cross and socket, but used workshop time and space to build them. Furthermore, the department gave invaluable help in providing scaffolding erectors, and — through links with industry — free transport for the pageant wagons to and from their farm in North Yorkshire. On a smaller scale, but no less appropriately, the Department of Metallurgy actually made gilt crowns for its play of the *Magi*, a play originally performed by the Goldsmiths' Guild.

Support from the departments was enlisted in three ways: by a portable exhibition on medieval drama; by advertisement in the University newsletter; and by direct letter to heads of department. The exhibition I always accompanied in order to answer questions and to make personal contact with interested parties. This method of advertising the project attracted many students, while the second and third methods were aimed at staff. In every case it was in the end personal contact which resulted in a department's joining in the project: it must be said, of course, that where a professor bothered to follow up my letter, the department was likely to be lively to begin with.

The individual drama groups — both university and city — took on a play on the understanding that they provided their own props and, if they

Figure 12.1. *The* Crucifixion *play, successfully staged by the Department of Civil Engineering. Christ's cross is dragged across the wagon and dropped into the concealed, supporting mortice.*

thought it necessary, extra scenery for their wagon: in other words the play was a production for which, apart from those aspects organized centrally, they took full responsibility. This medieval system of individual responsibility engendered a healthy competitiveness between groups, most of whom were determined to present no less successful a play than any other group.

Many different kinds of non-dramatic support were also given from outside the University. The Yorkshire Arts Association gave £Stg 100 specifically for publicity; Radio Leeds gave some air time to the production and Yorkshire Television gave it news coverage; Tarmac Construction Ltd saw to the transport of the wagons, free of charge; Leeds City Council supplied scaffolding for audience seating at no cost to us; and a local shroud factory undertook the sewing of the wagon curtains.

The aims of the Experiment

These were twofold: my aims in initiating the project, and the University's reason for supporting it. My purpose in initiating an authentic production of a cycle play was simply to prove that it was worth doing on its own terms, and to show that the York Cycle would be dramatically far more effective when so done than in the patronizing 'adaptation for a modern audience' presented triennially at York.

Most historians of the performing arts will agree that the attempted re-creation of original circumstances and techniques is necessary for the complete understanding of old works. More specifically, we cannot fully understand a play from the late Middle Ages unless we have tried to assess it on its own terms: and such an assessment eventually requires re-creation by authentic historical performance. In 1975 no such performance of a cycle play had yet been attempted.

Since the Middle Ages, circumstances of theatre have naturally changed: the average man in the audience now expects an indoor performance, by one professional cast, of a single play lasting from two to three hours, and probably still performed behind a proscenium arch. He also expects a certain style of acting, the result of communication with a seated audience in a building of a certain size. It is easy for even a theatre specialist to make an assessment of the mystery plays without appreciating their completely different circumstances, and to come to the conclusion that this earlier drama will not 'work', that a wagon is unsuitable as a stage, that the dramatic text is primitive — in short, that the audience will be bored unless the play is somehow adapted to fit their expectations. Against such claims there is no suitable rebuttal except performance: and the rebuttal is invalid unless the original circumstances of production are as far as possible recreated.

The York Cycle, besides being one of the most unified of the English cycles, is one for which much information survives on the practicalities of performance: and I could therefore be sure of following closely the original organization and staging techniques. In recreating the 'feel' of the streets of medieval York one could not, of course, change people's attitudes and beliefs: but over a period of many hours there is the possibility that those attitudes and beliefs may be suspended, at least to the extent that they are suspended in, say, the opera house.

If our twentieth-century attitudes could be suspended successfully enough, the whole process of mounting a cycle play could be assessed fairly accurately in medieval terms, so that some important questions might be answered. How big a wagon was needed? How much machinery was required? How long would it take to wheel a wagon on to each playing-area and set it up for performance? What was the effect of crowding 13 or more actors into a limited area? What sort of relationship would grow up between actors and audience? What would be the effect of a cast processing to the playing-areas? What effect on the audience would result from the various acting styles and (even more interesting) abilities of the different groups?

These, and many more questions that had raised themselves in the minds of scholars who had never seen a full mystery cycle mounted in a medieval fashion, might well be answered, at least in part, by a performance such as was envisaged for the Leeds Experiment, and indeed the project did answer many questions and shed much light on a number that could not be answered categorically.

The University supported the project because it was for a number of reasons a particularly appropriate contribution to the centenary celebrations of 1974-75. To begin with, the University Centenary was an occasion so concerned with making the community feel its involvement with a large civic university — *their* university — that some large-scale event had to be found in which academics and members of the community could participate on equal terms: the York Cycle allowed precisely this. Secondly, it had to be an event which was not obviously the prerogative of either academics or non-academics as a class. It was notable that at our first meeting with prospective participants, at which I, the academic instigator, outlined the proposals and asked for support, one comment was 'So this is an academic exercise, then?', a question which, if answered simply in the affirmative, would have killed the project there and then as a collaborative effort. And rightly so. Since I was able to prove to the questioner that it was in fact a *dramatic* exercise, his doubts were removed.

Thirdly, in the event, the celebratory aspect of the Centenary was enhanced by the ceremonial nature of the plays. It is not only that the plays present the greatest story ever told, and do it on a suitable time scale so that the dramatic experience is somehow commensurate with the story dramatized. That is, of course, true, and is perhaps the most striking aspect of the plays to someone who sees them without previous knowledge. But there is another reason, inherent in the mode of performance: namely, that a procession — necessarily a *religious* procession in this case — is itself a ceremony, and the performance therefore does not take place only when plays are being acted at the various stations. In practice, the spectacle begins the moment the first cast sets out for the first station, and ends only when the final procession is over. Interestingly, the non-academics were no less at home in this than the academics: for although a university does maintain a tradition of academic ceremony, in practice this is a very small part of an academic's life even if he regularly attends degree-ceremonies (which, indeed, very few do).

These aims did not change as the project advanced. They were however presented to the participants in a variety of ways and with different emphases according to their different areas of involvement. The local drama groups, for example, were told of the gala nature of the occasion, and the more experienced groups such as the Swarthmore Centre were attracted by the dramatic challenge it presented; some University departments, such as Colour Chemistry, had theatre-oriented professors who recognized the research potential of the experiment, while other heads of department realized that to contribute would be good for their department, at the very least in terms of public relations or internal staff-student relationships. As a result, the individual's view of the experiment varied considerably, according to his approach to it, his expectations, and his feeling of satisfaction in relation to those expectations. Although the results of the project were sometimes surprising, it would in general be fair to say that the project was so wide-ranging and took place on so many levels of hope and achievement that few people, if any, were dissatisfied with the event when it took place. On the contrary, such a project is bigger than the sum of its parts, and the sense of achievement is therefore bigger than expected.

The administration of the Experiment

Realizing from the start that we could not proceed without the support and resources of local drama groups, I held a preliminary meeting specifically for these groups. Some 30 societies sent representatives, and a few others expressed interest. Not all of these groups decided to join in, of course, and eventually 12 town drama groups performed in the cycle. I followed a separate recruiting procedure in the University of Leeds, mainly because I could not necessarily take for granted the same dramatic knowledge and expertise as in the practising drama groups. Eventually, 20 groups from Leeds University took part. It is perhaps worth mentioning that these groups were almost equally divided between the arts and the sciences, with the Administration and the Library also included. Of the remaining four groups, three came from local training colleges and one from the City and University of York.

These figures are however slightly misleading since they conceal a more integrated collaboration. Members of the University are also members of the community in their spare time: and so, for example, RoCo church drama group had a Medical School lecturer as one of the disciples in the play of *Doubting Thomas*. Conversely, many of the University groups co-opted experienced help from drama societies: the School of Education, for instance, invited a member of the Swarthmore Drama Workshop to produce their *Way to Calvary*. Departments collaborated — such as History and Economics who combined to produce *The Last Supper*; and so did local societies, such as Wellington Hill and St Aidan's drama groups, who stepped into the breach when a University department backed out, as it were, of the *Entry to Jerusalem*.

There were several reasons why groups decided not to take a play, or abandoned it at a later stage. Among the non-University groups a tight budget was a major factor in most cases, with groups unable to commit their time to a production which would bring them no income; of these groups, some of the more lively took stalls in the accompanying fair and made them pay (see below). Another reason given was pressure of other productions to which previous commitment of actors had been made. A third reason was probably some distrust of the unfamiliar conventions of medieval drama performed in a medieval manner. (It would be surprising if some groups did not take fright at the novelty of doing something for the first time: but it is of course impossible to be sure, since this sort of reason would never be admitted.) One difficulty experienced particularly by the local drama societies was that, while actresses are much easier to find than actors, all the plays demand a predominantly male cast. Among the University departments, lack of personal motivation in the man to whom the production was delegated was probably the main cause. It is also possible that in all cases the language offered some obstacle, but this was probably rare. (We performed the cycle in Purvis's modernized text, for a variety of reasons: but it should be pointed out that my production of the Wakefield cycle in 1980 used the original Middle English text with no percentage increase in groups backing out.)

In medieval York each play was produced by a particular trade guild, the whole being overseen on behalf of the City authorities by a group of responsible men. The City imposed through them a certain amount of discipline concerning such matters as the quality of the acting and the practical efficiency of a production which had to be moved around to an extremely tight schedule; one assumes that some overall control may also have been imposed over such matters as costuming, although no information on this survives. At Leeds I followed the general scheme of this organization, partly because it seemed reasonable to assume that the best way of organizing the event then was likely still to be the best way now, and partly in order to *show* that such was the case. The organization necessarily differed in some ways, however: discipline was vital but I depended on competitiveness, not fines; musicians, wagons, costumes and publicity were provided centrally; and because we naturally no longer share a common medieval mode of drama production I had to act not simply as organizer but as overall artistic director, imposing certain limitations on the producers and giving them information and advice on the medieval aspects of their plays.

Thus, while the individual plays were produced by drama groups from the City and University of Leeds, there was a clear artistic direction from myself (aided by specialists in staging, costume, music, etc) and an overall organization (myself, supported by the organizing committee from the Medieval Centre). I have already mentioned that correspondence between the subject dramatized and the guild acting it was a feature of the medieval organization: and it is worth recording here that in 1975 individual plays were offered where possible to groups for whom they were in some way specially suitable. *The Creation of the World*, for example, was undertaken by the Department of Physics; Leeds Co-operative Society, a department store, performed the *Temptation of Adam and Eve*; Chemistry produced the *Transfiguration*; the Department of Civil Engineering took responsibility for the *Crucifixion*; and the *Death of Mary* play was requested by the drama society of St Mary's Church, Whitkirk.

Such correspondences were not merely fanciful in the Middle Ages: in all cases the guild had a purely practical advantage in the production of the play, and it was sensible, as well as symbolically appropriate, that the plays should be thus disposed. While this reasoning has always seemed obvious, another reason for such correspondence emerged in the course of the 1975 production — namely, that the very appropriateness of the play for certain groups helped to give those groups a sense of purposeful corporate identity which supplied a strong motivation for performing that particular play, and performing it well. The civil engineers in 1975 realized that they had a task which needed their special expertise, just as the York Shipwrights in earlier times had a task specially suited to them in the building of Noah's Ark. In a large-scale collaboration it is vital that individual groups have this sort of motivation where possible.

Another way in which I tried to recreate the original circumstances of the York Cycle was in the setting. Ideally, of course, one would like to take over the city of York, ban modern traffic from it for a day, and use the medieval playing-places. That way, we should learn a great deal. As it is, no modern setting will otherwise give the exact 'feel' of the space originally available, acoustics, and so on. Nevertheless, much can be learned from the re-creation of important elements. It seemed to me necessary to give the feeling of a holiday atmosphere; to restrict the space available to the wagons in a way which would define the audience-areas and acting-areas in a clear cut way; and to make sure that these areas were crowded not merely with audience so that the modern reverential theatre hush did not prevail. The limiting of space was especially necessary because the plays were performed in the University's pedestrian precinct, where there is considerably more space than in the narrow streets of York.

The principal way in which all this was done was to line the procession route with fair-stalls, which defined a rather narrow corridor as the processional route in which everything happened. The stalls were a success in a number of ways: they were colourful; they drew crowds who would never have come merely to see a play; they offered an alternative attraction for the spectators, thus stimulating the actors to greater efforts; they provided such necessities as tea and other refreshments; they supplied souvenirs of the occasion, including programmes, etc; and they offered active participation to those who did not wish to take part in a play. From a financial point of view participation in the fair was well worthwhile; the stallholders paid a £Stg 5 refundable deposit as a guarantee of their attendance, and were then free to make as much money from the stall as they could.[11] This meant that there was competition for customers, so that the stalls were made as attractive as possible and thus formed a colourful, living setting for the plays. Many charities took stalls, too, so that some worthy causes were served in a venture in which the community at large was in evidence.

In addition to the fair, there were other non-dramatic attractions, in the form of wandering freelance minstrels, a dancing bear, tumblers, Punch and Judy (post-medieval, but immensely successful in terms of the medieval spirit of entertainment), and others. It is appropriate here to mention the Department of Metallurgy again, which — not content with performing a play — ran an alchemist's stall and did a roaring trade making and selling lead charms guaranteed to turn to gold within three days. In such ways do academics and the community at large get to know each other.

Results

The assessment of the project was a long process, and it will not be possible to give much detail here. What is offered is a brief explanation of the results in terms of the aims outlined above.

☐ The York Cycle at Leeds showed that medieval drama on this scale and performed in a medieval mode can be an enormously exciting theatrical experience. The performance took the York Cycle out of the realm of 'literature'; it showed that the true scale of the original is not only acceptable to a modern audience but that it is far preferable to the abridged versions of the cycles offered elsewhere; and it showed that the plays as total entertainment can be entirely successful, both dramatically and in other ways. The medieval dramatists, in other words, were right.

☐ More specifically, the production answered fairly emphatically some of the questions of recent years. We know now that it takes only a few seconds, not five minutes, to prepare a wagon for a play once it has arrived at a station. We know that crushing 13 people on to a small wagon for the *Last Supper* is no disadvantage: on the contrary, the very limitation of the space helps to focus both the presentation of the play and the audiences' perception of it. We know that the audiences establish a relationship with each successive play that is stable yet dynamic (they move closer to or farther away from the wagon according to their involvement with the action). We know that the audiences' reactions depend partly on the circumstances obtaining at a particular station (the three audiences were quite different from one another, and the actors had to play differently at the three stations). And we know that cumbersome stage machinery need not necessarily have been used in plays requiring special effects. The answers to more generalized questions were just as interesting: the power of the drama is such that the audience stayed to see an interesting story even when the actors were weak or inaudible; despite the length of the entire Cycle, even quite young children demanded to stay and watch it all; and, in some ways the most interesting and unexpected result of all, the sight of pageant wagons moving in procession, surrounded by a cast of actors, is stunningly effective, affecting and ceremonial.

☐ Finally, the overall artistic success of the venture was largely responsible for its success also in the field of public relations. During the two days of the performance well over 4000 people came as audience to a University campus which they do not normally enter; some 500 actors and almost 300 others from the University and the City of Leeds collaborated happily and fruitfully; moreover, the University benefited internally, since the collaboration within the University necessary for such an unusual event brought together members of the University who would not normally meet, let alone collaborate.

It will be clear that in respect of the aims detailed above the project was a success. Precise assessment is hardly possible, unfortunately, since assessment as such was not our aim and we did not have the resources to record data in parallel with the main business of organization. It is, however, possible to see some of the long-term results of the project, and thus to evaluate the importance of it as an influence on current thought in certain areas.

To begin with, the dramatic results have borne fruit. The University of Toronto mounted the York Cycle on pageant wagons in 1977, 12 plays from the Wakefield Cycle were played on wagons in the pedestrian precinct in Wakefield the same year, and in 1980 the complete Wakefield Cycle was performed at the same place, processionally but on fixed stages. These productions have by now convinced many scholars of the rightness of processional performance: more importantly, the dramatic success of these productions and their financial viability have convinced audiences and promoters to the extent that we may look forward to further productions of this kind.

Secondly, the type of large-scale collaboration of town and gown pioneered in 1975 has been approached since then and could be repeated at any time that conditions are right. In fact, the two Wakefield productions have shown an interesting progression along these lines. In 1977 it had been noticeable that the initiative and medieval expertise came from the University of Leeds: by 1980, although the same experts were invited to participate, the incentive for the production came from Wakefield itself.

Finally, the plays had a lasting effect on Leeds University. It goes without saying, probably, that the effect of so many people from the community coming into the University for a weekend was felt to be a step in the right direction: indeed, the occasion was marked by a visit from the Lord Mayor of Leeds, who watched some plays in the company of the University's Vice-Chancellor, thus symbolically sealing the knot of collaboration represented by the performance. Since then the University has held two more Open Days, in the last of which over 7000 townspeople visited the University in a single day to see how the University operated and what its members did there. So successful have the Open Days been that another is envisaged for 1983.

The performance of the York Cycle at Leeds in 1975 started something, then, that was obviously beneficial to the University and the community: and while few productions involve quite as many people as a mystery cycle there are a good number of alternative projects which could be used to the same effect: for example, some of the larger Renaissance plays, royal entries, the more complicated masques, or, as a longer term venture, the running of a radio station.

The Leeds Experiment was not only a dramatic and academic success: it proved that academic leadership of the community can work in practical terms and that artistic collaboration between town and gown may be achieved with very little cost and to lasting mutual benefit.

BASIC REFERENCE DATA (1975)

IA. The host institution

Name: University of Leeds

Date founded: The Yorkshire College of Science was founded in 1874, and became a constituent College of the Victoria University (Manchester) in 1887. It received its Charter as the University of Leeds in 1905.

Internal organization: Large, red-brick university structure. Seven faculties: Arts, Education, Economic and Social Studies, Law, Science, Applied Science, Medicine: subdivided into 83 departments.

Number of academic staff: 1025

Number of students: 7071 undergraduates; 2762 postgraduates

Catchment area: The whole of the British Isles. The largest group of students is from London and SE England; next, from West of the Pennines; next from Yorkshire and Humberside; then overseas.

Designated responsibility for off-campus activities: Responsible for university adult education in West and North-west Yorkshire.

Income: On the University's general revenue account was £Stg 18.6 million, including: grants from HM Treasury £Stg 14.7m; academic fees, £Stg 1m; grants and contracts for research £Stg 2m.

IB. The host centre

Name: Graduate Centre for Medieval Studies (now Centre for Medieval Studies)

Date founded: 1967

Internal organization: Director and Deputy Director at head of the Centre's Board of Studies. The Board is made up of the teaching and potential teaching members of the Centre.

Number of academic staff: Officially nil. In practice, 41 members of staff of other University departments (see note 8, below).

Number of students: 8

Catchment area: British Isles, North America

Designated responsibility for off-campus activities: NA

Income: Nil

II. The innovation/system being studied

Name: The Leeds Experiment

Date: Initiated in November 1974, and performed on 17-18 May 1975.

Nature: The first production of a Mystery Play Cycle for 400 years to use the medieval organization and staging techniques.

Internal organization: 36 plays (each with its own producer), stallholders, entertainers; an executive committee of 7: all of these responsible to the director.

Number of academic staff: The director and 6 of the executive committee were academic. 24 producers belonged to Leeds University or other higher education institutions. About half the performers, stallholders etc were academics.

Number of non-academics: One of the executive committee, 12 producers, and about half of the performers, stallholders etc were not academics.

Income: Cash grants: £Stg 300 from University Centenary Celebrations Committee, £Stg 100 from Yorkshire Arts Association, plus aid in kind from numerous organizations. £Stg 100 *profit* from sale of tickets, programmes, etc.

Income as proportion of institution's total income: 0.002 per cent.

NOTES

1. Although this chapter is the result of a collaboration, it is necessarily written from the point of view of the director of the performance discussed. The use of the first person singular therefore refers throughout to Jane Oakshott, the principal author.

2. Usually known as the Towneley Cycle but ascribed by some scholars to Wakefield. For reasons of publicity the production of the complete cycle in Wakefield (1980) was also called the Wakefield Cycle.

3. This play was formerly known as Ludus Coventriae but does not come from Coventry. It appears to be an East Anglian touring script compiled from a variety of sources and probably performed in the round.

4. York (1951) as part of the Festival of Britain celebrations.

5. A passion play written on the continental pattern for performance in the round. The play lasts approximately nine hours, divided into three separate Days. The first modern performance was in 1969 by Bristol University Drama Department, directed by Neville Denny.

6. The Leeds procession route was long enough for only three 'stations' as opposed to the 12 of medieval York. 36 out of a possible 48 plays were performed, giving a narratively complete Cycle: but unfortunately some plays, including the Marian group, had to be omitted.

7. Stations One and Three had raked seating for spectators, but crowds also gathered in front of these scaffolds and to the sides of the wagons, so that there were standing audiences at all three stations. It is to those standing that I refer throughout when discussing 'audience'.

8. Now the Centre for Medieval Studies. The Centre is an association of the medievalists in the University, offering an MA in Medieval Studies. It was set up by Professor John Le Patourel in 1967 on the understanding that it would cost the University nothing. Until the Centre was offered a room in 1981, it was 'two square feet on the French Department noticeboard'. The weekly drama meeting was held officially to carry out work on a Catalogue of Medieval European Drama, but the York Cycle production is only one example of other projects which the regular meetings stimulated.

9. At least one service department, having no students to justify the use of a departmental budget, requested a guarantee of payment from the Centenary Celebrations budget: but this in no way affects the fact that they were willing to give valuable staff time and energy to the plays.

10. Lectures given include Meredith, P, *The Leeds Production of the York Cycle in 1975* (given at Toronto University in September 1976, at a session sponsored by Records of Early English Drama and the Graduate Centre for the Study of Drama); and Oakshott, J, *Waggons Roll!: or, The Director's Report on the Leeds Experiment* (given at the University of Western Michigan, Kalamazoo, in May 1979, during the 14th International Congress on Medieval Studies). Written material is sparse; but many of the Leeds findings are repeated in Parry (1979), and much of Carpenter's perceptive review of the 1980 Wakefield production (Carpenter, 1980) could have been applied also to the 1975 performance of the York Cycle.

11. The original plan had been to charge the stallholders a £Stg 5 fee as rent: but the City's Charter of 1626 forbade this within a six-and-two-thirds mile radius of Leeds market.

REFERENCES AND BIBLIOGRAPHY

There is almost no published material on the Leeds Experiment (see note 10, above); we include reference to the official programme of the event here because it mentions a few of the aims and methods discussed in this essay. The works by Smith (1885) and Purvis (1957) are editions of the original and modernized text, respectively, of the York Cycle. Of the many scholarly books on medieval English plays we have chosen those by Kahrl, Kolve, Tydeman and Wickham as being — in their very different ways — the most useful for the general reader. Only Kolve's work is concerned exclusively with the mystery cycles. Purvis (1969) is a fascinating introduction to the York Cycle, and is included here for the variety and interest of the material discussed: but the reader is warned that many of the views expressed by Purvis are no longer accepted by scholars.

Carpenter, S (1980) Towneley Plays at Wakefield, *Medieval English Theatre*, 2(1), 49-52

Denny, N (1973) Arena staging and dramatic quality in the Cornish Passion Play, in Denny, N (ed) *Medieval Drama*, pp 125-53, Stratford-upon-Avon Studies No 16, Edward Arnold, London

Johnston, A F and Rogerson, M (1979) *Records of Early English Drama: York*, 1014 pp, Toronto and Manchester University Presses

Kahrl, S J (1974) *Traditions of Medieval English Drama*, 157 pp, Hutchinson, London

Kolve, V A (1966) *The Play Called Corpus Christi*, 347 pp, Stanford University Press, Stanford, Cal

Parry, D (1979) The York Mystery Cycle at Toronto, 1977, *Medieval English Theatre*, 1(1), 19-31

Purvis, J S (1957) *The York Cycle of Mystery Plays*, 384 pp, The Society for the Promotion of Christian Knowledge, London

Purvis, J S (1969) *From Minster to Market Place*, 89 pp, St Anthony's Press, York

Rogers, B (1969) Preview of the Cornish Cycle Production, *The Times*, 7 July 1969, p 8

Smith, L T (1885) *York Plays*, 635 pp, Clarendon Press, Oxford

Tydeman, W (1978) *The Theatre in the Middle Ages*, 310 pp, Cambridge University Press, Cambridge

The University of Leeds (1975) *The York Cycle of Mystery Plays* (programme for the performance of 17-18 May 1975), 12 pp, The University of Leeds, Leeds

Wickham, G (1959) *Early English Stages 1300 to 1660*, vol 1 (1300-1576), 472 pp, Routledge and Kegan Paul, London

Subject index

Author index